LIVING
with the
Locals

LIVING
with the
Locals

Early Europeans' Experience
of Indigenous Life

JOHN MAYNARD & VICTORIA HASKINS

NLA Publishing

NATIONAL
LIBRARY
OF AUSTRALIA

Published by the National Library of Australia
Canberra ACT 2600

Books published by the National Library of Australia further the Library's objectives to produce publications that interpret the Library's collection and contribute to the vitality of Australian culture and history.

Indigenous and Torres Strait Islander communities should be aware that this book contains images and names of people who are now deceased.

National Library of Australia Cataloguing-in-Publication entry

Creator: Maynard, John, 1954- author.
Title: Living with the locals : early europeans' experience of
             indigenous life / John Maynard and Victoria Haskins.
ISBN: 9780642278951 (paperback)
Notes: Includes bibliographical references and index.
Subjects: Europeans--Cultural assimilation--Australia.
             Europeans--Australia--Attitudes--History.
             Indigenous peoples--Australia.
Other Creator:
             Haskins, Victoria K. (Victoria Katharine), 1967- author.
Dewey Number: 994.02

Editor's note

Quoted material has been reproduced as it appears in the sources used.

Commissioning Publisher: Susan Hall
Editor: Joanna Karmel
Designer: Stan Lamond
Image coordinator: Celia Vaughan
Production coordinator: Melissa Bush
Indexer: Sandra Henderson
Printed in Hong Kong by Australian Book Connection

Find out about National Library of Australia Publishing at publishing.nla.gov.au.

Disclaimer

The usage of Aboriginal clan, group or language group names in this book is not authoritative or definitive in terms of orthography or location. Wherever possible, the names used here have been taken directly from the archival and other source material drawn upon in this publication. In many instances, these sources offer variations and distortions of Aboriginal group names, according to the individual's opinion, whether informed or not, who wrote them down. Where we have found it appropriate to refer to present-day names for Aboriginal groups, we have used the Australian Institute of Aboriginal and Torres Strait Islander Studies (AIATSIS) 'reference name' as defined by the AUSTLANG resource: austlang.aiatsis.gov.au.

Contents

Aboriginal artist Tommy McRae's depiction of
William Buckley's introduction to the Aboriginal people after
his escape from the convict settlement at Port Phillip.

Living with the Locals

From convict escapees William Buckley and James Davis to shipwreck survivors, boys John Ireland and William D'Oyley, and the gothic Eliza Fraser, the stories of the white men and women who cut loose, or were cut loose, from colonial society and made new lives with Aboriginal people have exerted something of a hold on the Australian imagination. In this book, we set out to retrace the stories of some of the individuals who found themselves living with Aboriginal people, sometimes voluntarily, sometimes involuntarily, and, in several instances, for decades, during the initial stages of the European presence on the continent. Here, we present a compilation of these individuals' incredible stories, based on the rich documentary, literary and pictorial sources held in the National Library of Australia. Many of the stories, especially in their original form, resemble a 'Boys' Own' adventure, or a *Ripley's Believe It or Not* tale. But these are about real people and events, and this book is an attempt to unravel and re-examine what we can from the sources we have.

Importantly, too, we hope to illuminate some kind of Indigenous insight into the stories, traditionally told wholly from the white perspective. In spite of the flaws, the biases and the sensationalist additions, the accounts of the white men and women who lived closely with Aboriginal or Torres Strait Islander individuals and communities over months and years remain ethnographies of incalculable value today. They provide a glimpse into Indigenous lifestyles and views of the world at the very point of first contact between the Indigenous people of the country and the British colonists, and some insight into their perspective on the world of the colonists at the time.

From this angle, the white men and women who lived with Indigenous people, regarded by the wider colonial society and sometimes by themselves as 'captives', look more like refugees. They tended to be in rather desperate straits when first found by Aboriginal or Torres Strait Islander people, and in pressing need of food, shelter and companionship, which they by and large received from their startled hosts. Indigenous communities typically adopted these Europeans, by treating them as reborn kin, family members returning from the realm of the dead. As historian and journalist Keith Willey notes, in the first stages of the colonial encounter white people were seen as:

> perhaps frightening and even to some extent unpredictable, but at least beings, who could be fitted into the local scheme of things, explained in terms of the local people's own experiences, if not assumed to be related to them by kinship.

Thus, Indigenous people could make sense of these strange pale-skinned people who appeared out of nowhere in their territories, when it was well understood that nobody would conceive of encroaching upon other peoples' land, let alone leaving their own country. It was an interpretation that would have saved the lives of many of those lone, lost strangers who were discovered by Aboriginal people.

But we have had to read against the grain of much of the contemporary material. Written and published at a time when white attitudes towards Aboriginal people and culture were highly negative, the literary record relating to the experiences of white people among Aboriginal people was demeaning, derogatory and, in many instances, openly racist towards Indigenous people and culture. Aboriginal and Islander culture was portrayed as childlike and primitive at best, and at worst as brutally savage. Writers were often further disappointed by the consummate failure of those white people who lived with Indigenous people to exert their authority over them, and the tone of much commentary was persistently patronising and insulting to both parties. In 1923, Archibald Meston, a former Queensland Protector of Aboriginals and self-proclaimed expert on 'wild white men', opined:

> It was somewhat unfortunate that the wild blacks had to form their first estimate of the white man on such types as Buckley, Davis, Fahey and Bracefell who were actually far below the average aboriginal in intelligence, and still further below him in dignity, honesty, courtesy, and self respect ...

But clear enough is the evidence that the white man, in contact with the savage soon loses his veneer of civilisation ... sure proof that the primeval savage wild man in all of us is terribly near the surface. Put the average man in a wild rage, with a weapon in his hands, and watch the result.

Most confronting in the various accounts is the persistent, indeed obsessive, fixation on violent 'warfare' and cannibalism. The colonial accounts were geared to an audience eager for sensationalist and titillating exposes of the customs of 'savages' that contrasted with what they believed about their own society. Such lurid depictions of Indigenous life and customs can be read today as virtual propaganda, justifying wars of genocidal extermination and the removal of Indigenous peoples altogether to make way for 'civilisation', while the 'ordeals' of the civilised among the barbarians provided also a kind of cathartic function for an insular settler society not entirely confident of the legitimacy of their claims on a continent. Even today, claims of 'traditional' Indigenous patterns of lethal violence and cannibalism based on these kinds of accounts can be (and sometimes are) mobilised to justify divisive race politics. In the late 1990s, politician Pauline Hanson provided a stark example of such usage of claims of Aboriginal cannibalism. For us, as an Indigenous and a non-Indigenous historian respectively, making sense of these often disturbingly graphic accounts has required some careful reading of the details and a healthy degree of scepticism, in order to retrieve some understanding of the Indigenous laws and protocols governing social relations that the white guests may have been witnessing.

In our discussions of the various accounts, we have been struck by the common complaint that those who returned to white society would not willingly share much of their experiences (which, in turn, draws attention to the fact that this literature is dominated by second-hand, and even third-hand, accounts). Given the prurient badgering they were subjected to, it is unsurprising that so many of the Europeans who lived among Aboriginal people were taciturn. But perhaps their reticence was also a way of protecting the cultural integrity of the people who had sheltered and befriended them: at the very least, a mark of respect for the Indigenous appreciation that not all knowledge is open and available for sharing. The majority of the individuals that we have looked at were consistent in keeping their silence on Aboriginal religious and spiritual beliefs, in particular, subjects that remain sacred and secret today.

Over the millennia during which Indigenous people occupied the continent before British colonisation, there were strangers who came to shore and lived among them, but their stories are long lost to us. Of those who have lived with Aboriginal people since 1788, a mysterious character by the name of Sammy Cox (also known as Samuel Emanuel Jervis) has been claimed by some writers to have been the first known white person. Supposedly the orphaned son of a British noble, Cox was taken on a voyage to the South Seas by his uncle, but fearing that the uncle planned to abandon him on an uninhabited island and take possession of his large inheritance young Sammy snuck away from the shore party when the ship anchored in Van Diemen's Land in 1789 and hid (the island had been named by Dutchman Abel Tasman in 1642 but would not be colonised by the British until 1803). According to the story, Cox was found by a group of Aboriginal people

they treated him very kindly, making a 'mi-mi' of boughs and a soft bed of rushes for his accommodation

with whom he remained for some 23 years, until 1812, when he met and became associated with a white family named Cox (from whom he took his name). In later life, Cox, who worked as a gardener, lived on the grounds of flour miller Thomas Monds. Monds recorded Cox's stories in a letter to the newspapers in 1890, when Cox was old and destitute, and wrote of how the boy Cox had at first been afraid of the Aboriginal people and had tried to swim out from the shore:

> However in this he was mistaken for the blackfellows could swim better and faster than he, and they soon overtook him and brought him to land. They were much astonished at the colour of his skin, and made a great fuss over him. However, they treated him very kindly, making a 'mi-mi' of boughs and a soft bed of rushes for his accommodation, and fed him upon the best of fish and kangaroos.

The story was immediately greeted with disbelief, but over the years it has continued to surface. More recently, historian Andrew Piper set out to debunk Cox's story, finding that Cox arrived in Hobart in 1825, and that he had been convicted in 1828 and again in 1835 for assaulting a boy 'with intent to commit an unnatural offence'. But he found nothing that could corroborate the claim that Cox had lived with Aboriginal people.

We are on surer ground when it comes to the experiences of the very first convicts at Port Jackson in 1788. The new settlement was not bound by walls and there was little restraint on the convicts who 'were everywhere straggling about', as First Fleet officer and chronicler David Collins recorded, so that it was difficult to tell when people had disappeared. There were multiple escapes from the colony over the period to 1810 by both convicts and soldiers, some of whom took refuge with Aboriginal people.

The earliest of these runaways who can be identified with certainty were four convicts who got away from the Rose Hill settlement on a September night in 1790. John Tarwood (or Turwood), George Lee, George Connoway and John Watson had escaped on a punt and had then taken a small boat, used by a harbour watch-house, in which they intended to sail to Tahiti.

Five years later, Captain William Broughton was forced past Sydney Harbour in a storm and sailed north to take shelter in Port Stephens, where he recorded his surprise on discovering four white men living with the Aboriginal people. He brought them back to Sydney, where Collins described their appearance with some disdain: 'four white people, (if four miserable, naked, dirty, and smoke-dried men could be called white,) runaways from this settlement'. But the tales of their lives at Port Stephens, with which they apparently regaled 'crowds both of black and white people' back in the Sydney settlement, suggested they had lived well enough in the previous five years.

The men 'spoke in high terms of the pacific disposition and gentle manners of the natives', Collins noted:

> Each of them had had names given him, and given with several ceremonies. Wives also were allotted them, and one or two had children. They were never required to go out on any occasion of hostility, and were in general supplied by the natives with fish and other food, being considered by them (for so their situation can only be construed) as unfortunate strangers thrown upon their shore from the mouth of the yawning deep, and entitled to their protection.

Collins was unimpressed by the men's insistence that the Aboriginal people considered them to be relatives returned from the dead:

> They told us a ridiculous story, that the natives appeared to worship them, often assuring them, when they began to understand each other, that they were undoubtedly the ancestors of some of them who had fallen in battle,

and had returned from the sea to visit them again; and one native appeared firmly to believe that his father was come back in the person of either Lee or Connoway, and took him to the spot where his body had been burnt. On being told that immense numbers of people existed far beyond their little knowledge, they instantly pronounced them to be the spirits of their countrymen, which, after death, had migrated into other regions.

Broughton had asserted that 'one or two of the men had married but left their wives and children with no regret'. He could have been mistaken on that count, for two years later, Tarwood and Lee—who could speak the language of the Port Stephens people, the Worimi—were among a group of convicts who seized one of the colony's best boats, the *Cumberland*, and set sail. A search party led by John Shortland was sent to Port Stephens to look for them, but while that party did make the highly fortuitous discovery of the mouth of the Hunter River, they failed to locate the runaways.

In 1800, a group of 15 convict mutineers took a boat north to the new Hunter River port. Nine were recaptured, but the remaining six joined an Aboriginal camp on the present-day Throsby Creek, living on food 'provided by the friendly natives' and eventually establishing their own pumpkin and maize farms. The number of Europeans in the camp grew with more escapees from passing boats, and eventually two returned to Sydney, but, apart from a soldier's fleeting glimpse of a man he believed to be a European 'attired in a jacket and trousers' among a group of Aboriginal people, nothing further was heard of any of them again by the colonists.

Meanwhile, in 1796, a group of convict fishermen had been shipwrecked, also in the Port Stephens area. The Aboriginal people who found them took it upon themselves to escort them most of the way back to Broken Bay. On their return, the convicts had startling news to report: their Aboriginal hosts had somehow conveyed to them that a white woman was living with Aboriginal people.

A party of volunteers was sent out to the northern reaches of Broken Bay to find the woman, presumed to be one of the convict escapees from the earliest landing of the First Fleet and, 'if possible, to bring her away unless she preferred the life she now led, upon which more than three years' experience of it would certainly enable her to decide'. Ten days of searching proved fruitless, however, and the woman, whoever she might have been, was never found.

This elusive white woman was an early exemplar of what would become something of a theme in this history. Titillating rumours of a strange white woman detained against her will would be followed by repeated search parties being sent out to find and rescue her. These often also entailed violent 'reprisals' against Aboriginal people encountered in their quest and, even more often, provided opportunities to explore and survey country as yet unknown to the colonists. The most well-known of these in Australian history concerns the mythical 'White Woman of Gippsland', believed to be a shipwreck survivor held captive in the Gippsland region of the Port Phillip District during the 1840s. Neither the woman herself, nor very much at all in the way of convincing evidence of her existence, was ever found, but the story exerted a continuing fascination, with multiple theories as to the identity of the supposed captive, or the source of the rumours, still being current today.

It seems a trying ordeal for a woman ... but in those days most of the females were hardened and indifferent to what fate had in store for them

In fact, among the Europeans who are known definitely to have lived with the locals, only a rare few were women. We may ask why that was: were white women less inclined to take their chances among Aboriginal people, or were Aboriginal people less inclined to take them in? In an unusual oral history account, a white woman who had been taken captive by Aboriginal people in retribution against her husband was held for about three weeks but was otherwise unharmed. The speaker (herself a white woman) explained that such an experience was not necessarily all that traumatic:

> It seems a trying ordeal for a woman to be forced to live three weeks with wild blacks, but in those days most of the females were hardened and indifferent to what fate had in store for them, that ... they were more like men and it was a common occurance for stockmen to exchange their wives with one another or sell them for a pound of tobacco or a keg of rum.

Nevertheless, in this case (which took place in the midst of frontier conflict in northern New South Wales), a massacre of Aboriginal people followed the woman's rescue. To harbour a white woman (whether captive or willing) was inviting attack once the colonial project of expansion was underway. At a time when Aboriginal girls and women were regularly kidnapped and traded by white men, potent sexual anxieties fuelled the colonial urge not only to find and rescue white women, but to wreak terrible revenge upon their captors. All this needs to be taken into account when we consider the experiences of those few known white women to have lived with Aboriginal people.

In the chapters to come, we have attempted to disentangle the mythologies and prejudices that surround the literary representations of the white men and women who lived with Aboriginal people to find out as much as we can about what their experiences were and how they themselves felt about their Aboriginal hosts, and, of course, what the Aboriginal people thought of them.

We have chosen to focus on those individuals about whom there is enough material, in both original and secondary sources, to glean an informative narrative account of the time they spent living with the locals. A full reference list of all sources used for each chapter is provided at the end of the book.

Where appropriate and for ease of reading, we have used the names and spellings used by contemporary writers for distinct Indigenous communities, but we caution readers that these designations may not have currency or credibility today (see Disclaimer at the front of this book). Likewise, some of the terminology used in original accounts and quoted here, as well as some of the claims made by particular writers, may be found offensive by our readers. We have worked hard to moderate and contextualise the information gleaned from the original accounts without losing the historical insight they provide into colonial mentalities, and apologise in advance for the shock that such accounts can still generate.

Our main focus and concern has been on trying to recapture what living with the locals was really like for these European individuals. The fact is that, in the main, they were treated with great kindness, compassion and care by their Indigenous hosts. And therein lies a great tragedy of the Australian historical experience. The wild white men and women were witness to the beauty and richness of Indigenous culture in this country that no other outsiders would ever see. For us, these men and women are our eyes into another world on the cusp of an incredible upheaval. We hope that we have done their stories justice.

I

John Wilson—'Bunboé'

A few years after the arrival of the First Fleet in 1788, the Sydney settlement began to expand as ex-marine soldier-settlers and emancipist convicts took allotments of land along the Hawkesbury River. The local Aboriginal people, whose traditional yam beds along the river were being taken over by the settlers for corn and potatoes, fiercely resisted the taking of their country and, by the mid-1790s, there was open warfare in the district. There is no doubt that, in spite of the intensity of the conflict, numbers of white men and youths were attracted to life with Aboriginal people and that the Aboriginal people were seemingly willing to accept them.

In February of 1795, ex-convict John Wilson met with an expeditionary party of officers along the Hawkesbury River and informed them of the 'ill and impolitic conduct' of the settlers towards the Aboriginal people, and that the Aboriginal people planned to take revenge against three settlers—Doyle, Forrester and Nixon—having already attacked and wounded two others whom they had mistaken for Doyle and Forrester.

John Wilson was already known to the officers of the First Fleet by then. A Lancastrian sailor who had managed to fall foul of the law in Wigan, a coal-mining town in Greater Manchester, England, Wilson had been sentenced to

The rich
Aboriginal estate.

seven years' transportation in October 1785. He had stolen ten pence worth of cloth, just short of a hanging offence, but enough to have him transported to New South Wales on the *Alexander,* one of the ships of the First Fleet.

Four years after his arrival, his sentence having been served, Wilson had unexpectedly gone to live with the Dharug people along the Hawkesbury. Judge-Advocate David Collins described Wilson as 'a wild idle young man' who 'preferred living among the natives ... to earning the wages of honest industry by working for settlers', and declared that it was only the Aborigines' 'mental inability' that allowed him to presume upon their hospitality.

It may be that the Aboriginal people wanted Wilson to act as their interpreter and intermediary with the white authorities. During the time Wilson had associated with the Aboriginal people, Collins reported, he had developed a kind of pidgin language and so came to understand:

> something of what they wished him to communicate; for they did not conceal the sense they entertained of the injuries which had been done to them.

DAVID COLLINS ESQ.

Perhaps Wilson intended his representations to the officers he had met on the Hawkesbury River to be a way of persuading the authorities to formally punish the renegade settlers to appease the Dharug. But despite Wilson's willingness to warn the British about the intended revenge attack, Collins' remarks at the time show that they viewed his apparent sympathy for the Dharug with suspicion and fear.

First Fleet officer and colonial chronicler David Collins in 1804.

The very fact that Wilson chose their company was enough to concern the British. Collins wrote:

> As the gratifying an idle wandering disposition was the sole object with Wilson in herding with these people, no good consequence was likely to ensue from it; and it was by no means improbable, that at some future time, if disgusted with the white people, he would join the blacks, and assist them in committing depredations, or make use of their assistance to punish or revenge his own injuries.

White convict and working-class men allying themselves with the Indigenous people and so jeopardising the success of British settlement was an unwelcome notion.

The officers directed Wilson to accompany Charles Grimes on his exploration of Port Stephens, to act as an intermediary between the expedition party and the Aboriginal people. It was there that Wilson possibly saved the life of Grimes, in a strange incident in which Wilson shot a man who threatened the expedition leader. The Aboriginal people had initially appeared to welcome the Grimes party, performing a dance 'joined hand in hand, round a tree, to express perhaps their unanimity', but then, as one individual drew Grimes aside and poised a spear at him, Wilson shot the man twice.

After returning to Sydney with the Grimes party in March 1795, Wilson went back to live with the Dharug, this time accompanied by ex-convict William Knight. Collins' assessment was that Knight must have been 'thinking there must be some sweets in the life which Wilson led' and was 'determined to share them with him'. It was with Knight that Wilson shook the Sydney folk in August that year by coming into town with a group of Hawkesbury Aboriginal people and trying to abduct two young white girls. The two white men were quickly captured and taken to the cells. The abduction attempt was followed immediately afterwards by two days of 'severe contests' between the Aboriginal people in the township, in which much blood was shed and many wounds inflicted. Nobody was actually killed, indicating some kind of ceremonial Law business. It was also possibly this event that enabled Wilson and Knight to escape and rejoin the Dharug.

It is difficult to interpret this incident. The officers apparently presumed that Wilson and Knight were being obliged by their Aboriginal hosts to pick out young wives for themselves from among their own race, on the bride-by-capture model. (The early colonists were convinced that this was traditional Aboriginal marriage custom, although some historians suggest they might have been, in fact, witnessing gender relations in disarray brought on by the impact of the patriarchal British themselves.) The situation could be more complex than that, considering the state of 'open war' that existed on the Hawkesbury by May 1795. The attempted abduction, which purportedly was carried out with the assistance of the Aboriginal people accompanying Wilson and Knight, could have been intended as a forthright declaration of revenge for the taking of Aboriginal girls by white settlers. Not only were there many Aboriginal girls and young women living in the Sydney settlement by then, but the abduction of Aboriginal children along the Hawkesbury was so widespread that, when soldiers were sent out there that year with orders to 'destroy the natives wherever they are met with', the direction was qualified with explicit instructions that those children 'domesticated' by the settlers were to be spared.

By February of the following year, 1796, the colonists were certain that Wilson and Knight had joined the Hawkesbury Aborigines who were attacking the settlers on the river, led by the legendary guerrilla warrior, Pemulwuy. It was supposed that the two white men were taking a lead role in directing the attacks, and the governor of the colony exhorted the settlers along the Hawkesbury to 'use every means in their power' to capture the two men if they could, 'that they might be so disposed of'. At the time, the settlers were given strict orders to no longer allow any Aboriginal people to visit or stay on their farms, the familiarity with 'the sweets of a different mode of living' being the reason, so Collins believed, for their aggression. The officers' worst fears had been realised in Wilson's and Knight's defection to the Aboriginal people, as they had, Collins reported, shown them how muskets were useless once discharged (it was a time-consuming and fiddly process reloading them) and had therefore 'removed that terror of our fire-arms with which it had been our constant endeavour to inspire them'.

Collins reported that Wilson was known among the Aboriginal people as 'Bun-bo-é', but that 'none of them had taken his [name] in exchange'. By 1795, the Aboriginal people on the coast around the Sydney settlement, led by Bennelong and Barangaroo, had been living among the white people there

Page 229. Vol. 1.

Portrait of Bennilong, a native of New Holland, who after experiencing for two years the Luxuries of England, returned to his own Country and resumed all his savage Habits.

The gentrified Bennelong on his
return to Australia from England.

for a few years, and the officers regarded the practice of name exchange to signify cordial relations between black and white, so the absence of any Dharug individual named 'Wilson' was a sign in the authorities' eyes that the Aboriginal people had not really accepted Wilson at all.

Collins also recorded that Wilson had been able to 'persuade' the Aboriginal people that 'he had once been a black man, and pointed out a very old woman as his mother, who was weak and credulous enough to acknowledge him as her son'. The 'natives who inhabit the woods are not by any means as acute as those who live upon the sea coast', Collins declared, and hence Wilson's ability to fool them. (Collins surmised that Wilson must have got the idea of this trickery

For a white man to freely choose the 'miserable' lifestyle of the Aboriginal people living in the bush was quite confronting

from the outlandish tales told by four escaped convicts from Port Stephens on their return to Sydney. This view did not make sense, since these escapees had returned after the officers' encounter with Wilson on the Hawkesbury.) Collins, a man who believed that white people's lifestyles to be of much greater comfort, asserted that the coastal people who frequented Sydney town despised and looked down upon the people of the interior:

> valuing themselves upon their friendship with the white people, and erecting in themselves an exclusive right to the enjoyment of all the benefits which were to result from that friendship.

For a white man to freely choose the 'miserable' lifestyle of the Aboriginal people living in the bush was quite confronting.

In May 1797, Governor Hunter issued an order that Wilson, along with three other white men, all apparently runaway convicts (John Jeweson, Joseph Saunders and Moses Williams), turn themselves in to the authorities within a fortnight to be given full legal protection, or otherwise:

> if taken, will be considered not only accessory to the death of those natives who may suffer in the unlawful plunder already mentioned, but as accomplices

with them in the mischiefs and crueltys so frequently committed by them, and be liable to be immediately executed without the form of a trial, having by their unlawful conduct forfeited the protection of those wholesome laws under which they have been born and bred.

Two of the men, but not Wilson, turned themselves in and were brought to trial the next month, but there was no proof or at least none for which they could be subjected to the penalty of death. Collins fumed that:

there was not any doubt of their having associated with and instructed the natives how to commit, with the least hazard to themselves, the various depredations which the settlers had sustained from them.

For reasons we will never know, Wilson 'surrendered himself to the governor's clemency' at the end of that year.

Wilson told the governor that he had travelled a hundred miles or more in all directions from the settlement and seen many strange birds and animals (including, famously, a 'pheasant'—a lyrebird), as well as 'a very expansive tract of open and well-watered country' to the north-west of the head of the Hawkesbury River. Governor Hunter decided that rather than attempt to imprison Wilson again, he would instead try to 'make him useful even in the mode of living with he seemed to prefer'. In January 1798, Wilson was appointed as one of two guides to an expedition party of four newly arrived Irish prisoners and an armed guard, sent out by the governor to, believe it or not, look for China.

This adventure followed on the heels of the audacious convict escape to Port Stephens, some 100 miles north of the Hawkesbury, in the governor's ship, the *Cumberland* (see page 6), and the foiling of another planned mass escape soon afterwards. Wilson's group included some recent arrivals, Irish rebels—'lawless and turbulent people', according to the governor, who had 'completely ruined' the English convicts and, as Hunter had learned from the thwarted escape attempt, had somehow acquired the idea that it was possible to travel overland from the colony to China, or to some other colony where they would not have to work. Wilson himself had spoken of once coming across more than 50 bleached skeletons in the bush, surrounded by European knives, shoes and other articles: he had been told by Aboriginal people that they were the remains of white men who had perished of hunger and thirst.

So Hunter decided he would send a group of four of the most discontented of the new prisoners to see and experience the reality of the country's geography, in the company of 'two men, long accustomed to the woods and intimate with many of the natives'—one of them being Wilson—so that when the convicts 'repented' of their attempt, they could be returned to 'tell their own story'. There was a slight delay to plans when the four convicts originally chosen to be a part of the expedition were discovered to have a plan:

> to kill their guides and go on alone. The conspirators were flogged and four more volunteers selected. As a precaution four soldiers were added to the party.

The journal Price kept is a rich source of early British observations of mysterious animals such as the wombat and the lyrebird

It would have been a rather risky enterprise considering that Wilson himself had already shown how a white man could live quite happily in the Australian wilds. But the governor correctly assessed Wilson's reliability in convincing the convicts that bush life would not be to their liking. After only seven days, the four convicts were complaining of their sore feet, the heat and the rugged terrain. They asked to return to the settlement, and were sent back with the armed guard to Parramatta.

Wilson, 19-year-old John Price (a personal servant of the governor and the expedition's scribe) and a man named Roe (possibly the second guide or a sentry) decided to press on to explore the country further inland. No doubt this exploration party was the real reason the governor ordered the expedition— had not Wilson indicated, in his description of the land to the north of the Hawkesbury River's head, that he knew a way through the formidable forested mountains to the west? The three men continued on to the junction of the Wollondilly and Wingecarribee rivers in the Southern Highlands region of New South Wales, some 160 kilometres south-west of Parramatta.

The journal Price kept is a rich source of early British observations of mysterious animals such as the wombat and the lyrebird, and of the rich country through which they travelled. Price noted their encounters with Aboriginal people, who seemed very cordial and eager to help them, presumably already acquainted to some extent with white people:

> We saw a great many kangaroos and emews, and we fell in with a party of natives which gave a very good account of the place we were in search of; that there was a great deal of corn and potatoes, and that the people were very friendly. We hearkened to their advice; we altered our course according to their directions. One of them promised he would take to us to a party of natives which had been there; but he not coming according to his promise, we proceeded on our journey as he had directed us.

The governor's annotation on Price's journal indicated that the place to which Price referred was a fabled colony of white people that 'some artful villain' had told the new Irish convicts about, 'where there was abundance of every sort of provision without the necessity of so much labour'. The origins of this story could conceivably be traced to the runaways living at Port Stephens, but the Aboriginal people's corroboration here can be questioned: perhaps Wilson (presumably the interlocutor) had falsified their response for his own purposes, or perhaps the Aboriginal people were being agreeable in the hope that they could move the party through their country quickly. In any case, they did not find the fabled colony by following the directions they had been given, but they did find an encrustation of salt at a cave at the junction of the Nepean and Bargo rivers—a find of significance for the early colony, which was dependent on imported salt to preserve meat.

In the course of their journey, as Price recorded, the small party came across another Aboriginal group who fled from them:

> Wilson run and caught one of them, a girl, thinking to learn something from them, but her language was so different from that one which we had with us that we could not understand her. We kept her all night, but she cried and fretted so much that the next morning we gave her a tomahawk and sent her to the rest of the natives, which were covered with large skins which reached down to their heels.

Following pages: A view of Parramatta in 1812, already resembling a British estate.

Collins recorded that the party had hoped the Aboriginal men might come to rescue the girl, providing an opportunity to ask them about the country, but that they did not appear. One wonders what the frightened young Aboriginal girl endured over that night in the bush.

Within another week, Price and Roe were ill but 'Wilson was well and hearty'. By offering to make a canoe to cross a river, shooting strange birds that Wilson said he had never seen the like of before, and providing them all with kangaroo dinners, Wilson struck the young Price as something of a superman:

> I thought that we must all have perished with hunger, which certainly would have been the case had it not been for the indefatigable zeal of Wilson to supply us with as much as would support life.

Exhausted, hobbling on bleeding feet (for their boots had simply fallen apart), the two men staggered back into the settlement at Prospect (30 kilometres north-west of Sydney) with Wilson.

In the wake of this journey, a return trip was hastily organised, with the specific purpose of finding more information about the salt hill. This expedition was led by Quartermaster Henry Hacking, accompanied by Wilson and another man, as well as a scribe who wrote the journal for the expedition, but did not record his identity—assumed by some to again be Hunter's servant, John Price. This expedition travelled for some three weeks south-west by south from Prospect for about 140 miles, the route closely following that of the present-day Hume Highway, and going inland as far as Mount Towrang where they looked out across the Goulburn Plains. 'They did not, however, meet a single native in all their journey,' wrote Collins, '(a proof that the human race was but thinly scattered over the interior part of this extensive country).'

This was quite a reassuring idea for the British colonial authorities, who were continuing to grapple with Aboriginal leader and resistance fighter Pemulwuy. There is an irony in how John Wilson, from being a threat to the colony, became an instrument of the colonial project, taking the British further inland than they had ventured before and encouraging them in their hopeful belief that expansion into these lands would be unhampered by Aboriginal resistance.

After his return from the second expedition, Wilson disappeared and returned to live with the Dharug. Yet, if they had ever accepted him as one of their own, as historian Grace Karskens writes, the Aboriginal people on the

A representation in bronze of Aboriginal resistance
leader Pemulwuy, by sculptor Masha Marjanovich.

Hawkesbury by now had shifted their understandings of the white people—no longer seeing them as returned relatives and subject to the rules and law of their culture, but as 'strangers, aliens outside the Law ... and invaders'.

her friends took an opportunity, when he was not in a condition to defend himself, to drive a spear through his body

It was the officer, Collins, who recorded in 1800 that the British heard Wilson was dead. With his customary aristocratic archness, Collins wrote that Wilson had attempted to take 'against her inclinations a female to his own exclusive accommodation', whereupon:

> her friends took an opportunity, when he was not in a condition to defend himself, to drive a spear through his body, which ended his career for this time, and left them to expect his return at some future period in the shape of another white man.

Historians since have accepted this story, which fits with the image of the renegade, the idle and macho white man (although Eric Willmot, who fictionalised the story of Pemulwuy based on his reading of the historical sources, has his Wilson killed by whites in an attack on an Aboriginal camp). If the way Wilson died is true, we might imagine that on his return to the Dharug, Wilson had become either so degraded or so arrogant that he did not recognise or care about offending the people with whom he lived. In turn, they saw no need to punish him in ritual combat, but simply despatched him in the act—a form of summary justice. But we should also take Collins' gleeful reporting of the circumstances of his death with a little of that salt Wilson had discovered.

Opposite: An Aboriginal family on the move;
Aboriginal groups travelled light and moved with speed.

Wilson's Aboriginal Life

Almost nothing about Wilson's experiences of Dharug life and culture is known. Unlike accounts of later 'wild white men', Wilson's story was never put into print, and so we are largely limited to the views of David Collins. Collins was not only hostile to Wilson, but showed little interest in the Dharug people (who were then known to the colonists as the 'wood natives'). While Collins recorded observations of Aboriginal culture around the Sydney settlement, he knew much less about the Hawkesbury people inland, offering only random snippets about them, such as their 'invariable rule never to whistle under a rock'.

From Collins' description of Wilson before Governor Hunter at the time of his surrender at the end of 1797, it appears that he had been incorporated into the Aboriginal community to some extent. Collins noted that Wilson wore only an apron of kangaroo skin, 'which he had sufficient sense of decency remaining to think proper', and that his shoulders and chest bore scarifications in the Aboriginal manner, 'which he described to have been very painful in the operation'.

William Buckley— 'Murrangurk'

William Buckley, the original 'Wild White Man', is one of the most famous of all those Europeans who lived with Aboriginal people. His is a household name for many Australians. The story of the convict escapee who lived for 32 years with the Wathawurrung people of the south-eastern Victorian coast, famously unaware that he had been altogether forgotten and abandoned by his fellow colonists, functions as a kind of parable of Australian colonialism—our own Robinson Crusoe, an oversized, hairy Gulliver of the Antipodes. His story also represents a distinctively Australian taste for the ironic. Buckley stands most powerfully for a colonial enterprise marked by loss, failure, inadequacy; and the way in which the colloquial phrase 'Buckley's chance' (meaning no chance, against preposterous odds) has become indelibly, if wrongly, linked to his survival story only reinforces the point.

There are several early accounts of Buckley's story, written from interviews with the man himself. The main account was published in 1852 by Hobart-based John Morgan, 'journalist-pamphleteer', who wrote that Buckley had asked him to publish his story, at a time when both men were in very difficult financial circumstances. C.E. Sayers, in his introduction to Morgan's account, republished in 1963, believed that Morgan had 'lavishly embellished' the illiterate Buckley's

William Buckley—
'Murrangurk'—with his
weapons and cloak.

27

story. What is more important to consider than just what Buckley recounted (or is claimed to have recounted) is what he may have chosen not to reveal.

The consensus of numerous white people who met Buckley after his return was that he was a particularly ignorant and stupid man, and painfully reserved. Their attitude seems to have arisen largely out of frustration that Buckley would not talk about the Aboriginal people or his life with them. Nineteenth-century Tasmanian historian James Bonwick concluded that Buckley must have retained no knowledge of his time with the Aboriginal people. What these observers may have failed to comprehend was that Buckley was determined to withhold the knowledge he had, perhaps to protect his Aboriginal family and community, perhaps out of respect for their taboos.

Buckley was an individual who genuinely respected and adhered to the culture and religion of the people who had taken him in

We can be sure that there was much more to Buckley than the eye could see and, considering that he had acquired an education, completed an apprenticeship and also served valiantly in the military, as well as successfully gaining acceptance and living within a completely different culture for 30 years, the claims he was of low intelligence are rather unlikely. It is not inconceivable that Buckley was an individual who genuinely respected and adhered to the culture and religion of the people who had taken him in.

Born around 1780 into a farming family in Cheshire, England, Buckley joined the army as a young man. In 1802, he was tried and found guilty of possession of stolen goods by the military authorities, though Buckley protested his innocence.

Buckley was transported on the *Calcutta* and arrived in October 1803 at Port Phillip, the planned new British penal settlement on the south-eastern coast of what was then known as New South Wales. After eight months, the British decided the region was 'unpromising and unproductive' and withdrew to Van Diemen's Land to help establish the new settlement of Hobart there instead. By that time, Buckley was long gone.

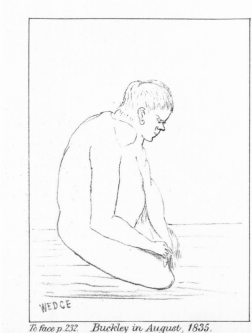 

To face p.232. *Buckley in August, 1835.*   *Buckley on Indented Heads.*

Sketches of Buckley by surveyor John Wedge, who saw him the day
after he presented himself to John Batman's party. Wedge recognised
Buckley as an escaped convict, but argued for his pardon.

About three months after his arrival at Port Phillip, Buckley had made his escape from the convict settlement one night, in the company of three other men (one of whom was shot in the process). Their idea was to head north to Sydney, maybe in the hope that they could somehow get back to England from there. They crossed the Yarra River, made the Yawong Hills and eventually reached the bay. They continued along the sea front for several days, but hunger and exhaustion were sapping them. Far across the bay, the dispirited men could see the anchored *Calcutta*. They built a fire and tied their shirts to trees to draw attention to themselves in the hope of rescue, but without success. After six days, Buckley's two companions decided to retrace their steps around the bay back to the settlement, leaving Buckley behind.

Buckley set off walking along the coastline, living on shellfish and berries. Eventually, he came across a large rock with a high overhanging bluff that kept the place in shade. He decided to stay here, a place he later discovered was known as Nooraki. He built himself a comfortable shelter from branches and seaweed, and settled in.

One day, Buckley was startled to hear voices. Above him on the bluff, looking down, were three Aboriginal men 'armed with spears, and [with] opossum skins thrown over their shoulders'. He summoned up his courage and came out to meet what he assumed would be a quick death. The Aboriginal men were immediately struck by Buckley's size and were obviously taken with him. They grabbed 'both my hands, they struck their breasts, and mine also, making at the same time a noise between singing and crying'. After a feast of crayfish, the Aboriginal men wanted Buckley to follow them. Still deeply wary but fearful they would harm him if he refused, he reluctantly agreed.

It was nearly dark when they reached the men's small camp of two little huts. The next morning, Buckley's new companions indicated that they were to set off again but, feeling somewhat bolder, or more desperate, he adamantly refused. After some discussion, they consented and left, one of the men returning unexpectedly shortly afterwards to give the nervous Buckley a 'basket' (probably a woven bark container) of berries before heading off again.

Eventually, some days after leaving the hut, Buckley came across a large lake and, following the river that flowed from the lake back to the sea, he managed to find his old seaside haven at Nooraki. Buckley remained alone there for the next three months.

As the winter began to set in, Buckley decided he had had enough of his solitary life. He decided to follow the bay around and try and attract attention of a ship, not knowing that the British had left by then. Buckley walked for days, becoming weaker and weaker through lack of food and water. Beside a stream, he came across a large earthen mound with an upright spear protruding from the centre. He removed the spear to use it as a walking stick and continued on to a large lagoon, where he collapsed in the sight of two Aboriginal women. The women immediately went off to get some assistance. When they returned with some men, the men rushed up to him, and, in the same manner as the first three men he had met had done, seized him by the arms and hands and 'began beating their breast, and mine'.

There is an interesting account of Buckley's discovery from a woman reported to have been Buckley's Aboriginal wife, whose story was recorded at Framlingham mission station in the late nineteenth century by the superintendent. Purranmurnin Tallarwurnin recounted that an Aboriginal man had found Buckley's gigantic tracks and, believing him to be a stranger and an enemy, had followed them to find 'a strange-looking being lying down on a small hillock, sunning himself after a bath in the sea'. The Aboriginal man left and later returned with a group of men who warily approached him. But Buckley took no notice of them at all and, for a while, did not even move:

> They were very much alarmed. At length one of the party, finding courage, addressed him as muurnong guurk (meaning ... one who had been killed and come to life again), and asked his name, 'You Kondak Baarwon?' Buckley replied by a prolonged grunt and an inclination of the head, signifying yes ... They made a wuurn of leafy branches for him, and lit a fire in front of it, around which they all assembled. He was then recognised as one of the tribe.

the people he had encountered believed him to be the returning, reborn spirit of this warrior

Buckley had inadvertently made a strong bond between himself and this Aboriginal group. The spear he had taken had come from the grave mound of a man who had been killed in a fight with a rival group. As Buckley would quickly come to understand, the people he had encountered believed him to be the returning, reborn spirit of this warrior. They mixed up a pulpy concoction of water and gums and fed it to him from a wooden bowl, then brought him some 'large fat grubs', which he found 'delicious'. As he gratefully ate, Buckley noticed that they were calling him 'Murrangurk'.

On waking in the morning, Buckley was frightened by the sight of the women covered in blood from their face, scalp and legs: they had been wailing all night and 'lacerating their faces in a dreadful manner'. At this time, Buckley was totally unacquainted with the Aboriginal processes of grieving and, in this case, of dealing with the return of someone from death.

After travelling some miles and crossing the Barwon River, his rescuers took him to their main camp, where evidently over a hundred men greeted them.

People surrounded Buckley:

> beating their breasts and heads with their clubs, the women tearing off
> their own hair by the handfuls. I was much alarmed, but they made me to
> understand these were the customs they followed.

Buckley would come to learn that 'as they believed me to have been dead, they were lamenting the sufferings I must have undergone when I was killed, and perhaps, until my reappearance again on this earth'.

Buckley settled into his new surroundings. One day, one of the men arrived at the camp with a young man who invited them all to visit his encampment. The next day, at the site of their hosts, it became apparent that Buckley was being placed back into the care of his own family—the late Murrangurk's brother, wife and son—and a great corroboree took place, with Buckley being treated to a roasted possum dinner (his first red meat meal since parting with his convict companions) and given a possum skin rug. And so Buckley embarked fully on his new life.

Buckley's early attachment to his adoptive family is reflected in his account of the death of his brother-in-law—Murrangurk's brother—that would set the path for his life among the Aboriginal people. One of the men had been bitten by a snake, and died instantly. A highly ranked individual, the man was given the honour of a platform burial high in the treetops. Immediately after this event, Buckley's group were set upon by a much larger group who sent a spear right through Buckley's brother-in-law. It transpired that their attackers were avenging the man who had died (a relative of theirs), his death being blamed on Buckley's brother-in-law, who was killed for the crime, with other members of his family also being killed. Buckley recalled that:

> for several hours my tears flowed in torrents, and, that for a long time I wept
> unceasingly. To them, as I have said before, I was as a living dead brother,
> whose presence and safety was their sole anxiety. Nothing could exceed the
> kindness these poor natives had shown me, and now they were dead.

Despite his brother-in-law's killer's insistence that Buckley should now join the killer's family, Buckley refused to surrender his brother-in-law's spears and took flight from the scene as soon as he could. He ran into another friendly group who were greatly alarmed at the news of Buckley's friend's death and immediately set off to take revenge, resulting in the killing of three members of the other group and the subsequent cremation of his brother-in-law and family at the scene. Buckley returned to the site and paid his respects:

> finding the ashes and bones of my late friends, I scraped them up together, and covered them over with turf, burying them in the best manner I could, that being the only return I could make for their many kindnesses.

For the next several months, 'sick at heart', Buckley reverted to his former existence as a loner. Now a proficient hunter and gatherer, he built himself a more substantial dwelling on a good location on the Karaaf River where edible roots grew in abundance, and set up a weir to trap the multitudes of bream in the river. After several months on his own, Buckley was overjoyed to hear familiar voices cry out, 'it is me'. He came out to meet two men, two women and several children from his old, original family, who were overjoyed to see him again. The men were especially impressed with his fish trap; they 'could not contain themselves for joy, patting me on the back, and saying I deserved three or four wives for my invention'.

After some time, in another intertribal altercation, the killing of a young man upset Buckley and he took himself off again. Some months later, however, his family rejoined him and decided that it was time that he was married.

Of marriage, Buckley recorded that 'I was not in any way consulted, being considered a sort of instrument in their hands to do with as they might think proper'. His chosen wife was a young widow, aged about 20. Buckley described her as 'tolerably good looking, after a fashion, and apparently very mild tempered'. With some humour, he noted that the cost of the wedding, including the ring, feast, wedding dress and his own dress-suit did not cost much! The marriage turned out to be short-lived. Only months after taking up together, several men entered Buckley's hut and removed his wife, although she went willingly. The following morning, Buckley went to argue his case with the intruders but 'did not make a very great fuss about my loss—if there was one—but endeavoured to whistle it down the wind gaily'. Some in his group wanted him to take 'the usual revenge', but Buckley refused, 'and in the end, she was speared by another man, with whom she had been coqueting, and to whom she had also played falsely'.

Following pages: Aboriginal and white men on a kangaroo hunt together:
'They place themselves at particular spots and distances, so as to drive them into
corners like flocks of sheep, and then they spear them without difficulty'.

One day, Buckley was unexpectedly joined by a young woman who had run away from her clan. This unnamed 'amiable young lady friend' would remain his companion for some considerable time. His friend was possibly the woman, Purranmurnin Tallarwurnin—a Buninyong woman. She said that, whenever ships appeared on the coast, Buckley 'never sought to make himself known to any of them', though he helped the Aboriginal people by demonstrating the use of items that washed up after the occasional shipwreck.

Buckley was now completely contented with his life. He expressed his pride in his ability to hunt, fish and provide ample food for them both. He recalled killing a *Koorman* (seal) and that they both:

> found the flesh very good eating, and my female friend enjoyed the repast with great gusto: greasing herself all over with the fat, after we had made the most of the carcass, which might well be compared to bacon.

Buckley looked back on this period thoughtfully in the account Morgan published:

> I had led a different sort of existence, and how easy it is for the human being, as well as every other, to change his habits, taste, and I may add, feelings ... I look back now to that period of my life with inexpressible astonishment; considering it, as it were, altogether a dreaming delusion, and not reality. Perhaps there is no one living who can cast his mind back to so many years of his past life with such a multiplicity of extraordinary sensations, as have fallen to my lot to experience.

Eventually, this idyllic time came to an end. Buckley's companion was visited by her own group and she was persuaded to leave with them. Buckley, lonelier than ever, turned his thoughts to returning to white society, and he was stirred when he encountered a group of Aboriginal men who were carrying a flag. They told Buckley that there was a ship at anchor in the bay and that when all of the white men on it had gone ashore in long boats, they had swum out to the ship, scaled the side, and took the flag along with other items they thought might be 'serviceable' (such as rope, and glass bottles to sharpen their spears with). The crew on returning had fired a number of shots into the bush and shoreline, and then moved further out into the bay.

In Morgan's account, Buckley stated that the Aboriginal men wanted him to return with them to act as a decoy to entice the men from the ship back to the shore 'so as to get them into our power, with the vessel, boats, and cargo also', but that he had persuaded them against this, arguing that if they returned the crew would fire upon them and they would all be killed. Instead, a few days later, Buckley went to have a look for himself. Finding the ship at anchor, he built a fire hoping to attract the crew but his efforts were 'useless'—Buckley supposed that the crew suspected he was trying to decoy them and he could not call out to them 'having lost all my English language'. When a group of men from the ship set out in a longboat towards a small island just off the beach, Buckley tried to run up the beach to get closer to them, but they 'shoved off' before he could get there 'only laughing at my violent gesticulations and unintelligible cries; little thinking who I was, or that I was any other than I appeared to be in my native dress':

> Forgetting this all, I reproached them to myself very bitterly, thinking them worse than savages, thus to leave me in my misery. Instead of their having been guilty of inhumanity, I should have remembered the possibility and probability of their firing upon me—and particularly after the act of robbery before mentioned.

A few months after the first incident, Buckley discovered a large battered boat on the shore, in all appearances one having belonged to a whaler. There were oars, blankets, ropes and mast. He learned that at least two men had initially survived the beaching of the boat, but had been killed by another Aboriginal group. On another occasion, Buckley came across a large cask or barrel filled with some kind of alcoholic beverage. He broke up the cask for the iron hoops and dispersed them among the local people.

But Buckley's time with the Aboriginal people was coming to an end. He was out gathering vegetable roots with some others when they spotted two young Aboriginal men approaching with coloured handkerchiefs attached to their spears. Buckley stated that it was 'evident they had met with civilised people; and on coming up, it was explained that they had met three white, and six black men, they had never seen before'. According to Buckley, the two men explained that they planned to gather a large group to attack and murder the newcomers to secure their provisions. On hearing of this plan, Buckley immediately set off to warn the newcomers that they were in danger. The new arrivals belonged to John Batman's party, which was looking for a site for a new settlement: the group consisted of a number of Aboriginal guides and some white men, but Batman himself had gone, leaving the men to set up a camp under the charge of a man called Gunn. It may have been in Buckley's interest to construct such a story so as to enhance his own position and to be looked upon favourably for any past misdemeanour. At the time, his concern that, on revealing himself to the white men, he could well be punished for his escape all those years before, was weighing heavily upon him. James Bonwick, the colonial historian, concluded that Buckley probably made up the story of a planned attack.

On reaching the campsite, Buckley initially sat back and took in the camp, but allowed himself to be spotted by the Aboriginal men in the group. In *The Illustrated Australian News* of 1869, Buckley is described as then boldly walking into the camp, seating himself down and placing his spears and hunting weapons between his legs:

> On being observed he caused great surprise and no small alarm. His gigantic stature already referred to (his height being nearly six feet six inches), enveloped in a kangaroo skin rug; his long beard and hair of thirty three years' growth; his spears and club, all tended to create the mixture of astonishment and apprehension with which he was regarded.

The white men in the camp were completely bewildered by the sight of him. They tried to make sense of his extraordinary height and background. He was obviously white but deeply tanned. At first Buckley could not speak a word of his former language when they asked him questions. He was then offered a piece of bread, and was able to repeat what it was called, whereupon he was given clothing, tea, biscuits and meat.

The next day Buckley showed the men a tattoo with his initials on his arm:

> they saw the imprinted letters W. and B. They were marks common enough among sailors, and not uncommon then with soldiers … Suddenly his own name came back again. He plunged forth 'W—William; B—Buckley'.

The group initially assumed he was some long lost shipwrecked sailor and afforded him every kindness. As Buckley's understanding of the language returned, he soon came to realise that these white men were intending to stay in the country, and were under the belief that they had made a contract:

Above: An artistic rendition of John Batman's famous
treaty—the Aboriginal men and women of the area would
have had no idea of the meaning of the transaction.

Following pages: Waiting for the appropriate moment,
William Buckley introduces himself to Batman's party.

with several of the native chiefs, with whom—as they said—they had exchanged all sorts of things for land; but that as I knew could not have been, because, unlike other savage communities, or people, they have no chiefs claiming or possessing any superior right over soil.

Buckley for his part was already anticipating and comprehending what the future would bring:

> if any transactions had taken place, it must have been because the natives knew nothing of the value of the country, except as hunting grounds, supplying them with the means of present existence. I therefore looked upon the land dealing spoken of, as another hoax of the white man, to possess the inheritance of the uncivilised natives of the forest, whose tread on the vast Australian continent will very soon be no more heard.

Shortly after, John Batman returned by ship and was most surprised at the appearance of Buckley. Batman asked many questions and undoubtedly formed his own opinion on the benefit of having someone like Buckley as a go-between with the local Aboriginal people. Buckley advised Batman on materials he could provide the local people, 'and these were distributed at a great Corrobberree we had that night'.

if any transactions had taken place, it must have been because the natives knew nothing of the value of the country, except as hunting grounds

Buckley would now be observer to the immediate imprint of a permanent settlement being established. He was promised Batman's support in gaining a free pardon from Governor Arthur for his ongoing assistance in the development of a colony, particularly as an interpreter. He was asked by a member of Batman's party, John Wedge, to join him on an exploration of the interior. Buckley later reminisced that he guided Wedge through some familiar country over the next two days, with Wedge being 'surprised and delighted with the magnificence of its pastoral and agricultural resources'. On their return to the main camp, Buckley was overjoyed that correspondence had arrived by ship to inform him that he had been granted a full pardon.

Batman's encampment moved shortly after and re-established its base of operations on the banks of the Yarra River (and would, of course, in time become the city of Melbourne). Buckley was subsequently employed by explorer Joseph Gellibrand as 'Interpreter, at a salary of fifty pounds a year, with rations'. He was able to guide Gellibrand's group through the country, reconnecting to Aboriginal people he knew so well. Gellibrand later recounted in the *Port Phillip Journal*:

> We started very early in the morning under the expectations that we should see the natives; and, in order that they should not be frightened, I directed Buckley to advance and we would follow at a distance of a quarter of a mile. Buckley made towards a native well and after he had ridden about eight miles, we heard a coo-ey, and when we arrived at the spot I witnessed one of the most pleasing and affecting sights. There were three men, five women, and about a dozen children. Buckley had dismounted and they were all clinging around him, and tears of joy and delight running down their cheeks. It was truly an affecting sight, and proved the affection which these people entertained for Buckley ... Among the numbers was a little old man and an old woman, one of his wives. Buckley told me that this was his old friend with whom he had lived and associated for over thirty years.

Buckley was able to take a prominent role in later distributing food and articles to the local people. He also took up the case of wrongs being done to Aboriginal people, including an Aboriginal woman who had been captured and tied up by a shepherd. The woman broke free during the night and had made her way to Buckley for protection. Buckley complained to Gellibrand and the perpetrator was reprimanded and dismissed from the company's service, and ordered back to Van Dieman's Land. Gellibrand for his part commented very favourably on the Aboriginal women, writing that the 'women and especially the young ones, are modest in their behaviour—they all appear to be well disposed'. But Buckley was beginning to be an unpopular employee, seen 'as having too great an influence over the natives'. He resigned but remained with Batman until the arrival in 1836 of a new commandant, Captain William Lonsdale of the King's Own Regiment of Foot (Buckley's 'old corps'), who took him into his service as an interpreter and attendant.

Working for Lonsdale, Buckley was able to arrange the employment of some Aboriginal people within the settlement, carrying loads of goods for which they were paid in food. However, relationships were quickly becoming very strained. The new commandant's soldiers had an unnerving impact on the Aboriginal people, who were 'very much alarmed' at the sight of the red coats, 'associating the colour with something very dreadful'. Indeed, within the surrounds of the settlement, there was an escalation of violence and reprisal between white and Aboriginal people. Two stockkeepers had been killed in response to 'their attempting to ill-use some native women'. In retaliation, some white men took it upon themselves to seek revenge on any Aboriginal people in the vicinity: 'a native was seized, and although merely suspected, he was tied to a tree and shot; the body being thrown into the Barwin River'.

Buckley was part of the party sent to apprehend the guilty white man for this crime, but, while committed and sent to trial (in Sydney), the man was acquitted, as no person could prove the identity of the deceased. Buckley was also involved in arranging for over 100 Aboriginal people to be present at the parade for Governor Bourke's visit, and he accompanied the governor on an excursion of the interior where they met with numerous groups of Aboriginal people. All of these people were assured:

> by the Governor, that if they came to the settlement, and avoided committing any offences against the white people, they should receive presents of all kinds of useful articles.

Sometime later, Gellibrand and George Hesse from Hobart had disappeared in the interior. Buckley was encouraged to join a group attempting to find them, but he suggested that it was a far safer proposition for him to go off alone in search of the missing party. Buckley's offer was ignored and the group set off, after engaging 'several blacks to go with them, who strange to say, they furnished with fire arms'. Meanwhile, Buckley gained permission to set off on his own, but there was an attempt to keep him at bay. While his horse had been tethered, someone had severed 'all the hind sinews of his legs' and Buckley had to go back to Geelong to procure another horse before again setting forth. He was alarmed to discover at a Mr Reibey's station that news had been received that the heavily

Opposite: An older Buckley,
under the title of 'The Wild White Man'.

NEWS LETTER OF AUSTRALASIA;

OR

NARRATIVE OF EVENTS: A LETTER TO SEND TO FRIENDS.

WILLIAM BUCKLEY,

THE WILD WHITE MAN.

WILLIAM BUCKLEY, whose extraordinary adventures have inseparably connected him with the history of this Colony, was the first Englishman who acquired an intimacy with the natives of Port Phillip, among whom he became a denizen. He was born at Macclesfield, in Cheshire, in the year 1780. His father was a small farmer. After having received a slight education from his grandfather, he was apprenticed to a bricklayer. Discontented and rambling in his disposition, he conceived a desire for military life, and presently enlisted in the Cheshire militia, from which he subsequently volunteered into the 4th regiment of foot. After his return from a campaign in Holland, he fell into dissipation and disorder, and becoming amenable to the law, was sentenced to transportation. He was at first employed on the fortifications at Woolwich, but as the plan was projected of forming a penal settlement at Port Phillip, then only known by name, he was drafted out with 366 other convicts, and shipped in the *Calcutta*, which arrived at Port Phillip Heads on the 9th October, 1803. Being a mechanic, he was set to work at the building of a magazine; but forming with some companions the wild project of escaping, and finding the way to Sydney, he and three others contrived to break bounds. One of the four was shot, and retaken; the other three travelled, without provisions or arms, save some that they had stolen, and their pannikins, completely round the Bay, until they saw the ship lying on the opposite side of the Heads. Their courage here failed them, and they anxiously made signs for a boat to reconvey them to the settlement; but being disappointed, the other two decided on retracing their steps, Buckley determining to remain and shift for himself rather than return to captivity. In the course of his wanderings he underwent extreme suffering, having no superfluous clothing, and no implement by which to construct a habitation, or to procure and prepare food. He was at one time reduced to the eating of raw shell fish, which he gathered on the beach. He met with a party of natives by whom he was kindly treated, being declared, according to one of their superstitions, as a returned deceased relative. He was accordingly at once received into a family, and remained with his new friends for a long time, occasionally leaving them in disgust of their frequent and sanguinary conflicts, but always returning. He was allotted a lubra, and formed *liaisons* with two or three others. In the course of his residence with the aborigines, he became conversant with their dialects and customs, to the entire oblivion of the language and usages of his former life. On one occasion when he abandoned his tribe, after a disastrous war, he settled alone on the banks of the Saltwater River, and subsisted on bream, which he caught by means of a weir, and cured by drying in the sun: a device that gained him great reputation among his black friends when they found out his solitary dwelling, and became his guests. When Batman and his party arrived in 1835, Buckley helped to deter the natives from robbing the ship, and endeavoured to introduce himself to the new comers, but then found that he had lost all knowledge of the English language, and could only shew that he was a European by the letters W B branded on his arms. Presently, however, he re-acquired the language in the same way as he had at first learned the aboriginal tongues, and was engaged by Batman, as interpreter, at a salary of fifty pounds a year. This was after Batman's pretended purchase of land from the natives, a proceeding which Buckley characterised in his narrative as a hoax; justly remarking, that not only would the natives have no conception of what was intended, but they had no recognised chiefs whose acts in such a matter would be acknowledged by the people. Mr. Wedge, one of Batman's party, interceded for him with the Governor of Van Diemen's Land, and succeeded in procuring a pardon, in consideration of his services. This was thirty-two years after his escape from the penal settlement at Point Nepean. He afterwards engaged with Mr. Gellibrand; and when Captain Lonsdale was sent over from Launceston as resident magistrate, became interpreter to the Government, at a salary of sixty pounds a year. He obtained leave to visit Tasmania, as constable in charge of an absconder, being dissatisfied with his position, and left in the *Yarra Yarra*, on the 28th December, 1837, never to return. He alleged that the settlers were constantly thwarting him in his plans of conciliation, by committing outrages upon the natives, and by interfering with his negotiations; and says that his position became dangerous, owing to his being distrusted by both parties. He asked the Governor of Tasmania for a grant of land, but as this request could not be granted, he was made assistant storekeeper, and afterwards gate-keeper, at the Female Nursery. On the abolition of the latter office, in 1850, he was discharged with a pension of twelve pounds a year, with a bonus of forty pounds from the Victorian Government. He married in 1840, and had one daughter. He died on the 2nd February, 1856.

Buckley was an ungainly figure, about six feet five inches in height. His mind appears to have been little more than a blank, and his actions to have been little more than those of a mere animal. During his residence with the natives he sank to their level, without a solitary effort to advance their condition, or to alleviate his own. And on the arrival of the new colonists he was to them nothing but a savage. Of course due allowance must be made for the privations he underwent; for the want of all intercourse with white people for thirty-two years; and for the debasing influence of association with savages. That even his own narrative, as edited by Mr. Morgan, interesting and *vraisemblable* as it is, and favourable to himself, gives not a single evidence of any attempt to enlighten his black companions, or to do any thing else than live from day to day as a mere animal. All the records of the time describe him as an ungainly barbarian, devoid of intelligence, and feared as a savage rather than trusted as an interpreter. The portrait given above is drawn after that taken during his life for the illustration of Mr. Morgan's memoir, with modifications, by Dr. Ludwig Becker, who had frequent opportunities of observing Buckley in his lifetime, while residing in Tasmania. To Mr. Morgan's memoir we are in great part indebted for the facts contained in the present sketch.

GEORGE SLATER, PUBLISHER, 94 BOURKE STREET EAST, MELBOURNE.

COUNTRY AGENTS:—Ballarat, Humffray, Brown, Huxtable; Beechworth, Ingram; Castlemaine, Vale, Sandifer; Dunolly, Divers & Co.; Geelong, Franks and Jackson, Brown; Maryborough, Divers & Co., Spooner; Sandhurst, Sparkes Warrnambool Atkinson. Additional Agents wanted.

Walker, May & Co., Printers.

armed search party had shot a 'native and his daughter'. For Buckley this was 'inexcusable murder':

> for there was not the least reason to believe that the poor people who had been so mercilessly sacrificed, had had anything to do with the death of either Mr. Gellibrand or Mr. Hesse, neither was it known at that time whether they were dead or alive. This affair gave me great pain, because, from my long association with the natives, I thought such destruction of life anything but creditable to my countrymen; but on the contrary, that they were atrocious acts of oppression.

The mystery of the disappearance of Gellibrand and Hesse has never been resolved, but Buckley admitted he had lost a good and loyal friend in Gellibrand. From this time, Buckley was to find that people were dismissing his authority and knowledge of the local Aboriginal population. There were people in the colony that wanted Buckley out of the way. Buckley for his part did not hide his disgust. Historian James Bonwick reported that co-founder of Melbourne John Pascoe Fawkner had written to a newspaper, stating that Buckley:

> soon displayed a spirit of antagonism to the whites, and, in fact, stated one day, when hard pressed, that he should rejoice if the whites could be driven away, he did not care how, so that the aborigines could have the country to themselves again.

Buckley decided it was best to leave the colony, 'where my services were so little known, and so badly appreciated by the principal authorities'. But the relocation may not in fact have been a choice for Buckley. According to an article published in 1869, Buckley was 'supposed to sympathise with the blacks more than the settlers liked, especially in regard to some cases of outrage perpetrated by white men against the native women', and was therefore 'removed from Victoria and sent to Hobart Town, where he got a pension of twelve pounds from the Tasmanian Government'.

Once he was gone, there was nobody to speak up on behalf of the local Aboriginal population. His departure in December 1837 marked the end of Buckley's connection with the Aboriginal people with whom he had shared so many experiences. He lived out the remainder of his days in Van Diemen's Land, marrying an Irish widow (whose husband, ironically, had been speared and killed near the Murray River, on an overland journey to Sydney) in 1840, and working as a storekeeper at the Immigrants' Home and later as the gatekeeper at the Female Nursery.

William Buckley died in 1856, at the age of 76. In the final assessment, Buckley was bound by the strict codes of Aboriginal cultural knowledge and behaviour within which he had been accepted, and honourably carried all of the valuable cultural knowledge to his grave.

An Aboriginal man scales a tree in pursuit of possums.

Buckley's Aboriginal Life

Buckley explained to Morgan how the people who befriended him—described variously and confusingly in his early accounts as the Wallawarro, Woddowro or Watowrong/Watourong—'did not seem to think it at all surprising' that he was unable to converse with them at first:

> my having been made white after death, in their opinion, having made me foolish; however, they took considerable pains to teach me their language, and expressed great delight when I got hold of a sentence, or even a word, so as to pronounce it somewhat correctly; they then would chuckle, and laugh, and give me great praise.

As he came to learn the language, he discovered that one of the men he had escaped with had also been found by Aboriginal people, and treated kindly likewise, but after some time, it was said, the man had been killed, for 'having made too free with their women'. Buckley, in contrast, evidently entered very deeply into Aboriginal life and was accepted to the extent of even being provided with a wife. In Morgan's account, he frequently expressed his deep sense of gratitude to those who had taken him in, and wrote warmly and sympathetically of their lives and customs.

RETRIBUTIVE JUSTICE

Of the diverse aspects of Aboriginal life and culture that Buckley purportedly described in his accounts, it was the details of violent intertribal interactions that have persistently interested readers most, with some historians regarding these as evidence of the violence of traditional Aboriginal culture. Closer examination of his recorded accounts reveals that this was not the chaotic violence of warfare but rather a highly ritualised form of conflict resolution under a shared Law— one might see this as the application of the death penalty, with all and any deaths occurring outside of the Law being considered the work of sorcery requiring retribution. As Buckley explained, the Aboriginal people he knew 'have an odd idea of death, for they do not suppose that any one dies from natural causes, but from human agencies'.

The complexity of such retributive, ritualised justice can be seen in a close reading of some of the earliest conflicts Buckley described that occurred around the time of his entry into Aboriginal society. After being welcomed back by his brother and family, a great fight broke out between 'two tribes'. Buckley saw a woman of the people who had brought him back to his brother killed, and then ceremonially burnt, before they all departed, leaving Buckley with his new relations.

Seven or eight men of the opposing group rose and hurled spears but Buckley's champion 'with great dexterity ... warded them off'

In another incident, Buckley described a drawn-out conflict involving his own group and another group he described as the Waarengbadawa. The Waarengbadawa had arrived unexpectedly with some 300 men, covered with red and white ochre, and initiated a challenge. While the women and children ran and hid (taking Buckley with them), the men smeared themselves with clay. Initially, one man from Buckley's group ventured forward singing and dancing. Seven or eight men of the opposing group rose and hurled spears, but Buckley's champion 'with great dexterity ... warded them off, or broke them every one, so that he did not receive a single wound'. A Waarengbadawa individual then rose and threw a boomerang within a mere three yards of Buckley's champion, who 'avoided the blow by falling on his hands and knees'. A shout went up from the enemy gathering, at which both men embraced and then 'beat their own heads until the blood ran down in streams over their shoulders'.

Buckley stated that this was just a prelude to the main drama, which commenced with a shower of spears and boomerangs being hurled in both directions. When a man from Buckley's clan was felled by a spear right through the body, a 'war cry' was raised by another of the clan and the women grabbed their clubs and rushed in. The ensuing fight went on for two hours, a 'frightful' scene with men and women covered in blood. Two women from Buckley's party were killed before the Waarengbadawas retreated 'to recover themselves'.

During the night, the 'hostile tribe left the neighbourhood'. A group of men from Buckley's tribe ambushed them as they slept, killing three men on the spot and wounding several more. The Waarengbadawa fled, leaving the wounded behind, and Buckley's people celebrated their victory by bringing back the bodies to be brutally beaten and mutilated.

Buckley's observations (as recounted by Morgan) must be tempered by the fact that Buckley was not allowed to participate nor was he part of the 'ambushing' party. He had explained that he 'was always kept in the rear' in tribal fights and that he 'could not then understand what all these quarrels were about'. For some time, Buckley laboured under the conception that he himself was the source of the conflict: 'These continual contests alarmed me, for the contending parties were always pointing toward me, as if I have been their origin'. It is remarkable that for such a prolonged battle involving 300 armed Waarengbadawa men, his group should have apparently suffered only three deaths (the two women and the speared man, if the latter indeed died) and even more startling that his group were able to successfully ambush such a large group in retaliation.

My visits were always welcomed, and they kindly and often supplied me with a portion of the provisions they had

Buckley may have acquired a position of some respect among the local people as well. He recounted how he had by now:

> seen a race of children grow up into women and men, and many of the old people die away, and by my harmless and peaceable manner amongst them, had acquired great influence in settling their disputes.

He went on to say he had prevented many of their 'murderous fights' by taking away their weapons just before they began a battle, an intervention that was permitted by the people on both sides in such disputes and recognised as 'well meant'; indeed:

> My visits were always welcomed, and they kindly and often supplied me with a portion of the provisions they had—assuring me, in their language, of the interest they took in my welfare.

This is an interesting account which, if true, indicates that Buckley had been given a ritual role in intertribal dispute resolution.

Charles Barrett, author of *White Blackfellows,* writes that 'Buckley could never become reconciled' to the practice of cannibalism and that 'it horrified him as a dreadful custom, and he would not share in the occasional cannibal ceremonies held by his tribe'. In Morgan's account, Buckley purportedly described various instances where the partial remains of individuals killed in hand-to-hand combat were roasted and consumed (apparently sections of thigh flesh), although he pointed out that 'it is proper to explain', that many such 'cannibal ceremonies ... are performed out of what they consider respect for the deceased'.

What Buckley possibly observed was a funerary practice as explained by the medical doctor and anthropologist, Herbert Basedow. Basedow recorded that in Central Australia, after cremation of a great warrior or highly significant individual, it was the custom to:

> cut portions of the soft parts from a dead warrior's body, whether he be friend or foe, and to eat them. The belief is that by so doing the brave qualities of the departed soldier will be kept among the tribe and will not be taken away by the spirit when it migrates to the ancestral hunting grounds.

He concluded that this practice 'is another reason why the Australian Aborigines are often referred to as cannibals, but the title is unmerited'. Today, the assessment by historians and anthropologists is fairly uniform that Aboriginal people did not practise cannibalism, in the sense of either eating human flesh for sustenance or to strike fear, at all.

BUNYIPS

Morgan recounts Buckley's story of the 'notorious tribe' known as the Pallidurgbarrans, who he insisted were actual cannibals, but that all of these 'copper coloured people with protruding bellies' were engulfed and destroyed by a huge fire. In his analysis of Buckley's narrative, Tim Flannery concluded that:

> the Aboriginal people who were educating Buckley about their environment made no clear division between myth and material reality; instead both were interwoven in a seamless view of the world. I think that in his discourse on the Pallidurgbarrans and the bunyip, Buckley is describing life through the

experiential eyes of his Aboriginal family—and this includes the phenomena at the edge of their social universe. There is not the slightest impression that Buckley is reporting anything but what he sensed was true, yet for the modern reader there is equally little doubt that bunyips and Pallidurgbarrans are mythical beings.

Buckley insisted he had seen the bunyip, although only its back, which, he recounted, appeared to be covered in feathers. He stated that Aboriginal people were in dread of the creature, who they believed carried supernatural powers to cause 'death, sickness, disease, and such like', and that the plentiful supplies of eels in some lagoons were there for the bunyip's consumption. On sighting a bunyip, his people, Buckley said, would throw themselves flat on the ground 'muttering some gibberish' (presumably a chant) or beat a hasty retreat away from the water. He stated that he had on several occasions attempted to spear the creature, although he did not alert the Aboriginal people to his intentions, as 'it would have caused great displeasure'.

We might surmise that the bunyip stories that flourished across south-eastern Aboriginal cultures operated as a kind of cultural mechanism ensuring adherence to important laws and customs, although what we can make of Buckley's apparent boast of his clandestine attempts is less clear—perhaps these, too, were embellishments for the sake of Morgan's readers.

HUNTING TECHNIQUES

Buckley soon grasped that each individual clan was spiritually connected to its own country and that the group moved to a new location every few months, following the seasons, before exhausting the food supply. In contrast to the notion that Aboriginal people were aimless wanderers, Buckley recounted that his people set up camp near a large lake called Yawangcontes and there they built huts made of reeds and stone and remained there 'for many months; perhaps for a year or two'.

Buckley was taught how to throw the spear accurately, 'and handle the tomahawk very adroitly'. He took part in kangaroo hunts: 'they place themselves at particular spots and distances, so as to drive them into corners like flocks of

Above: Aboriginal men fishing under torch light in their canoes, in Gippsland in the 1840s.

Following pages: An idyllic night scene of Aboriginal people fishing, while others are already enjoying the harvest.

sheep, and then they spear them without difficulty'. He was taught how to skin kangaroos and possums with mussel shells. The skins were stretched and dried in the sun, and sinews were used for sewing the skins together as rugs.

Buckley also learned how to catch and spear eels in the lakes and rivers. At night, the hunters took fire torches into the water with one hand while holding their spears ready to strike. The eels were almost hypnotised by the torches and languidly approached the hunters allowing themselves to be taken. The fish were roasted between 'thick layers of green grass on the hot ashes'.

Buckley described in great detail the teamwork involved in the capture of the much sought-after possum:

My brother-in-law, as he considered himself to be, had shown me how to ascertain when these animals were up the trees, and how the natives took them; this was, in the first place, by breathing hard on the bark, so as to discover if there were any opossum hairs left attached to it when the animal ascended. This found, he next cut a notch in the bark with his tomahawk, in which to insert his toe, and then another notch, holding his tomahawk in his mouth after making the incision, and so on upwards; by this means climbing the highest trees, and dragging the animals out of their holes, and off the branches by their legs and tails, then throwing them down to me at the foot; my business being to kill, and carry them. At the former I was tolerably expert, so that he often cried out from aloft, Merrijig; which means well done. We lived in clover at this place, getting plenty of opossums, and a very excellent root, which when roasted, I found as sweet as a chestnut, and as white as flour.

Buckley told of the Aboriginal method of firing the bush to procure food and encircling their prey with fire. In this way, they gathered cooked kangaroos, wombats, possum, snakes, lizards, frogs, rats, mice and wild dogs. *Norngnor* (wombats) were caught by sending young children feet first down into the tunnels. On touching a wombat's fur, they would yell loudly to the adults above who would immediately start digging down to grab their prize.

Indeed, Buckley provided a wonderful insight into the richly varied food sources available to the Aboriginal groups at particular times, including the swans and the bountiful harvest of their eggs. At another time and location, he described the intricate and delicate nets that were made to catch 'great quantities of shrimps'.

Buckley described the manufacture of tools, such as the stone axe:

The heads of these instruments are made from a hard black stone, split into a convenient thickness, without much regard to shape. This they rub with a very rough granite stone, until it is brought to a fine thin edge, and so hard and sharp as to enable them to fall a very large tree with it. There is only one place that I ever heard of in that country, where this hard and splitting stone is to be had. The natives called it karkeen; and say, that it is at a distance of three hundred miles from the coast inland.

Opposite: Aboriginal men hunting birds and possums.

In Morgan's account, Buckley explained that the only way to procure the much-valued stone was for a party of heavily armed men to make the dangerous trip inland. However, taking into account the many criss-crossing Aboriginal trade routes we now know existed across the continent, it is reasonable to assume that trade would have been the more obvious way the stone was procured. As Buckley did not accompany the men on any of these trips and so could not offer any genuine firsthand accounts, perhaps he did not fully understand the process.

MARRIAGE PRACTICE

Buckley was particularly observant of marriage practice, realising that differing tribal gatherings were not solely for the purpose of exchanging food and undertaking ceremonial activities, 'but for the very laudable purpose of *bringing out* their very elegant, amiable, marriageable daughters to be seen and known, and of course, courted'. He noted that the tribal groups mostly consisted of groups of between 20 and 60 people and held no man as the singular chief of the group. Men who were the 'most skilful and useful to the general community [were] looked upon with the greatest esteem'. Regarding marriage, there were very tight restrictions observed and they:

> contrive to keep a tolerable account, by recollection, of their pedigree, and will not, as I observed before, knowingly marry a relation—except where two brothers happened to be married and one dies; in that case the survivor claims the widow; in fact, as many wives or widows as he has left behind him.

BURIAL RITUALS

Buckley described burial rituals, in which the deceased were buried, wrapped in their skin cloaks and lying on their sides. A ring of fire sticks was erected around each grave, with digging sticks laid on top for women and spears for men: 'They have an idea that they will want them when they come back to life again'. On one occasion, Buckley witnessed a very different approach, for the burial of a highly regarded man. A stout tree, not too high, was selected. Between branches about 12 feet off the ground they installed a wooden platform, covered with bark. On this flooring, the body was placed, wrapped in a blanket with the face 'inclining toward the setting sun, and over it was placed some more bark and boughs, and then logs as heavy as the branches would bear; all this being done to protect the body from the birds of prey.'

In the brief account recorded by George Langhorne in 1837, Buckley related how the Aboriginal people had some forewarning of the European arrival. Explaining that there were two 'Beings' that the people respected, one who was 'the author of all the songs which he makes known to them through his sons', Buckley elaborated how the other:

> is supposed to have charge of the Pole or Piller by which the sky is propped—
> Just before the Europeans came to Port Phillip this personage was the subject
> of general conversation[.] it was reported among them that he had sent a
> message to the Tribes to send a certain number of Tomahawks to enable him
> to prepare a new prop for the Sky as the other had become rotten and their
> destruction was inevitable should the sky fall on them[.] to prevent this and
> to supply as great a number of Iron Tomahawks as possible—some of the
> Blacks repaired to Western Port and stole the Iron work from the wheels of
> the Sealers cart—It is about 25 years since I first saw an European Tomahawk
> among them—on enquiring where they obtained it—they informed me that
> while I was absent some distance in the interior some white men had rowed
> up the Barwin in a Boat and had left the Tomahawk at the place where they
> landed[.] on visiting the spot I observed the place where the Strangers had dug
> to procure water.

A similar account was recounted by the Wurundjeri elder Barak, who had met Buckley in his childhood. Barak stated that his people had learnt that the eastern prop of the sky was rotting and that 'if presents were not sent to the old man in charge he would not repair it, the sky would fall, and everybody would be killed ... this news filled the land with consternation'. We could interpret this evocative legend as a way of explaining the actions of Aboriginal people in taking what materials they could salvage or steal from the European newcomers, presumably to trade back along the people further inland. (Barak referred to traditional stone axes being sent eastwards towards the site of invasion, whereas Buckley spoke of the new European tomahawks left on the shore.) The prophecy also suggests a prescience on the part of the Aboriginal people about the seriousness of the threat that the British posed to their world.

3

Thomas Pamphlett, Richard Parsons & John Finnegan

In 1823, the cutter *Mermaid*, carrying an exploring group led by Surveyor-General John Oxley, dropped anchor in Moreton Bay. When the ship first appeared, large numbers of Aboriginal people gathered on the shore waving and calling out to them. Through a telescope, the party on the ship sighted a powerfully built and lighter-skinned man among the Aboriginal people, his naked body painted decoratively with red and white ochre. They immediately launched a small boat and went ashore to meet him. In his published narrative of the expedition, John Uniacke, a guest of Oxley on the expedition, captured this extraordinary moment:

> While approaching the beach the natives showed many signs of joy, dancing and embracing the white man, who was nearly as wild as they. He was perfectly naked and covered all over with white and red paint, which the natives make use of.

The painted white man was Thomas Pamphlett.

The amazing life journey of Pamphlett (also known as James Groom) is forever tied with two other men, Richard Parsons and John Finnegan. These three convict mariners blown off course (as they claimed) were the first white men known to live with the Aboriginal people of the Moreton Bay area in present-day Queensland.

Some 13 years earlier, in 1810, Pamphlett, a 22-year-old bricklayer from Manchester, had been brought before the court to face charges of stealing five pieces of cloth. He faced additional charges of stealing a horse and was sentenced to hang for this crime, but the sentence was commuted to transportation to the colony of New South Wales.

Pamphlett proved to be a serial offender, resulting in him being sent to Coal River (Newcastle), a destination for the more difficult convicts. After a conditional pardon from the governor in 1820, Pamphlett returned to Sydney with a wife and three children in tow—no details are known of who his wife was or how he came to meet her. Married life did not settle him though and, after moving to the Hawkesbury River district, Pamphlett was convicted of robbing a house. Sentenced to seven years at the Port Macquarie convict settlement, he was let off because it was deemed that he was not of sound mind.

Over the next three or four years, Pamphlett worked as a timber-getter, and it was due to this experience combined with his boat-handling skills that he was chosen in 1823, along with three other men (Parsons, Finnegan and ticket-of-leave convict John Thompson), to sail 50 miles south of Sydney to the South Coast to transport cedar back to the settlement. The four men disappeared, assumed lost at sea.

As Pamphlett later explained to Uniacke, the group of four men had left Sydney in a large open boat—part-owned by ticket-of-leave convict Parsons—with a good supply of pork, flour and rum, intended to be used as an exchange for cedar they would cut at the Five Islands (Illawarra). They were only eight miles from their destination when a violent storm hit. A gale blew for five days before they could again raise their sails. The men believed that they had been driven well south and were somewhere in the vicinity of Van Diemen's Land. With no compass, they set a north-west course by sheer guesswork to bring them back to the Illawarra. The small crew steered the boat by the sun and continued on the course for 21 days when, to their great relief, land was once again sighted.

The men were suffering from exposure and lack of water, and had suffered greatly, none more so than Thompson, who died soon after they had spotted land. The three survivors were afraid to go ashore because they could see large numbers of Aboriginal people around fires and, despite their desperate condition, sailed on.

Some days later, the group found a site at which to anchor, with a freshwater stream emptying into the bay. They anchored and Pamphlett swam a quarter of a mile to shore, towing a keg with him to replenish their water supplies. It took him an hour and a half and when he got ashore and reached the stream, he 'drank like a horse'. Finnegan and Parsons beseeched him to return to the boat as the wind had begun to whip up, but Pamphlett called out to them to let the boat run ashore instead. It was pounded to destruction on the shoreline by the heavy seas, and they were now well and truly marooned.

They followed a trail into the bush and, having seen and followed an Aboriginal woman and a child, emerged on another beach where they saw a small Aboriginal boy 'throwing spears at foraging crows'. Seeing the intruders, the boy fled into a small hut from within which a man, obviously his father, emerged and, grabbing a spear standing next to the hut, took hold of his child. A woman also appeared and quickly threw the child up onto her back, ready to flee. Pamphlett called out to the family to stop. To their complete astonishment the man turned and answered in perfect English, 'What do you want? Do you want to kill me?', before hastening after his wife and child. This, recounted Pamphlett, led the three men to believe they must be near an English settlement, though later they 'could never account for this Moreton islander's being able to speak English, while the natives of Moreton Bay appeared never to have seen a white man before'. Uniacke, taking down this account, noted that Matthew Flinders had visited the region in 1799, but decided that Pamphlett in his muddled state must have imagined that the man spoke to him in English.

Pamphlett stated that the men still held the belief that Sydney was to their north, but it is possible that, from the very beginning, the three men might have planned an escape from the colony in their substantial and well-provisioned boat, and were attempting to sail north for Asia when their plans came unstuck.

The men had come ashore at an island off the present-day southern Queensland coast, Moreton Island, or Moorgumpin, part of the wider Quandamooka region of the Indigenous people of Moreton Bay and its islands. From this initial encounter, the men would be assisted and cared for by a number of small groups of people in their mistaken quest to continue north to find Port Jackson.

Pamphlett described how the three were at first surrounded by a group of curious men as they devoured the cakes of flour and water they had made from the last of their provisions, cooked over a fire they had made (he did not explain exactly how he had made a fire). The white men gave their observers some of their food, a gesture that undoubtedly signalled friendship to the Aboriginal men, even as they discreetly spat it out when they thought the newcomers were not looking. Pamphlett described how nervous he and his companions felt:

> Their number now amounted to about twelve; and they began to feel us about the breast and shoulders in a manner that greatly alarmed us: we therefore prepared to move again, as soon as we had finished our meal ... They had nets on their backs, with which they made signs that they would catch fish for us; but when they found we were obstinate, some of them prepared to accompany us, and one or two of them took up our bags of flour to carry for us. We proceeded about a mile with them, when we came to another set of huts, into which our conductors invited us; and on our consenting, they appeared quite happy, dancing and singing around us ... In the morning, after having breakfasted on some of our cakes, we again set out, accompanied by our kind friendly natives, who brought us down to the beach, and again seemed very anxious that we should return the way we came, but they did not offer to use any kind of force.

After some days of travelling northwards without seeing anyone, the three white men took an Aboriginal canoe, left on the beach by two men they saw going into the bush. As it was not large enough to hold the three men and all their bags of flour and food, Parsons and Finnegan left Pamphlett and used the canoe to reach what they believed was the mainland. Two days later, just as Pamphlett was despairing that he had been abandoned, he saw Finnegan come into shore with an Aboriginal man in the canoe, the man making signs that Pamphlett should get into the canoe with them:

> Finnegan now told me that nothing could exceed the kindness with which they had been treated by the natives, who had lodged them in a large hut by themselves, and given them as much fish as they could eat, but that they could not before persuade the natives to let the canoe come over for me; and it was only by accident that he was now enabled to come with the native I had seen, who was going to visit his friends on the island.

Crossing with Finnegan, Pamphlett saw Parsons and 'a number of natives waiting on the beach, and were received by them with many demonstrations of joy'. The Aboriginal people welcomed them ashore (at Amity Point on present-day Stradbroke Island, Minjerribah), gave the pair 'several roasted fish' and 'placed us in a very large well-built hut by ourselves, and supplied us with fish, water, &c. very liberally'. The white men remained here for some ten days or so, during which time they continued to be treated 'most hospitably', to the extent that Finnegan announced that 'the blacks were so friendly that he wished to remain with them, sooner than encounter the difficulty and danger of attempting to return to any of our settlements'. But he finally relented and agreed to accompany the other two men who were intent on reaching Sydney.

They had only covered some ten miles when an altercation erupted within the small party. Finnegan had been given the responsibility of keeping their firestick alight and, when it went out, Parsons, evidently a man with a short temper, vented his wrath upon the unfortunate Finnegan, striking him with an axe handle and threatening to kill him. Finnegan promised to go back to the nearest 'native camp' and relight the stick.

Not unexpectedly, Finnegan did not come back. The other two men pressed on, but mangrove thickets stopped any hope of further progress. Parsons and Pamphlett gave up and marched the hours back to their original camp with the people at Amity Point, finding Finnegan along the way on a fishing expedition in the company of two Aboriginal men. That evening the three men were back in their hut together enjoying a meal of fresh fish and fern root, supplied by their hosts.

Parsons and Pamphlett then decided to make a seagoing canoe, but Finnegan refused to assist them. The result of this had an immediate impact on the Aboriginal group where a sense of group work ethic was bound to the collective and common good for all. The Aboriginal people were clearly annoyed at Finnegan's reluctance and laziness, and attempted to make him take an axe. As he continued to refuse to assist, they would not give him food, while providing Parsons and Pamphlett with plenty. Finnegan had to find his own food as best he could. The statement was quite plain: 'we do not support those who do not support the group'.

After three weeks, the canoe was completed and Parsons and Pamphlett were ready for departure. Their hosts were delighted. '[They] would not allow us to

Aboriginal tools, utensils and weapons
from the Moreton Bay region.

W.G.MASON

launch it,' Pamphlett told Uniacke, 'but did it themselves; and when they saw it afloat, with Parsons and me in it, their joy and admiration knew no bounds: they leaped, danced, and roared, following us up and down the beach.' Assured that the canoe was serviceable, the two men came back on shore, whereupon the Aboriginal people 'rolled the canoe up again on the beach, not allowing us to touch it'. It's hard not to get the impression that they were anxious for their guests to leave, and wanted to take no chances of something happening to the canoe.

> *when they saw it afloat, with Parsons and me in it, their joy and admiration knew no bounds: they leaped, danced, and roared*

The next day, with Finnegan refusing to join them, Parsons and Pamphlett set off, their canoe holding a quantity of fresh fish given to them by the Aboriginal people. But Finnegan was quickly made aware that he was no longer welcome:

> We had not proceeded above a quarter of a mile, when the natives, perceiving that Finnegan did not accompany us, hastily launched a canoe, and two of them embarking, he was by the rest forced to follow, when they paddled quickly towards us; but we had gotten around a sand-bank that lay off some distance from the shore. They therefore pulled to the bank and made Finnegan land on it, where they left him, and went back to the huts. As he was unable to swim, he would have drowned when the tide rose, if we had not pulled back for him, as we immediately did.

They made it across Moreton Bay to another island (Peel Island, or Chercrooba) as the Aboriginal people had directed them, and from there to the mainland. Here they decided to abandon the craft and push on along the beach on foot. After three days, they came to a wide river they were unable to ford—the present-day Brisbane River—and trekked upriver to find a safe spot to get across. Their slow progress through swamps, thick scrub, mud and saltwater creeks forced the men to turn back, all but exhausted from their efforts. Their food intake during that month had largely consisted of fern roots.

On their way back, they found two canoes alongside the river and met with an Aboriginal fishing party who kindly gave them 'a good meal of fish', but who

Examples of the roomy Aboriginal huts in the Moreton Bay region.

were not inclined to continue to support them: 'the next day they seemed anxious that we should leave them; and upon our not doing so, as readily as they wished, they made an attempt to seize our canoes'. The men hastily departed and paddled out to the middle of the river, continuing on their way back to the river mouth.

On reaching the river mouth, they discarded one of the canoes and Pamphlett paddled the other close to shore while Parsons and Finnegan walked along the shore of the bay. At present-day Hays Inlet, Pamphlett was ferrying Parsons across, intending to return for Finnegan who was waiting on the shore of Pine Creek, when they saw Finnegan paddling towards them in another canoe. It was full of fresh fish. Finnegan had discovered the haul on the beach and had quickly helped himself and followed the two others. They beached at Clontarf Point and took the fish to some empty Aboriginal huts nearby, where they kindled a fire with their firestick.

It was not long before the men whose catch they had taken (and who had evidently seen Finnegan rowing off) turned up—about ten men in one canoe— and their commotion attracted the attention of the owners of the huts at Clontarf Point, who also came running. After a diet of little other than fern roots for several weeks, the three men were ready to resist losing their stolen goods, and prepared for a fight, Pamphlett taking up his axe and Finnegan a stick.

The Aboriginal people, however, 'seemed at once struck with our miserable condition' and, instead of contesting the issue, quickly set about catching more fish with their nets for the starving men. Despite the three white men having stolen their fish, the evidence is clear that the Aboriginal people quickly forgave the perpetrators and even went so far as to provide them with both accommodation and more food than they could possibly consume. How different to European responses to any perceived wrongdoing by Aboriginal people, which usually resulted in near annihilation for an entire group on mere suspicion of stealing.

The men had stayed with their new hosts for some four or five days when Pamphlett proposed they leave. Finnegan remained behind (fearing that Parsons would eventually kill him) as a guest of 'the chief of the tribe', while the other two set off. But, being unable to find any food, they quickly returned and, for another month, the men stayed with these benevolent people. During this time, as Finnegan explained to Uniacke, the three men were distributed among different families in the group, he remaining with 'the old chief', while 'every one of the tribe contributed to our support, one bringing fish, another *dingowa* [fern root], and so on; so that we were as comfortable as we could expect to be in our situation'.

When the three decided they should continue on, their hosts—in contrast to those who had sheltered them previously—were reluctant to see them go, and went so far as to send four men after them to entreat them to return. They included a young man Pamphlett called 'the Doctor', who he had previously assisted by extracting part of a spear from a wound he had, and who had 'become much attached to Pamphlett' in consequence. But the white men, believing 'that they only followed us in consequence of our having promised them the axe and some other things, which we had not given them ... drove them away'. They were then 'overtaken' the next morning by a man and a woman from the same group, who insisted upon travelling with them for a mile or so, attempting again to prevail upon them to return.

After the Aboriginal pair left them, the three white men continued on and, after a while, came across an old, crippled man and three women with children, 'all eating fish, with which, on our arrival, they instantly supplied us'. Continuing on, they next met with yet another group, which to their surprise included 'the Doctor', who 'now urgently entreated' Pamphlett to return with him, to see him fight the man who had wounded him. At this point, Pamphlett gave in and agreed to go with his friend.

Meanwhile, Parsons and Finnegan travelled on together for another two days but were soon arguing. Finnegan was again convinced that the volatile Parsons intended to murder him. He took to his heels and fled. That night, 'he met a party of blacks crossing the river in three canoes'. They provided a man and his wife to escort him back to the main camp, where he found Pamphlett. Finnegan reported that he was 'again received by the old chief with the greatest kindness, he seeming quite delighted with my return'.

Finnegan was asked by the old chief to go to a ceremonial fight at some distance away and went willingly, but Pamphlett, protesting that his feet were sore, was allowed to remain behind. His reluctance to attend may have been resented because Pamphlett now found that the 'old man in whose hut I lived' suddenly would not give him any share of his catch of fish and, when Pamphlett asked for some, 'he refused me rather gruffly'. Pamphlett assumed he might have worn out his welcome and decided his best course of action was to depart and, taking his axe, set off to try and locate Parsons. He was then quickly overtaken by four of the young men of the group:

> who made use of every persuasion in their power to entice me back, to which
> I at last consented, the more readily as each of them brought two spears, and
> I was not quite certain what use they would have put them to, had I persisted
> in my refusal.

He dutifully returned, giving up any further effort to count the days and having no idea for how long Finnegan had been gone.

One evening, as Pamphlett lay back 'by the fire':

I heard some natives shouting on the beach and calling me; upon which I rose and walked slowly towards them; but what was my astonishment and delight, when I saw a cutter under full sail standing up the bay, about three miles from where we stood! I instantly made towards her with all speed I could, followed by a number of the natives.

Hailing the ship, the *Mermaid*, as it came to anchor near the shore, Pamphlett was taken on board and washed and clothed. Within another couple of days, Finnegan had heard word of the vessel's arrival and turned up, walking out to meet the Europeans on a long sand bank on the opposite shore, and was taken to the *Mermaid* in a whaleboat.

An artist's rendition of the discovery of
Thomas Pamphlett by John Oxley's expedition.

Despite their earlier entreaties for him to stay, the Aboriginal people were willing to help Pamphlett to get back to the ship and be reunited with his people. Perhaps he had finally given the axe he had promised them. In Uniacke's detailed account, there is one incident of 'pilfering' that occurred when one of the ship's two felling axes disappeared, while one of the crew was onshore cutting timber. Uniacke described how the Europeans initially tried to demand that the Aboriginal people show them where they had hidden the axe. When the old man who promised to take them to it fled into the bush, they gave up, but the next morning:

> we found a number of them on the beach, abreast of the vessel, shouting and elevating the axe, which, on my going on shore, was delivered to me by the old man who had shown such speed the evening before. So this incident, instead of interrupting our good understandings, rendered our mutual confidence more strong; for several of the natives ventured on board that day for the first time, whereas they had always before refused to do so with signs of fear. From this time forward not a single day passed, on which we had not ten or twelve of them on board at a time.

They were 'very curious', Uniacke recorded. But it took a long time before they could be persuaded 'to eat any thing with us'—again, intriguing, considering how generous the Aboriginal people had always been in feeding the three men.

> However, when they once began [eating with us], it was by no means an easy matter to satisfy them. Our cats and goats struck them with particular astonishment. We could not prevail upon them to approach the latter, of whose horns they seemed to have a great awe. They were, however, continually caressing the cats, and holding them up for the admiration of their companions on shore.

Meanwhile, Surveyor-General John Oxley was exploring the area in the company of Finnegan. They looked for Parsons, but eventually had to return to Sydney without him, leaving a message in a bottle for him.

Oxley, having suggested to Governor Brisbane that a settlement should be established at Moreton Bay, returned to the area nine months later, complete with 30 convicts who were promised early release in exchange for being the first convicts to go to Moreton Bay. Arriving in late September 1824, Oxley, almost immediately upon landing and somewhat miraculously, located Parsons. Parsons had only been back there for a month or so, his northwards trek having failed when the heat got too much for him. Oxley recorded his astonishment in recognising alongside Parsons:

> the venerable old man so often mentioned as the kind protector of Pamphlett and Parsons [Finnegan] ... When Parsons was about to get into the boat, the old man, his kind protector, evinced the strongest remarks of attachment towards him; and could not be persuaded he would ever see him again. After we left the beach he followed us for some time alone, and waved many an adieu.

According to a newspaper interview with Parsons published just after his return to Sydney, as the ship was about to set sail, the people came on board to give him a fishing net 'in order as they told him to get his living in the country he was going to'. Such solicitude for his well being is a striking sign of the humanity of those who had helped him. As the writer of the article concluded:

> These facts, especially such as relate to the disposition of the natives, we consider important, as they shew that by avoiding harsh treatment in the first instance, many misunderstandings [may] be avoided between the whites and the blacks.

On their return to Sydney, author Chris Pearce has found that Finnegan, who was still serving time, was assigned as a ship hand. He was granted a ticket of leave in 1825 and acted as a government guide for at least three years. As no further record has been found of him in the colony, he may have made his way back to Britain. Parsons worked as a bullock driver on the South Coast, served a further sentence on Norfolk Island and died at Goulburn in 1864.

Pamphlett had expressed ambivalence at the time of his return, telling Uniacke that the treatment he and his companions had received from the Aboriginal people 'had been so invariably kind and generous, that, notwithstanding the delight I felt at the idea of once more returning to my home, I did not leave them without sincere regret'. For a time, he stayed out of trouble, but Pearce reports that in 1826 he was accused of stealing 200 pounds of flour. Pamphlett was sentenced to seven years at the newly opened penal colony at Moreton Bay, where the irony of his position must have surely crossed his mind. He saw out his seven-year sentence in pretty much exemplary fashion. In the last year of his sentence in 1833 he made a failed escape attempt and was, rather surprisingly, freed anyway. If it occurred to him to go back to the people who had sheltered him before, he did not do so, but instead returned to Sydney, where he died three years later.

Pamphlett, Parsons and Finnegan's Aboriginal Life

Although the three men were evidently kindly treated by the Aboriginal people they lived with, the extent to which they had been accepted into Aboriginal society was not particularly great. In the original accounts, they did not ever provide a name for any Aboriginal individual (apart from 'the Doctor') or group they met, and they did not appear to have learnt any of the language of their hosts. There is nothing to indicate that any of them were taken for relatives returned from the dead, although their exceedingly generous treatment might indicate they were regarded with some respect.

BODY DECORATION

Pamphlett told Uniacke that while they lived with the Aboriginal people, he and Finnegan were:

> regularly painted twice a day, and were frequently importuned to allow
> themselves to be further ornamented by scarifying the body and boring
> the nose; but on their signifying that they did not wish it, the natives
> always desisted; nor was any violence used against them during their
> whole residence.

Oxley recorded that everyone in the group over the age of six had the cartilage of their nose perforated, the operation being performed by the same person ('the Doctor') 'whose office is hereditary, and confers some privileges, such as receiving fish, &c, from the others'. They wore no clothing, but the clans were distinguished by different body paint, those on the north side blackening themselves with charcoal and beeswax, those on the south side wearing red, and other groups daubing white over black. Uniacke described giving them strips of red cloth and bunting to decorate their heads, which 'much gratified' them, and some scarlet tail feathers of a black cockatoo, which 'nearly produced a quarrel among them'. He also remarked that some articles of clothing that the whites had given to the Aboriginal people had been taken off and hidden in their camp; 'nor did we ever see any article again after they once became possessed of it'.

DIET AND FISHING METHOD

In his account of that time and of the following months to come with the people they would meet in their trek northwards, Pamphlett delivered many intriguing insights into the life of the people of the region. The people of the islands and mainland of Moreton Bay were a marine-orientated group who relied heavily on fish and shellfish for their diet:

> they never travel without fire, the moment the fish are out of the water, they commence roasting and eating them, which they do without cleaning or any other preparation; and when they have satisfied themselves, should any remain, they carry them home for their women and children, who have been employed during the day in procuring fern-root, which they call *dingowa*, and a part of which they give to the men in exchange for fish.

Uniacke described the fishing method he observed. The men, he wrote, who carried a pair of hoop nets each that they had woven from the kurrajong shrub (native hibiscus), went out in parties of equal numbers to walk along the shoreline looking for fish. Once they had spotted some, a 'little boy' crawled on his hands and knees into the water while the party divided into two lines one on each side of him. As soon as the fish were near enough to the boy, he would throw a handful of sand to 'distract their attention', as the men rushed into the water, forming a semi-circle around the fish and drawing their nets close together: 'In this manner they are seldom unsuccessful, and frequently catch more than they can consume'.

THE CAMPS

The clan with whom Pamphlett was living at the time he was discovered by Oxley consisted of about 30 men, 16 or 17 women, and about 20 children. They had a main camp further up the river and several permanent camps, three or four miles apart, which they migrated to when fish became scarce in one place. The huts in the camps were substantial:

> Their huts are built of long slender wattles, both ends of which are stuck into the ground, so as to form an arch about three feet and a half or four feet high. These are strongly interwoven with rude wicker-work, and the whole

An Aboriginal man with his fishing net.

is covered with tea-tree (*melaleuca armillaris*) bark, in such a manner as to be quite impervious to rain: thus forming a spacious and commodious hut, capable of containing from ten to twelve people.

Uniacke noted that there was a 'chief' who 'appeared to possess an unlimited authority over them'—a tall middle-aged man with two wives, one of whom had the role of collecting food from the others in the group. 'The chief possesses nets both for fish and kangaroo, but seldom uses them except for his amusement. Neither does his head wife ever go out to gather fern-root with the rest of the women.'

WOMEN

There is no indication that either Pamphlett, Parsons or Finnegan were able to take a wife. Perhaps the remarkable hospitality they were shown had something to do with keeping them at a distance from the Aboriginal women. They seemed to have been treated throughout their time as special guests, with an expectation of their eventual departure.

The women specialised in gathering fern roots, which they carried in their woven string nets. Like the women of the Sydney region, they had the joints of their little finger removed, an operation performed by the same man who perforated noses. Pamphlett's account was glowing in its estimation of the women and their position in Aboriginal society. He emphasised that:

during his residence among these natives (nearly seven months), he never saw a woman struck or ill-treated except by one of her own sex. Indeed, save among the women, he never saw a quarrel in that or any other tribe he met.

He told Uniacke that at first the white men were not allowed to approach the huts where the women lived, and that every night a number of younger men slept in front of their hut to keep watch: 'But they afterwards became less vigilant, and we used to pass through their huts among the women as we pleased'. There was also some discussion between Pamphlett and Uniacke on the merit of the local Aboriginal women, Uniacke writing:

The women that I saw were far superior in personal beauty to the men, or indeed to any other natives of this country whom I have yet seen. Many of them are tall, straight and well formed; and there were two in particular whose shape and features were such as no white woman need have been ashamed of.

Later, in a newspaper interview, Parsons said that on his journey northwards the Aboriginal people he met had, for the most part, avoided him when they saw him and, if he could not 'entice' them to come to him, he would 'get hold of one their children, and caress it':

> This stratagem usually succeeded. They would then come and offer him fish and be very friendly. At all times he found the men very jealous of their women, who often were not allowed to present any thing; for the men would give it [food] themselves to him. This feeling he describes as pervading the whole tribes he fell in with, to a greater or less degree.

Parsons further told the reporter that he 'was never in any danger from the natives except once', when he attempted 'a little familiarity' with a girl or woman, and 'a great number of the natives started up, and in a menacing attitude called out to him to let her alone'.

LAW AND PUNISHMENT

Both Finnegan and Pamphlett left accounts of Aboriginal intertribal warfare and fighting. When these accounts are re-examined closely, they are more likely to have been matters of Law and punishment, or something akin to the chivalrous accounts of medieval knights at a sporting jousting event, rather than some all-encompassing war. At Clontarf Point, Pamphlett was well positioned to see a fight between the Doctor and a man of another group who had wounded him in the knee with a spear when he was out hunting. Pamphlett had previously assisted the young man by removing a splinter from a broken spear in his leg, cementing a friendship between them. When recovered, as we have seen, the Doctor had persuaded Pamphlett to accompany him to 'a great gathering of the natives, and witness the revenge fight or duel'.

Following pages: Aboriginal men netting schools of fish.

Pamphlett gave a detailed description of the event and arena:

The spot appointed for the combat was a small ring, about twenty-five feet in diameter, about three feet deep, and surrounded by a palisade of sticks. The crowd assembled to see the fight amounted to about 500 men, women and children; and the combatants, followed by those who were friendly to them, respectively, approached the ring in single file, and drew up in a regular manner on opposite sides of the circle. The whole assembly were well armed, many of them having five or six spears each. The two combatants then entered the ring, and having laid down their spears in opposite rows, point to point, began walking backwards and forwards, talking loudly to each other and using violent gestures, as if to inflame their passions to a due height. The women had previously been driven away, and the most profound silence reigned in the rest of the assembly. After about ten minutes spent in this way, they commenced picking up their spears with their feet, keeping their eyes fixed on each other, so as to prevent either from taking advantage of the other's stooping. In this manner they proceeded till they had each three spears, which they stuck in the ground, ready for immediate use. At the moment when they commenced thus picking up their spears, a tremendous shout burst from the spectators, who immediately relapsed into former silence.

In a similar fashion to a present-day boxing match, with the ring announcer and trainers in the centre of the ring and each corner, this Aboriginal main event began with a couple of friends or advisors speaking first for a few minutes before the hostilities commenced. The Doctor had the first opportunity to hurl his spear at his opponent, who deflected the flight of the spear with his wooden shield. The other combatant then had his turn, but the Doctor was also successful in dodging the missile. The third spear thrown by the Doctor felled his adversary to the ground with the spear piercing his shoulder right through. His two handlers raced to his aid, removed the spear and returned it to the Doctor. The tournament concluded at this point with loud cheering from all the gathered spectators.

This was not the formal conclusion of the event, as the following day the wounded man's group had an opportunity to lodge another challenge to avenge his defeat:

But it appeared that no one wished to do so, as each had now wounded the other, and a reconciliation took place between the two tribes, which was announced by shouting, dancing etc.: and a parcel of boys were selected from each party, and sent into the ring to wrestle; after which both tribes joined in a hunting expedition, which lasted a week; but my feet being sore, I was consigned to the care of the women.

Finnegan, who accompanied the tribal group to a contest while Pamphlett stayed behind, corroborated Pamphlett's description of the contests, but with some variations. He described how one-on-one combats took place in a circular pit, about 40 feet in diameter, and observed a preliminary bout between two female combatants complete with sticks:

> they appeared to be quite in earnest; and in five minutes their heads and arms, &c. being dreadfully cut and swelled, our woman was declared the conqueror, the other not being able any longer to oppose her. The victory was announced by a loud shout from all parties, and the amazonian combatants were immediately carried away by their respective friends.

Finnegan was at all times under the care of members of his tribal group (particularly, in the charge of the chief's wife) and was at one point introduced to a group of the 'chiefs', apparently causing 'great talking and laughing among them, from surprise at my colour and appearance. The king [Finnegan's host] then addressed them at some length, apparently asking them not to hurt me, which they gave me to understand by signs that they would not'. During this introduction, Finnegan had missed one of the main events but, on returning, witnessed a member of his group being carried from the ring mortally wounded:

> He was brought down to where I was, and placed on two men's knees, with some kangaroo-skins spread over him; the men, women and children howling and lamenting, much in the manner of the lower Irish. They supplied him with water from time to time, but his wound was evidently mortal, and in less than an hour he expired.

FUNERARY RITES

The body of the man killed during the fight described above was at that point skinned in a ritual procedure, which Finnegan could not closely observe. The fights continued and several men were wounded 'and another man of our party killed'. Later that evening, both of the dead men were placed in a large fire 'in which, as I judged from the noise as well as the offensive smell they were both consumed' (that is, by fire).

Finnegan's description of the funerary rites for the two men who had been killed recalls some of the details from Buckley's narrative, although again there was no mention of any anthropophagy. He described how the remains of the men were brought back to the camp and, despite efforts by the chief to prevent him from viewing them, he took himself to where the men's skins were stretched and drying over a fire:

> Several of the men and women were sitting round the fire under the skins, and now invited me to sit down with them, which I did. They then gave me some kangaroo-skin to decorate my arms and head, and seemed to wish me to sing to them; but on my making signs that it was not proper to do so while the remains of our friends were not buried, they seemed surprised, and afterwards told me by signs that they were much pleased at my refusal. After sitting with them about half an hour, the chief's wife came and brought me back to the hut. Shortly afterwards, all the men dressed themselves in kangaroo-skins, and one of them in an old rug jacket which I had, and with one or two of the women, held a consultation round the fire, each person having a fire-stick in his hand. After conversing about half an hour, two of the party separated from the rest, and having taken down the skins, set off at full speed through the bush; the rest followed, shouting and making much noise. After this I saw nothing more of the skins, nor do I know what became of them. In about three-quarters of an hour the party returned; and the man who had taken my old jacket gave it me back. The next morning we returned towards the Pumice-stone River by the same path which we had travelled to the fight, and the natives followed their usual occupations of fishing and hunting as if nothing had happened.

Apart from this account, Uniacke took nothing down from either Finnegan or Pamphlett about any secret, sacred beliefs, and stating that the men had not seen 'any thing like religious ceremony or prayer' during their time with them he concluded that the Aboriginal people did 'not stand in awe of either good or evil spirits'. As with other accounts of Europeans who lived with Aboriginal people, if the white men knew anything of Aboriginal spirituality they chose not to share it.

4

James Davis—'Duramboi' & David Bracefell—'Wandi'

James ('Jem') Davis and David Bracefell were convicts at the Moreton Bay penal settlement (in the location that is now Brisbane) in the late 1820s. The settlement was established for hardened and recidivist offenders as a way of dealing with runaways at the Port Macquarie penal settlement (founded in 1821). The Moreton Bay settlement was ruled by a much hated commandant, Captain Patrick Logan, whose death in 1830—reportedly killed by Aboriginal people while surveying the headwaters of the Brisbane River with a small party of convicts—was often attributed to the convicts themselves. Davis and Bracefell were just two of the many prisoners who absconded to the bush, rather than stay in such a harsh place.

Some have theorised that the convict Thomas Pamphlett, confined there between 1826 and 1833, with his tales of living in the bush with the generous Aboriginal people, encouraged a whole list of escapees from Moreton Bay. In 18 years of operation (1824–1842), over 500 of the 2,200 prisoners who passed through the Moreton Bay penal settlement escaped (many of them multiple times). Most returned after a short time, either being captured or returning voluntarily because of the threat of starvation. From the outset, it was hoped that the Aboriginal people in the area would be enlisted in apprehending and bringing back escapees, and they often did so, in return receiving food, tomahawks, blankets and fish hooks from the British authorities. No doubt the local Aboriginal people saw the runaways as trespassers and were more than happy to oblige by returning them. But, sometimes, runaways found shelter with Aboriginal people and were able to remain with them for many years. Davis and Bracefell were so fortunate. They did not escape together nor did they live with the same people, but their stories would become inextricably entangled with each other.

There is some debate about the origins of James Davis, but according to biographer Patrick Tynan he was the son of a Glasgow blacksmith and aged around 16 when he was tried in 1824 for theft. He was convicted and sentenced to transportation for 14 years. Less than three years after arriving in New South Wales in August 1825, he gained a further three years on his sentence

Moreton Bay, New South Wales, 1835

for a robbery committed at Patrick's Plains (now Singleton, New South Wales), probably while an assigned servant. Davis was sent to the four-year-old Moreton Bay penal settlement, but only six weeks after his arrival in February 1829 he took to the bush and joined an Aboriginal group. A member of the expedition that found him in 1842 recorded Davis' explanation:

> he had runaway because the men on his chain were cutting each other's throats, or knocking a mate's head in with the pick used on the roads, so that they might be sent to Sydney to be 'what they called hung.' Fearing for his own life at the hands of his comrades, he had managed to escape and take his chance of mercy among the blacks.

Davis had been taken in by Aboriginal people and would spend the next 14 years living with the local people, learning their language and adopting their cultural practices. He had gained acceptance because it was assumed he was a tribal family member returned to life, 'jumped up' as a white-skinned man. Presbyterian clergyman and journalist John Dunmore Lang, who spoke with

Davis not too long after his return to European society, described how Davis had gone from tribe to tribe, and had travelled as far as 500 miles north of Moreton Bay. In Lang's account, wherever Davis went, he was understood to be a long-lost person who had returned from the dead. Among groups who had never seen a white man before, his appearance caused a stir and was:

> an event of intense interest to the natives. They would gather round him in a crowd, and gaze at him for a time, apparently in silent awe and veneration.

All of these groups examined him in minute detail, Lang wrote, looking for some tell-tale sign that he was a returned member of their own group. At the moment when a family member recognised Davis as a deceased relative, there was a mixture of great excitement and mourning.

Should no one recognise you as a relative returned to life again, you are sure to be speared

Occasionally, some people failed to find any resemblance and 'he was usually asked who he had been, or what had been his name when he was a black-fellow, and before he died'. Lang remarked on the ingenuity of Davis in extricating himself from such sticky situations by replying 'that it was so long since he died, that he had quite forgotten what name he had had when he was a black man'. The local people were always satisfied with the answer.

Immediately after Davis' discovery and return, Commissioner of Crown Lands for Moreton Bay Stephen Simpson reported Davis' account to the Colonial Secretary. After Davis had travelled for some 100 miles after first escaping, he was taken in by 'the Doomgalbarah Tribe of Blacks near the Noomoowoolloo or Wide Bay River', who 'stripped him, but otherwise treated him kindly and claimed him as a relative'. About a year later, Davis 'left them and went on to the North', along the coast. He encountered several rivers, including the Condamine, which he followed inland until he eventually met with a large number of Aboriginal people:

> the Gigyabarah Tribe, about 150 strong: he was claimed as his son by one of
> the fighting men and has remained with them ever since; thinking it the safer

plan, as there is always considerable danger in encountering a new Tribe, for should no one recognise you as a relative returned to life again, you are sure to be speared.

Famously, Davis had been recognised and adopted by a senior man named Pamby-Pamby, as his long departed young son, Duramboi (meaning 'kangaroo-rat').

Meanwhile, David Bracefell (also known as Bracewell or Bracefield), who had been held prisoner at the Moreton Bay settlement since 1827—having been convicted at Middlesex Gaol Delivery of assault and given a sentence of 14 years transportation, and sent first to Hobart Town—had made good on his third escape attempt, on 8 February 1831. He, too, joined Aboriginal people, going into 'the protection of the warrior chief Eumundi' from the Carburrah clan of Lake Cootharaba at Noosa, as Tynan writes.

Like Davis, Bracefell had the good fortune to be recognised as a relative returned from the grave, with Eumundi claiming him as his son. He was given the name of Wandi, meaning 'great talker'. As the name suggests, Bracefell might indeed have been something of a braggart—he would claim to have assisted in the 'rescue' of Eliza Fraser but, on reaching the settlement with her, had been fearful of retribution and had withdrawn, leaving another white man, returned runaway John Graham, to claim the credit (see chapter 6). In May 1837, some eight months after Mrs Fraser's return, Bracefell was captured and taken to Brisbane in May 1837—but two years later he managed to escape again and returned to Eumundi's clan (after the death of Eumundi).

Bracefell's name, Wandi, also indicated a facility with languages. At the time of his capture, Bracefell could speak the language of his group fluently, as well as the dialects of four different groups, and his abilities in this regard would make him valuable to the colonial authorities.

In 1842, on the heels of the closure of the Moreton Bay penal settlement, Andrew Petrie, clerk of works at Moreton Bay, was commissioned to explore the coastline around the area as far as Wide Bay and, at the same time, to gather up convict runaways who remained at large. The party set off in early May, and the entry in Petrie's journal where he documented the party's landing at Noosa Heads gives a vivid depiction of colonial attitudes of the time. Having tried several times to make landing at different places but being unable to do so because of heavy surf, the party eventually found its way into a bay shortly after sunset, where a 'very heavy swell' confronted them:

> Before leaving the boat we were surprised to see twenty or thirty aborigines running along the beach, coming to meet us. I made signs to them to carry us ashore, and they immediately jumped into the water up to their arm-pits. I was the first who mounted their shoulders. They appeared bold and daring, and I immediately suspected that this must be the place where several shipwrecked seamen had been murdered by these black cannibals. Little did I think at the time that the one who carried me ashore was the principal murderer. The moment he put me off his shoulders he laid hold of my blanket, but I seized him and made him drop it. He then took hold of a bag of biscuit, and would have taken it away had I not taken strong measures to prevent him. There were no guns on shore, and those on board were not loaded, so I called for my rifle, and, loading it, kept them at bay, and at the same time made them carry our luggage on shore. We then gave them a few biscuits, and ordered them off to their camp, retaining the murderer and another, and kept regular watch all night, each of us taking an hour in turn. During supper I made enquiries after 'Wandie' (the bush name of the runaway Bracefield), and was informed by the natives that he was only a short way off.

Petrie sent a note to the runaway via two Aboriginal men on the expedition and asked them to bring Bracefell back.

They soon returned with him, as well as three men of his clan, including 'his adopted father'. Petrie noted that Bracefell could not recollect his language for some time but, when he could, his 'first expression was to thank me for being the means of bringing him back to the society of white men again'. Petrie also noticed that Bracefell was very anxious that he might be flogged for his escape, but Petrie convinced him that, if he joined their party and assisted them in mapping the country, 'things would turn to his advantage'. Bracefell agreed, and he and 'his friend, the blackfellow', provided Petrie with the names of some landforms, and helped them make contact with other Aboriginal people as they travelled on. It was at this point that the stories of Davis and Bracefell would intersect. In Harold Richards' biography of Davis, Bracefell also passed on information that he had received from 'his black friend, that there was another white man in the area, living with a tribe whose run was mostly on "a large water"'. The party then set out in search of this man, with Bracefell piloting their boat to the mouth of the Mary River at Wide Bay.

In his journal, Petrie described how he heard the sounds of a large gathering of people about half a mile from the camp they had made, and sent Bracefell and Ullappah, one of the Aboriginal men with the expedition, to investigate. They returned to report that there was indeed a very large gathering under way:

> Bracefield was sure there were some hundreds of them; he and the black
> were both much frightened; he told me he would require two more men with
> firearms. Bracefield informed me the man we were in quest of, Davis, or
> 'Duramboi' (his bush name), was sure to be with the tribe, on which I offered
> to accompany him and assist him in procuring him.

Bracefell insisted that two convict members of the party should go, not only because of the danger to Petrie, but 'if they succeeded in bringing him into our camp, something might be done for these men in the way of mitigating their punishment'.

On reaching the camp, Bracefell and Ullappah went among the people while the two convicts remained on the outskirts. Bracefell was recognised by many of the people there who told him that 'the white fellows had poisoned a number of their tribe'. Bracefell assured them that Petrie's party had come only to:

> explore the river and the country, and would not interfere with the blacks,
> provided that they did not meddle with the white men. If they did, there were
> a great many white men and firearms, and they would be shot immediately.

Meanwhile, Davis had taken the opportunity to hand himself over to the two convicts rather than to Bracefell, declaring to Bracefell that he had come to get him (Davis) just to get his own sentence mitigated—a not unjustified accusation. Davis refused to accept Bracefell's denials, until Bracefell 'got into a passion and sung a war song at him'. Petrie wrote:

> With that Davis bolted off towards us [the expedition camp], our men being
> scarcely able to keep pace with him. I shall never forget his appearance when
> he arrived in our camp—a white man in a state of nudity, and actually a wild
> man of the woods, his eyes wild and unable to rest for a moment on any one
> object. He had quite the same manners and gestures that the wildest blacks
> have got. He could not speak his 'mither's' tongue, as he called it ... all he
> could say was a few words, and these often misapplied, breaking off abruptly
> in the middle of a sentence with the black gibberish, which he spoke very
> fluently. During the whole of our conversation, his eyes and manner were

completely wild, and he looked at us as if he had never seen a white man before. In fact, he told us he had nearly forgotten all about the society of white men, and had hardly thought about his friends and relations for these fourteen years past; and had I or some one else not brought him from among these savages, he never would have left them.

Henry Stuart Russell, a member of Petrie's party, gave a vivid description of Davis' appearance:

> Derhamboi was wearing the necklaces and armlets usual among the natives, and as he frantically went on in the scream of his excitement, seeing that we were unable to understand a word he said, and could express himself in no other language: too impatient to submit to the dilatory relief of interpretation: flew off again into a satanic passion, wrenched off his bijouterie and set to tearing and clawing up the ground with his fingers, sinking his voice from the shrillest howl to a very Bedlamite whisper, accompanied by a wicked leer well suited to the change. A long time afterwards he told me that he had never been able to recollect what had passed! I think he was mad.

It turned out that Davis was trying to make them understand that they were in great danger if the party continued on (as Petrie had indicated they planned to do) as the Aboriginal people then gathering in such numbers were determined to take revenge on the white people. With the help of Bracefell interpreting, Davis explained the reason for the 'great gathering of tribes and fighting men': they were commemorating a recent mass poisoning of Aboriginal people carried out by shepherds on some sheep stations recently established not far from the southern end of the Bunya lands. Some 50 to 60 people died 'horrible' and 'agonising' deaths after eating arsenic-laced flour. Davis enacted for the transfixed party the scenes of the poisonings and the subsequent stalking and killing of two of the shepherds.

Davis further told the party that his adoptive father, Pamby-Pamby, 'had a white man's watch wrapped in grass, part of the *spolia opima* after the murder mentioned', which had been passed between all the tribes to 'wonder at it' before being returned to Pamby-Pamby. Asked to have his father bring the watch to them in exchange for a tomahawk, Davis agreed, but also asked to be allowed to return to the Aboriginal people for the night: 'and he would try and make it alright with them; he pledged his word he would return to us by daybreak'. Petrie allowed him to do so, in the company of Bracefell and Ullappah, although most of the party, Petrie recorded, did not believe Davis would return, or rather, he would return at the head of an attacking party:

> This made our party very timid, and I therefore took what I thought was the most prudent plan, which was to put everything in the boat and sleep on board, keeping a regular watch all night ... some of us did not sleep much, we were all prepared for them.

The whole encounter seems highly ritualistic. The next morning at sunrise, as arranged, Petrie had three musket shots fired as the signal for Davis to return, and he duly emerged accompanied by his Aboriginal father, 'very much afraid of us', who presented them with a European watch, belonging to a shepherd killed at the Kilcoy station some time before. Petrie gave the man a tomahawk in exchange, as promised. Petrie learned, probably from Bracefell, that Davis and Bracefell (who had been welcomed by the Aboriginal people) had made them

so many had hung about his neck; clung to his limbs, his legs, his arms, to stay him

believe that they would return to the gathering, and that Davis had made a long 'oration', reiterating Bracefell's account earlier in the day that white men had come to explore and intended no harm to the people but would shoot them 'all' if they were molested. Furthermore, Davis impressed upon them the terrible power of guns and, when the three shots were fired in the morning, 'they nearly all fled in the greatest consternation'. 'This,' concluded Petrie, 'terminated our manoeuvres with the natives.'

Davis' description of how he parted from his people that morning, before returning to Petrie's party, was recorded by Russell in his narrative of Davis' return published many years later:

> so many had hung about his neck; clung to his limbs, his legs, his arms, to stay him, maybe, yet from going farther away from them. How they kissed and moaned in low tones, for fear we should hear.

Russell was suspicious of Davis, noting that he had 'adorned himself afresh' with bracelets and armlets. Russell thought Davis' account of how he had successfully persuaded his friends that the white party was much more numerous and dangerous than they really were, in order to prevent them being attacked, was 'got up in order to curry favour with his new messmates, and I still believe that fear alone [of the British authorities] brought him in'.

Russell also gives us a most vivid description of the scene of Davis' departure from the Aboriginal people:

No sooner had our oars dropped into the water on Pamby-Pamby's withdrawal, than every tree by the water's side, in the bush beyond, below, this side and that side: every hiding place unnoticed but for what it now revealed, became alive with natives; some peering round the stout trunks, afraid to expose their bodies to a possible 'tolloolpil' (shot); others springing unexpectedly into view from some protecting limb aloft, while the dark scrub shot out hundreds of heads, young and old, piccaninnies and gins, whose habitual caution and jealousy of being seen by strange people had been put aside on such an occasion of grief and wonder,—thrust before our astonished eyes an extemporised tableau vivant, of which white man, methought, shall never see the like again.

Pamby-Pamby launched into a long, lamenting song, and then the people around him took up the refrain. Davis, 'shaking in every limb', thereupon launched into song himself, a translation of which Russell offered:

I came to you when young and driven like a dog from the doors of the 'makromme:' I told you of all my misery and my torture: I said, 'do to me as you think best, I am yours,' and I dropped as one dead again, for I was hungry, thirsty, weak and worn with looking behind for the hated ones pursuing: you came together, but all was to me as a fog: your voices were crying kill! kill! but there was little life to stamp out: you, Pamby-Pamby, knew me again: could I tell who I had been? You knew me father: you took me, you fed me, you gave me tabil (water) to drink, you gave me flesh to eat. Was I not your son? Beegie [the sun] had washed me back to you, and I was glad. But the great Commandant (pointing to the south) has sent for me, I must go: I will come back; when the moon has come back to you three times I shall be here.

The people followed him, singing, for some miles. Petrie's party made camp that night about 17 miles down river, where Davis was shaved, and given clothes to wear. Remarked Russell: 'as the effect always is upon blacks, so his appearance in stature was reduced to somewhat below the average white man's'.

For the rest of the journey, Davis, recovering his English language abilities, entertained the party with his descriptions of 'the manner of life and customs of the blacks', including demonstrating the way they hunted emu and kangaroo and climbed trees. 'His clothes were a great annoyance to him for some days.' He impressed upon them his great regret on leaving the Aboriginal people, and the way he told it convinced Russell that he shared deeply 'in the grief which had dogged his footsteps all the way back'.

The hostility between Duramboi and Wandi continued. Russell recorded that they kept far apart at night and during the day spoke only to each other 'in a quarrelsome fashion', the others having to intervene at one point to prevent them having a spear fight, which 'if anything, made matters worse for the rest of the cruise':

> One would sit in the bows, the other in the stern-sheets; both looked moody, and were plainly considering matters in doubt and disquietude as the distance day by day between Brisbane and ourselves diminished.

However, by the time they got back to Moreton Bay in May 1842 and once they were fully assured that neither would be going back into custody or taking a flogging, the men relaxed into their new surroundings. Petrie's son Tom remembered that, on the night of their return, some of the squatters asked the two men to perform Aboriginal songs and to 'tell them about the blacks':

> The two men sat down tailor-fashion as the natives do, and one had a couple of waddies and the other had boomerangs, and with these they beat time to their songs. The squatters kept them going for half the night.

This was the only time on record that Duramboi was known to have spoken in any way about his life with the Aboriginal people. Tom said that Davis had been happy to show the cicatrices on his body at first but, from a few months after his return, 'I don't think he would have shown his marks even to the King'.

Davis' return marked the onset of very fierce conflict between Aboriginal people and white colonists in south-eastern Queensland, which might be traced to the Kilcoy poisonings. Like other returned white men before him, Davis initially served as a guide for the colonists looking to expand their grasp on the country, including for an expedition back to the country where he had lived (and where stations were being abandoned in the wake of Aboriginal retaliation for the Kilcoy poisonings), during which time it is recorded that he met up with some people he had previously known. He and Bracefell were both 'attached' to the colonial police force while they served out the remainder of their sentences (their time with the Aboriginal people not being taken into account). The authorities intended they should be utilised as interpreters with the Native Police. During this time, as Tynan tells us, it appears that only Bracefell was employed as an interpreter for the police, while Davis served as a hutkeeper and blacksmith, and was reported to have been 'little better than an aborigine' himself. In 1844, both men were recommended for a ticket-of-leave (a permit to work for others or work for themselves), but Bracefell did not enjoy it for long, as he was killed by a falling tree branch while felling timber.

Davis was more fortunate. In 1846, he managed to secure some kind of reward for his efforts in volunteering to help search for a purported white female shipwreck survivor at Wide Bay. This woman was probably Barbara Thompson (see chapter 7), whose ship was actually wrecked some 2,000 miles further to the north. But, while Davis was unsuccessful in locating her, he did get the freedom he sought and enough resources to start up his own blacksmith shop at Kangaroo Point on the Brisbane River late that year.

It was some time after this that young Tom Petrie commented to Davis that he could make 'a lot of money' if he got somebody to write up the story of his adventures as Duramboi. Now a married man with his business well established, Davis had responded:

> I don't want to make money. I get enough now to keep me. If any one wants
> to know about the blacks, let them go and live as I did. I'll tell you a thing that
> happened the other day. A swell who lives in this town [Brisbane] brought
> another swell with him to see me, and said, 'Mr. Davis, allow me to introduce
> Mr. So-and-so to you, from Sydney; he has come all the way to see you, and to get
> some information about the blacks.' Do you know what I said to him? I said, 'Do
> you see the door there? Well, the sooner you get out of my shop the better, and if
> you want any information about the blacks, take your clothes off and go and live
> with them as I did.' And off they went with their tails between their legs, and I
> saw nothing more of them. No one will get anything from me about the blacks.

Davis also worked on occasion as an interpreter for the courts in a number of cases involving Aboriginal defendants and witnesses during the 1850s, and in 1861 Davis gave evidence to the Queensland Government's Select Committee

Opposite: The returned James Davis in 1872, now a
storekeeper of a crockery shop in George Street, Brisbane.

on the Native Police Force, by now notorious for the violence they had wreaked across the colony upon Aboriginal people for the previous 40 years. Startlingly, Davis firmly defended the Native Police and attacked the character of Aboriginal people in general: 'they are a lazy race, and not inclined for doing any good ... I would not trust them as far as I could throw a bullock by the tail'. But, when asked how he had been treated by those he himself had lived with, he stated simply: 'First-rate—nothing could be better'. Whatever complex motivations lay behind his undeniably hostile testimony, by this time Davis wanted no part in any further interactions between Aboriginal people and colonists on the frontier. The final question he was asked was whether he thought an interpreter for the outlying districts might be useful to 'keep the blacks quiet', to which he retorted that 'I don't think you could find an interpreter on this side of the country', and that he himself would not act as one, 'and I would speak the blacks' language with anyone'.

Although he continued to act as an interpreter in court cases until the 1880s, he became steadfastly obstinate in his refusal to talk to white people about his experiences among the Aboriginal people—as stated in his obituary, on the 'rare occasions' when he was 'willing to refer to his first adventures, at the first question he would abruptly stop in a snappish manner, and break off the conversation at once'. The writer, William Robertson, who delivered a series of radio lectures enthusiastically promoting Aboriginal culture during the 1920s and who claimed to have met Davis in his later years, did not like him at all, describing him as 'a grumpy old chap'.

Despite his reticence with white people, Davis may have maintained some of his personal connections. According to Fraser Island's local historian, Fred Williams, there were persistent rumours throughout his life that Davis used to periodically rejoin his Aboriginal family. Apparently, he had also arranged for his son by an Aboriginal woman, fathered during his life as Duramboi, to come and live with him and his wife in Brisbane, although the wife drove the youth away. It's not clear whether this was his first wife, Annie Shea, whom he married in 1846 and who died in 1882, or his second wife, Bridget Hayes, who he married the following year. In 1889, Davis died, as oddly as he had lived, following a bad beating by Bridget.

A perpetual enigma, Davis carried his memories and knowledge of the Aboriginal people to the grave.

Davis later in life—'a grumpy old chap'.

Davis' Aboriginal Life

After his return to European society, Davis was extremely reluctant to divulge anything of his life with the Aboriginal people and there are few recorded accounts of his time with them. Nevertheless, Davis had established himself within the social structure and had participated in ceremonial practice. His chest had parallel lines of ceremonial scars, his thigh had a scar of a spear wound and, below his right knee, there was a gash from a boomerang. He had learned to speak four or five different languages, and eventually he had acquired a wife and had a son.

When Davis was discovered by Andrew Petrie's expedition party, he demonstrated to them that, with the help of a length of vine, he could quickly climb up huge bunya trees; he could sing Indigenous songs (as well as Scottish songs), and he could 'throw a spear, a club, or a boomerang, with the best of them'. Tom Petrie recalled how, when his father met with some Aboriginal men of Davis' tribe years later, they remembered Duramboi with admiration:

> These men said they were very sorry when 'Duramboi' left them; they cried a lot, for they missed him very much. They all looked up to him. He was a great man to hunt for game, was always lucky in spearing kangaroo, and was a good hand at spear and boomerang throwing. He could also climb splendidly, using a vine as they did, and was so smart in capturing 'possums or honey. Then he was a great fighter.

MORTUARY RITES

Unfortunately, John Dunmore Lang's account of Davis' story in his book, *Cooksland*, published five years after Davis' return, was entirely taken up with a detailed description of what seems to have been elaborate funerary rites for warriors killed in battle, involving the consumption of portions of human flesh before their remains were preserved as relics, and offers very little about any other aspect of the culture of the people Davis lived with for many years. Lang took considerable pains to argue that Davis (who he called 'Davies') gave indisputable proof that 'in that part of the Australian territory the bodies of the dead, whether they fall in battle or die a natural death, are, with the exception of the bodies of old men and women, uniformly eaten by the survivors'.

Henry Stuart Russell, likewise, wrote in sensational and gruesome details about the supposed cannibalism among the Aboriginal people, complete with a story he claimed that Davis had told in mime for the amusement of Petrie's party, about Aboriginal women killing an old woman and then secretly feasting on her remains. (Russell also asserted that he had not believed either Bracefell or Davis' 'protestations of having kept their own hands clean of such defilement'.) It appears that Russell was considerably and imaginatively embellishing a description of what were funerary rites, to satisfy an audience eager to believe the very worst of those they sought to dispossess and eradicate from the face of the land. Given the horrific distortions these two writers gave of Davis' experiences, it is not surprising that Davis became so surly towards any who interrogated him.

THE KABI PEOPLE

Davis had named the people with whom he lived as the Gigyabarah people (Russell called them the 'Ginginbarah'), but many writers today identify them as the 'Kabi' or 'Gubbi-Gubbi'. There are descriptions of these people in the accounts of nineteenth-century writers such as Ebenezer Thorne, who wrote of the Noosa tribes in the 1860s: 'a fine race of men, among who are as finely formed and well-developed specimens of the race as are to be found elsewhere', characterised by 'a dignity of gesture, a firmness of tread, a litheness and gracefulness of motion' that Europeans associated with the image of 'gentlemen'. Similarly, nineteenth-century ethnographer John Mathew described the Kabi as carrying themselves like 'the lords of creation, stepping out with elastic tread and graceful bearing', as they gathered their food along the way—'opossums, bandicoots, honey, grubs, birds, and so forth'.

An Aboriginal man of the Kabi people, holding a club and boomerang.

5

John Ireland—'Waki'
& William D'Oyley—'Uass'

The story of the 'shipwrecked orphans', John Ireland and William D'Oyley, who lived with the Islanders of Torres Strait for nearly two years before their rescue in 1836, is hardly remembered today, but their story captured the white colonial imagination at the time. It was retold, almost immediately, in two separate books written by men who were part of the rescue party. A third appeared the year after, written by Thomas Wemyss and, in 1838, John Ireland himself published a version written for children (edited by Thomas Teller, a purveyor of sentimental 'orphan' stories), which was republished several times. An account also appeared in the first Australian children's book, *A Mother's Offering*, in 1841.

To our eyes, it is not a suitable story for children, but it definitely had a major impact on generations of young Australian readers. This was particularly true of Wemyss' book, whose graphic details of the initial massacre of the shipwreck survivors cemented an enduring colonial fixation with the shipwreck survivors being attacked and eaten by native cannibals. Much less acknowledged was the loving treatment that the two boys received from the families who became their guardians on Mer (Murray) Island, and for whom John Ireland sought some recognition in his account.

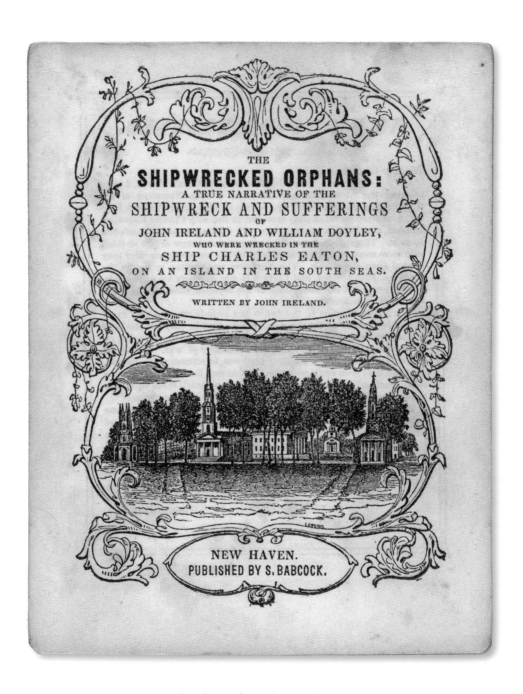

The title page from John Ireland's own
account of his experiences, published in 1845.

The story began with the shipwreck of a wooden barque, the *Charles Eaton*, en route to India from Australia in 1834, on the outer northern reaches of the Great Barrier Reef. On board were Captain Thomas D'Oyley of the Bengal Artillery and his wife Charlotte, their two youngest sons, George and William, aged eight and three respectively, and the boys' Indian nursemaid. The D'Oyleys had been in India with the British imperial army and were returning to Surabaya from Hobart. There were also two cabin boys, John Sexton (or a William Hill) and John Ireland, the latter a tall, thin boy aged 15, who came from one of London's outlying villages and had joined the crew on the ship's voyage from England.

The fate of the four boys, two of them born into privilege and two into much more challenging circumstances, would become entwined in the aftermath of the wreck. The ship struck the reef 'so violently that both the keel and the rudder were instantly knocked off and carried away'. One of the two lifeboats was smashed to pieces while being lowered into the wild sea. Some of the crew took the remaining boat, marooning the other survivors on the wreck. In his account of events, Ireland was damning of those sailors in the lifeboat: 'they

only thought of themselves, and made no attempt to assist those on board, but after getting what they could from the wreck, made off'. It took this renegade group more than 12 months to reach Batavia and alert authorities about the shipwreck.

Meanwhile, the survivors left on the wreck set about constructing a raft. The first they built would not hold all 30 people and there is a strong suggestion that the ship's captain and others, including the D'Oyley family, deserted during the night leaving those left behind, including John Ireland, to make a second raft, which took another week.

Ireland described how they drifted for several days on the raft 'up to our waists in water, and with a very small allowance of food', before on the fourth day encountering a canoe coming towards them, manned by ten to 12 'native Indians':

> As they came towards us, they extended their arms, which we supposed meant that they were unarmed, and wished to be friendly.

An Islander outrigger setting out to meet ships for trade.

The Indigenous men wanted to trade with the survivors, one of them being drawn to the raft's sail of white cloth. The others were 'very much pleased' with a mirror and a piece of red cloth. They had experienced contact with white men before (as far back as 1802, Matthew Flinders' party, on its circumnavigation of the continent, had met with Meriam Islanders who traded with them) and, like the people that William Buckley had met, were keenly interested in acquiring iron. Directing the survivors to get into their canoe, the men then 'commenced a strict search for iron and tools' and finding a 'few old hoops', loaded them into the canoe as well.

The Islanders went past several islands before landing on Boydang Cay, one of the innumerable small islands in the Torres Strait. From here, Ireland could see the mainland, but there were 'ominous signs' that the island was not inhabited, as there were no huts visible. With their rescuers accompanying them, the survivors set off walking around the island looking for water and food, but found none. Intensely fatigued, they collapsed. The Islanders began to behave alarmingly, 'grinning and yelling in a most hideous manner, as though delighting in the success of their schemes'.

As the exhausted survivors began to fall asleep, Ireland recorded that he noticed a man coming back up the beach from the canoe with a club in his hand. The Islanders placed themselves among the survivors, and, despite his unease, Ireland also fell asleep.

Soon after, Ireland was torn from his slumber by shouting and screaming, waking to the horrifying scene of his comrades being bludgeoned to death with clubs and having their heads hacked off with knives. Ireland was thrown into complete shock and confusion. When a large Islander, whom he later came to know as Biskea, approached him holding a carving knife from the ship, Ireland was terrified and struggled furiously with him. He managed to break free and ran into the sea, but, with darkness approaching, Ireland realised he would have to return to shore to stay alive. There are conflicting accounts of what happened when he returned to shore, but one quoted him saying that Biskea gave him food and water. Meanwhile, the other youth, Sexton, had been in the grip of another man, but his life too was spared. The two cabin boys were the only members of the group not killed—presumably, because they were not considered a threat.

Veronica Peek, who has written a lengthy and detailed blog based on her extensive research into the story of the *Charles Eaton* shipwreck, suggests that the Islanders probably considered the adult survivors as potentially extremely dangerous. Later testimonials and evidence indicated that these people had every reason not only to be mistrustful of white people, but to strike first. Wemyss conceded that the Islanders' actions were justifiable 'owing to the outrageous behaviour of European or American seamen', who were 'too apt to consider these poor beings in no other light than wild beasts; but this is from prejudice, and a misconception of their real character'. In a confessionary tone, Wemyss further stated they 'are an injured people, and like all other injured people, they have been traduced and vilified by their oppressors, by way of excuse for the injury done them'.

Following the attack, the Islanders built a large fire on the sand, before which the heads of the dead were placed in a row. In a somewhat gothic scene, the two youths sat huddled together next to the fire and, as Ireland wrote in his book, witnessed ritual cannibalism when the Islanders:

> cut pieces of flesh from the cheeks, and pluck out the eyes and eat them ...
> This, I afterwards learned, it was the custom of these islanders to do with their prisoners; they think that it will give them courage, and excite them to revenge themselves upon their enemies.

The boys' captors divided up the spoils they had taken from the dead men, but showed concern for the boys by covering them with a canoe's grass sail for the night. It was a long and disturbed night for Ireland and Sexton, who expected at any moment to be murdered.

the Islanders built a large fire on the sand, before which the heads of the dead were placed in a row

The next morning, the Islanders collected the heads and left in their canoes, taking the boys with them to another island, 'which they called Pullan, where the women lived'. On first landing at the island, John Ireland's spirits were lifted when he spotted the ship's dog and the young sons of Captain D'Oyley, who were being cared for by Islander women. George told Ireland that their parents had both been killed, along with all the others who left the *Charles Eaton* on the first raft.

On surveying the scene, John Ireland quickly understood the calamity that had taken place. Some canoes now sported the cabin doors that had been used in the construction of the first raft. He also saw pieces of clothing, including Charlotte D'Oyley's gown, and:

> Near the huts a pole was stuck in the ground, around which were hung the heads of our unfortunate companions. Among them I plainly recognised Mrs Doyley's, for they had left part of the hair on it.

George told Ireland that his little brother, William, had been in his mother's arms when she was killed, but was saved by one of the Islander women who rushed forward and snatched him up, while another woman had rescued George in the same way. Again, it seems the D'Oyley boys escaped because of their youth.

A few days after Sexton and Ireland reached Pullan Island, a ship passed the island at some distance, and Ireland tried to induce the Islanders to take the boys to it, but they refused. Only a week later, two ships were seen much closer to shore and this unsettled the Islanders:

> The natives seemed very much frightened at this, and were in the utmost confusion; they took us, and all the skulls, with the dog, and hid among the bushes until the ships were gone.

Ireland estimated that they spent about three months on the island. The island, which had at its centre a rare and plentiful supply of fresh water from a spring, was a well-known and long established base of operations.

Captives' skulls were the focus of rituals and ceremonies.

The boys were not given much food, but were expected to provide for themselves. Some of the men took them spearfishing in the canoes, but if the fishing was successful the boys were given only the entrails and heads—otherwise they ate only whatever plant food they could forage. Ireland recalled that 'We were sometimes so hungry as to be glad to eat the grass'.

The two older boys were:

chiefly employed in climbing trees, and breaking up fire-wood to cook the fish with; when they thought we had not gathered enough, they would beat us with their hands, and sometimes with the wood.

The two younger boys, George and William D'Oyley, having come from pampered lives in India, were especially ill-prepared for life in the wild. William, the three-year-old, began to aggravate everyone around him with his persistent crying. The people beat him and occasionally tied him up for several hours. Ireland once earned their wrath by untying the child and nearly lost his life in the process with a warning arrow whizzing inches past his head.

One day, the group on Pullan Island split into two groups, with John Ireland and William D'Oyley in one group and John Sexton and George D'Oyley remaining on the island with the other. The separation of the young D'Oyley brothers must have been truly traumatic in the wake of witnessing the deaths of their parents.

Ireland and William's party travelled north by canoe for many weeks, eventually arriving at Erub Island (Darnley Island) where they were welcomed as trading partners by the local people, who had several villages dotted across the island and who numbered around 400 people. The island was well watered and had an abundance of food. According to Peek, the Erub Islanders were wealthier than the people of the central islands who had the boys (the Gam le) and able to offer generous hospitality, while the latter maintained the equilibrium by adventuring in search of hard-to-get trading items, such as a calico sail they had taken from the first raft off the *Charles Eaton*.

John Ireland looked back on the Erub Islander people with great fondness, as he recalled that here, in the village of Bikar, they were treated kindly for the first time. They ate well for the first time, too, on yams, sweet potatoes, bananas, fish and coconut milk.

After about two weeks, when the trading and bartering was over, the two boys left with their canoe party and made their way to Sirreb (Marsden Island). Here, the boys were given new names—'Waki' for John and 'Uass' for William.

A week later, some Meriam Islanders arrived to trade with the Gam le. Among this trading group were a man called Duppa and his wife, Panney, who knew about the boys through a friend on Erub Island. It seems they travelled to Sirreb with the idea of rescuing the boys through barter. Duppa made an offer of two branches of bananas and the deal was done. Peek surmises that the Gam le people's willingness to hand over the boys for such a small payment might have been to placate the Meriam Islanders, with whom they had been at war.

The boys left with Duppa's party in a canoe bound for Mer, stopping on the way at Massid (Yorke Island). It was here that they reconnected with some of the Gam le men who had stayed at Pullan Island. There was no sign of John Sexton and George D'Oyley. Although openly hostile to Ireland, the Massid Islanders would not touch the boys as they were now under the protection of the powerful Duppa. When Duppa and his party arrived back on Mer, they were met by a large group of people excited by the appearance of the two white boys and full of questions. Duppa and Panney adopted Waki and Uass into their family, which included five other children, three boys and two girls.

Ireland (Waki) and William (Uass) took to speaking the Meriam language. Little Uass was given in to the special care of a man called Oby. 'This man soon got very fond of the little boy, as the child also became of him,' Ireland recounted, 'indeed he seemed here to have quite forgotten his father and mother.' Waki kept an eye on the little boy and when he was concerned about his state of mind would ask to be allowed to sleep in Oby's hut

A village scene by Harden Melville, artist on surveying expeditions in the 1840s, depicting the Erub Islanders who treated John Ireland and William D'Oyley so kindly.

with him, which 'made him much more happy'. Eventually Uass completely entered the Meriam world:

> As soon as he could speak their language pretty freely, he would go down to the beach with the other children of the island; and the effect of the sun on his skin became very apparent. In a few months he could not be distinguished by his color from the other children; his hair being the only thing by which he could be known at a distance, from its light color.

At one point, when the ship, the *Mangles,* came to trade, Waki's people prevented him from returning to the Europeans, out of concern for his safety. Ireland described in his account how Duppa painted him black 'as he usually did when a vessel came in sight', with a streak of red across his face, while Duppa's wife and daughters put ornaments around his neck and limbs, and hung tassels of plaited grass in his ear piercings. Waki then went out in a canoe with the Islanders to the ship, but a recently sprained wrist made him unable to take hold of a rope thrown down to the canoe. One of the crew held out some tobacco to Ireland and, when he asked him to lower one of their boats to enable him to get in, they did so, but they:

> put their pistols and naked cutlasses into it. When the natives saw that, they thought mischief was intended to me and to themselves; they immediately let go the rope, and paddled towards the shore. I stood up in the canoe; but Dupper took hold of me and laid me down in the middle of it. The boat rowed a little way after us and then returned to the vessel.

A few hours later, a boat from the ship came onto the island, but, while Ireland recounted that one of the Islanders went so far as to take little William down to the beach and 'beckoned to the crew to come and take him', the captain signalled that the Islanders should come to them. With both parties distrustful of each other's motives, a stalemate was reached, and eventually the boat returned to the ship without either boy.

In a recount by Phillip Parker King, Ireland apparently later said how he could have gone on board the *Mangles* in the boat first lowered for him had 'not one stood up in the bow with a naked cutlass, and the others flourished

Opposite: Harden Melville's depiction of Duppa (sitting, with an axe),
who took charge of the boys. Duppa's adult son, also called Duppa, stands
with a spear, alongside his wife Areg.

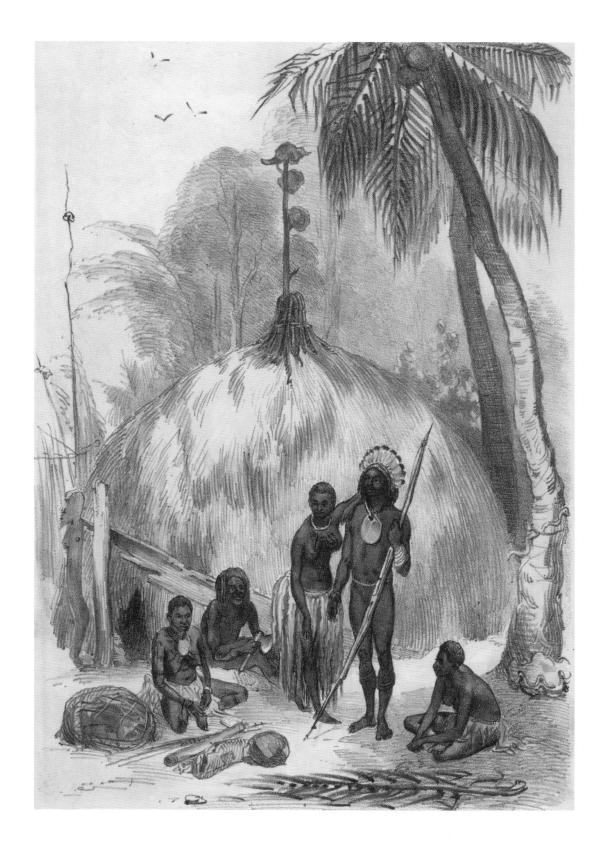

John Ireland—'Waki', & William D'Oyley—'Uass'

their weapons over their heads, which frightened the Indians so much that they pulled away on shore'. Furthermore, had the captain, W. Carr, offered an axe in trade for him as opposed to mere tobacco, both he and the child would have 'been given up immediately'. As it was, the Islanders knew that Ireland wanted to go back to his own people, but they feared he would not be safe in that vessel, saying, 'You shall not go there to be killed'. The departure of the *Mangles* left Ireland feeling depressed.

Around a year later, Duppa's family was looking after his brother's house, high on a hill, while he was away. It was from this high vantage point that Ireland first sighted the *Isabella* near the northern tip of the island. At this point, the two boys had been living in the Torres Strait for some 22 months, and Ireland was just 17 years of age.

The *Mangles* report published in *The Sydney Gazette* together with another report of the original shipwreck had resulted in the colonial governor directing Captain Charles Morgan Lewis of the *Isabella* to proceed to Meriam Island to find out who the Europeans there were. He was directed that if he should find any Europeans he should 'induce the natives to surrender them voluntarily, or to concert measures with the parties themselves, for enabling them to effect their escape'.

On arriving off the shore of Mer Island, the *Isabella* was approached by four canoes of men eager to trade tortoise-shell and coconuts for iron and axes, but the captain insisted that there would be no trading until the European youth was produced—at which point a canoe was sent back to the beach and within the hour had returned with Ireland in it, who as soon as some axes were handed over, came on board.

Ireland explained how he prevailed upon Duppa to let him get on board saying he did not intend to leave him but only wanted to procure some axes. Duppa, Oby and several others came on board with Waki and spent the night on the ship. The *Isabella* captain insisted that there would be no further trade until young William was brought aboard also. Ireland recounted that the following morning the Islanders 'made a great many excuses' not to bring Uass to the Europeans, saying that 'he was crying, and would not leave the women'. Ireland explained that there would be no trading until the child was brought on board and eventually, in the middle of the day, they brought William out to the ship too.

'At first, he seemed frightened at the strangers, and did not like parting with his old black friends,' Ireland recorded, 'but I did my best to pacify him, and he soon became used to the new faces.' The sailors gave the little boy some clothes to wear, and Ireland further commented that he looked strange in them and that they made him uncomfortable: 'I have the cap now in my possession'.

It must have been a very intense experience for both. At the time of their rescue, Ireland was described as being unable to speak English, except for a few limited sentences. Some felt he had completely lost his senses and was mentally impaired: the 'boy appeared almost stupefied'. Captain Lewis stated that he mixed English and the Islander language so much 'that he was, at first, scarcely intelligible'. But Waki was able to express emphatically that their Mer families had treated both him and young D'Oyley with 'parental kindness', and that he owed his life to Duppa.

Duppa was rewarded with linen and 'loaded with presents'. It was noted that he was well pleased, but whether that fully compensated in losing a boy he regarded as a son was not discernible. Young William D'Oyley was described, as he was handed from the canoe, as 'crying and [he] would not leave the black women, who had charge of him ... he could not speak a single word of English, but he spoke the native language with fluency'. The captain also spoke of the heart-wrenching parting of young D'Oyley from his carer, Oby:

> a young Indian, who seemed by his kissing him to be very sorrowful at the idea of giving him up. He, however, embarked in a canoe, and brought him alongside. The child was frightened, and cried very much at the idea of leaving his sable friend, whose neck he clung around and pointed to the shore.

In their last moments with the boys, Duppa and Oby 'were disconsolate at the idea of parting with their favourites'. They pressed the captain to come back to shore and visit them the next day, which he did—with two armed boats waiting to take action should the Islanders be planning an attack. On landing, however, he was 'immediately surrounded by upwards of one hundred Indians, who expressed great delight at the meeting, by hugging and caressing him, and

Following pages: An artist's oil painting of William D'Oyley's 'rescue'.
In reality, the little boy was very reluctant to leave his Islander family.

shaking hands'. A 'movement' in the armed boats frightened the women and children away, but at last they were persuaded to return by some of their men:

> who were evidently amused by their timidity; and an old fat lady gradually drew near and took Mr. Lewis's hand, and held it in one of hers, scratching the palm with the fingers of the other. Confidence being thus restored, the women and children were presented with handkerchiefs and toys, which seemed to delight them very much.

After some two hours with 'these friendly Indians', the captain and his crew, together with the two boys, embarked for Sydney, though not without some further stops to trade with Islanders and to retrieve items from European shipwrecks. The ship also carried in its hold the skulls of Europeans, presumed to be those of the *Charles Eaton* survivors, that they had managed to find in a raid on a ceremonial 'shed' on the island of Aureed, during which the crew 'destroyed everything that could be useful' to the Islanders to show their outrage and set fire to the whole island.

One account states that the captain of the *Isabella* took the young D'Oyley back to England to be reunited with members of his family, while another account reveals that a Mrs Slade of Sydney, known as a friend to the D'Oyley family:

> claimed the child from the Governor, Sir Richard Bourke, who after strict enquiries allowed her claim, and consigned him to her care. When the child was embraced by Mrs Slade, he called her 'Mamma,' the only word he could utter in English.

John Ireland concluded his narrative with a call to his child readers to learn from his story not only to 'avoid the savages of Boydan', but to recognise the humanity of the Islanders who treated him as one of their own: to 'lend a helping hand to civilize the kind natives of Murray's Island, and the Indians of Torres Straits'.

But Ireland's 'little message of friendship' (couched as it was in the patronising terminology of the time) was not destined to have any lasting impact, in stark contrast to the way in which the sensational horrors of the massacre of the adult survivors fed into a fearful European imagination, providing a justification for the slaughter of Indigenous people both on the mainland in the Torres Strait.

Ireland and D'Oyley's Mer Islander Life

There is no doubt that the two boys were very closely integrated into the society of the Mer Islanders, and raised as part of their world. Ireland's sympathetic account provided some insights into the everyday lives and customs of their guardians, though again, there was limited information about their spiritual beliefs, possibly because of the boys' youth, and perhaps because of their uncertain status as outsiders.

THE MER ISLANDERS' APPEARANCE

The Mer Islanders were described by other European adventurers of the time. Naturalist Joseph Beete Jukes, part of the surveying expedition of HMS *Fly* in 1843, described the Mer Islanders as striking people:

> The men were tall, well made, stout and muscular ... Their colour was a dark brown, approaching to black, the hair frizzled, but often dressed in short, close, pipe-like ringlets ... and looking frequently like wigs; none of them had lost a front tooth, neither were they cicatrized or tatooed, except a faint oval scar on the shoulder. The men were naked, but the women had a short petticoat of leaves, reaching from the waist to the knee.

In fact, many of the men did actually wear wigs, made from human hair and often covered in red ochre.

FOOD GATHERING AND HUNTING

Waki and Uass' enculturation into Islander life included participating in food collection and hunting (with large bows and arrows, sometimes poison-tipped). Duppa was a very patient teacher and parent and instructed Waki on 'how to collect shellfish and grow yams, bananas and coconuts'. Waki was given a piece of land to cultivate and his own large canoe from New Guinea. Their 'canoes have two masts opposite to each other, and a sail extended between them ... No boats can be better manoeuvred than these are by the naked savages', wrote Wemyss in his 1837 book.

With lessons, John Ireland became very proficient with the bow and arrow.

The Meriam Islanders used lighted torches to attract fish.

Wemyss also readily praised the Islanders' skills with their weapons:

They are very expert in archery, indeed the most skilful European archers fall far short of these athletic savages, whose amazing feats could not have been surpassed by the English archers of olden times. Their astonishing adroitness can only be attributed to their being accustomed to this exercise from their early youth. Even the boys when very young, amuse themselves, shooting with bows and arrows, suitable to their strength.

Ireland described the techniques of Islander fishing and harvesting:

Their usual way of catching fish is by spearing; but they also take the small ones with a kind of net, something like a sieve. One party disturbs the water, by beating it with long bamboo sticks, and so drive the fish towards the other, who then spear or net them. Lobsters are caught in the following manner: a party will get on a sandbank at night, some of them holding a bunch of lighted cocoa-nut leaves above their heads; the lobsters, seeing the light, leave their holes, and are then speared by the others.

Turtles abound on the islands, and are caught by the natives very dexterously. When they see them asleep on the water, a party of seven or eight go in a canoe, four of the party paddling very slowly and silently towards them, the others squatting on the fore part of the canoe, with a rope fastened to their arms, and only their heads above the side of the canoe. Upon getting near enough, the parties in the canoe suddenly leap out, and catch the turtle by the fins; by which they are then hauled into the boat.

BELIEFS AND WORSHIP

The Islanders practised a form of hero cult of four legendary brothers, and worshipped Malo (Malu). They performed ceremonies and magic as part of the worship of Malo. Ireland made no mention of initiation into the hero cult stage of Islander life and appeared to be completely unfamiliar with any of the rituals attributed to this belief system. He was, however, able to draw upon reflections of the use and perceived power of magic stones to change the weather at sea, and would explain to the captain of the *Isabella*, on which he eventually returned to the European world, how he believed the Islanders had managed to delay the ship's passage out of the Torres Strait by causing a gale that lasted for seven days:

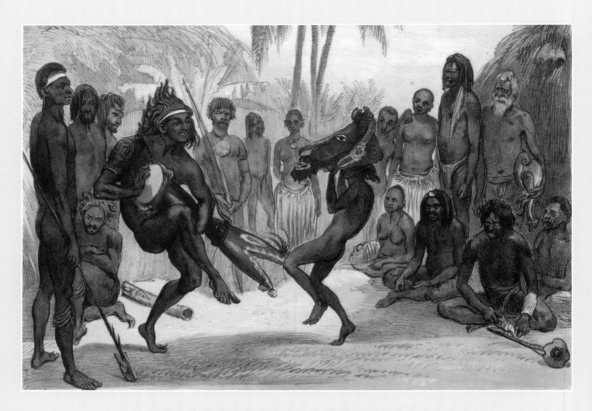

Erub and Meriam Islanders at a ceremonial dance performance.

when they wish the wind to blow hard, [the Murray Islanders] are in the habit of suspending a stone to the branch of a tree, by a string, and of vociferating loudly, and talking to it, and spitting on it, whilst they turn it about; which they suppose causes a gale. The stone is called by them Dow-yumbe.

The Islanders also held deep cultural beliefs about death. One evening, on the death of a near neighbour, Ireland heard the sounds of rattling shells and heavy breathing outside Duppa's hut. Duppa screamed out 'in a language ... quite different from that of Murray's Island, and then himself and all that were in the hut, hid their faces in the sand'. When the boy asked Duppa what the noise was, he replied, 'The spirit of the dead man'. The next day, Ireland heard the same noises and saw:

two figures, one red and the other white, with what appeared to be a fan over each of their heads ... The figures were very short, not larger than children of fourteen years of age. I was told that they were the spirits of their departed friends.

Ireland searched all the huts for evidence of items worn by the figures, but could find none.

According to Philip Parker King, Ireland had said that the Islanders called these spirits of the dead 'lammoors', which meant 'white men'. The Islanders believed that the lammoors were very powerful and, with their huge hands, could kill someone with a single blow.

COLONIALISM

The great majority of Islanders had at least one item made of iron (taken from wrecks or from trade with Europeans)

As with other Europeans who were taken in by Indigenous groups in this early colonial period, Ireland was a witness to the initial impact of colonialism on Indigenous life and experiences. At the time of the discovery of Ireland and D'Oyley, King recorded that the Islanders believed that white people lived 'always on ships, and possess no territorial home, and that they subsist upon sharks, porpoises, and dogs'. In the complex trading culture of the Islanders, the Europeans were valued as iron traders. Ireland recorded that the Islanders were 'very fond' of European items, particularly iron or 'torre':

> When they see a ship, they say directly, 'We will get some torre.' They think iron is found in the white men's country in large rocks; and that we merely have to break pieces off as we want them.

The great majority of Islanders had at least one item made of iron (taken from wrecks or from trade with Europeans) decorating their huts or being used as a tool. On one momentous occasion, Ireland came across Duppa trying fruitlessly to bend a piece of an iron bolt, by bashing it with a large stone. Ireland instructed him to place the iron in a large fire for softening. The Islander leader, amazed and very pleased with the result, quickly informed the others, 'and we were after this frequently employed in straightening or altering the shape of these iron articles, as it might suit the various fancies of their owners'.

John Ireland showed his adopted father, Duppa, how to use heat to soften and shape iron.

Recording that the Islanders gave European guns the same name as that they used for their bows, Ireland recounted how Duppa told him that some of their people had been killed by these guns, 'and they never could see what struck them'. Waki's knowledge of iron working was beneficial to his hosts but, unlike his predecessor at the early Sydney settlement, John Wilson, he couldn't explain to them the workings of the one thing they were most inquisitive about—the white man's deadly weapon.

POSTSCRIPT

In an important postscript to the story, in 1992, after a long struggle in the Australian courts, Meriam man Eddie Koiki Mabo with four other plaintiffs achieved the recognition that the Indigenous people of the Torres Strait islands held sovereignty over their own land in the face of British and Australian colonisation, and had never lost it. The 'Mabo decision', which recognised the potential of Indigenous native title, was a landmark in Australian history.

6

Eliza Fraser

The story of Eliza Fraser remains one of great intrigue, mystery and excitement—and fabrication. Unlike some others, the time Eliza Fraser spent living with Aboriginal people (on present-day Fraser Island and the wider Fraser Coast region of Queensland's southern coastline—named not for her but for her husband) was quite short, no longer than six weeks. In such a short space of time, it is not surprising that Fraser did not become closely integrated into their way of life. What is surprising, and rather far-fetched, is that the Aboriginal people she met with purportedly held her captive and abused and enslaved her. The story of her traumatic experiences would have a powerful and enduring impact in Australian culture. The idea of a white woman being captured by 'wild blacks' and held against her will grabbed the imagination and attention of the white Australian public then, and for many years afterwards.

In recent times, there have been important explorations of the ways in which Eliza Fraser's story entered popular culture from the very first sensational accounts that appeared in newspapers and pamphlets, and then in a full-length narrative by English journalist John Curtis (first appearing in *The Times* newspaper and then in an illustrated book in 1838), through the 1950s when Australian artist Sydney Nolan painted a series of elegiac artworks inspired by her story, to 1976 when Nobel Prize-winning writer Patrick White turned it into the novel, *A Fringe of Leaves*, and director Tim Burstall made a swashbuckling satirical movie about her. Most recently, the Fraser story has been the subject of a book-length study by Indigenous scholar Larissa Behrendt, *Finding Eliza*. The inconsistencies between the multiple accounts and the persistent arguments about the story's details, particularly about who actually 'rescued' her from the Aboriginal people in the end, have also been well documented. Was it the convict, John Graham, as officially recognised, or David Bracefell (Wandi), erstwhile comrade of James Davis (Duramboi)?

This chapter concentrates on disentangling various accounts to get a sense of how Elizer Fraser experienced her life with the Aboriginal people and how they too looked upon her. The Fraser story remains a source of resentment for the descendants of those with whom she lived because of the negative characterisation of their treatment of her. As the first white woman known to have definitely lived with Aboriginal people, Fraser followed in the footsteps of the mythical White Woman of Gippsland (see page 7) and many of the same kind of fears and anxieties about Indigenous people degrading and abusing white women can be seen coming to the fore in the way her experiences were represented. It has often been suggested that Fraser was somewhat deranged, accounting for the extremity of aspects of her narrative and her exaggeration of her ordeals for a market avid for tales of white women enslaved by savages.

Unlike convicts William Buckley and James Davis, Fraser came to Australia as a free person, and in this respect she had more in common with the D'Oyley orphans. In 1835, the *Stirling Castle*, a merchant ship, set sail from England for Van Diemen's Land, its main cargo listed as 900 barrels of ale. On board, along with the crew of 15 and a number of passengers, was Eliza Fraser, the wife of the captain, James Fraser. After a five-month voyage south, the ship berthed in Hobart and then continued on to Sydney where a number of the crew deserted, but replacements were quickly found and the ship duly sailed for Singapore on Sunday 15 May 1836.

Only seven days out to sea, the ship struck a reef off northern Queensland, to the east of present-day Bowen. Heavy seas pounded the ship and it began to break apart. The crew and passengers boarded the damaged ship's longboat and the smaller pinnace. Eleven people were in the longboat, including the captain

Survivor of the *Stirling Castle* shipwreck
Mrs Eliza Fraser, Captain Fraser's wife.

and his wife, as well as provisions they had managed to secure from the *Stirling Castle*. The pinnace, under the command of John Baxter, towed the heavily laden longboat, and they battled through the seas and reefs for five days, eventually landing at Cumberland Island. After making repairs to the boats, they set a course for the mainland. Most of the supplies, including the water, had been exhausted. In one version of the story, Eliza Fraser gave birth to a baby at sea, but the infant only survived for a few minutes. The survivors subsisted on water they could procure and small shellfish they scavenged off the numerous islands around them.

During a wild storm one night, the two boats became separated. Baxter had moved to the longboat, and the sole survivor of the pinnace, seaman Robert Hodge, would later come across a party of white men and be rescued. The longboat reached the northern shore of the island K'gari (later named Fraser Island) at the end of June.

The mode of trading was for the natives to throw a fish, and then the other party to throw some article of clothing by way of payment

The best sources for working out what happened next are not the many lurid accounts published and reworked multiple times but the statements Eliza Fraser and two other survivors provided a few weeks after returning to Brisbane. In her statement, Fraser explained that, when the starving crew members on the longboat saw smoke on shore, they 'became very mutinous' and threatened to throw the captain overboard if he prevented them from putting ashore. The captain 'endeavoured to dissuade them by telling them the blacks would murder them all', but was unable to stop them.

On landing, she continued, the Aboriginal people immediately 'came down in numbers, but were prevented at first from using any violence from the sight of our Firearms'. Curtis' published account explains that the survivors initially ate a kind of breadfruit and a 'berry of the gooseberry species, which, although sweet and refreshing to the taste, proved highly detrimental to health', indicating that they were foraging for themselves.

An illustration from the Curtis account shows Eliza Fraser
searching for water on a rock ledge, upon reaching land.

On the third day, a barter system started up between the survivors and the
Aboriginal people, with up to 150 people coming to visit at a time, generally
bringing 'extremely delicious' mullet: 'The mode of trading was for the natives
to throw a fish, and then the other party to throw some article of clothing by way
of payment'. As Eliza Fraser explained in her statement, 'we procured some fish
from them in exchange for articles of wearing apparel', having taken two trunks
of clothing from the wreck.

Harry Youlden, a crew member and one of the survivors, later gave this account:

> The natives were shy at first, and would not come near us; but if we moved ever so short a distance from the boat, they were very sure to carry off all they could lay their hands on ... The natives brought us a few small fish, that were very stale and forbidding; but hunger like ours is never dainty; so putting them on the fire, we ate them, half-cooked, with much relish.

It is hard to imagine what the local Aboriginal people made of these white strangers from the sea, with their inability to feed themselves and their seemingly inexhaustible supply of sewn clothing and bags, which they eagerly offered as currency for fish. The Aboriginal people showed no interest whatever in making use of the clothing they were given or had taken, instead quickly secreting the items away in the bush never to be seen again.

After the boat was repaired, five of the crew told the captain that they intended to walk back to Moreton Bay (perhaps thinking they were on a peninsula) rather than try their chances at sea again. It was now ten days after landing on the island and the dissenters, including Harry Youlden and Robert Darge, set off. Not long afterwards, the six who had remained (the captain and his wife, chief officer Charles Brown, second officer John Baxter, steward Joseph Corallis (sometimes spelled Carrallis or Corralis) and crew member Michael Doyle) had a rethink and followed them. The next day, Eliza Fraser recorded, they met with 'a numerous tribe of natives, who finding us unarmed took every thing from us with the exception of the clothes on our backs, beating us severely at the least resistance'.

Some two days later, Fraser and her party met with another group who now 'stripped us perfectly naked and forced us to follow them into their camp'. It was from this point, according to Fraser in her original statement, her enslavement began:

> We were now portioned off to different masters, who employed us in carrying wood, water and bark, and treated us with the greatest cruelty. With the exception of a small portion of Fish which we but very seldom got, all we had to subsist upon was a kind of Fernroot which we were obliged to procure ourselves in the swamps.

In his longer narrative, Curtis described how, following this final stripping, Corallis and Doyle left Fraser's group, and the rest of the survivors continued

An over-dramatised rendition of the *Stirling Castle*
survivors being stripped of their clothes.

on. Seeing a large group of Aboriginal people, painted either red or black to indicate their tribal affiliations, they took cover in the bush, but were driven out with fire. To their surprise, their captors then supplied them with water and fresh fish. They were further astonished to see among them the survivors from the first group who had gone ahead (with Youlden and Darge), and Corallis and Doyle also. The account implies that there had been discussions between the various clans or wider groups in the area about what to do about these people wandering about in their country, and that they had launched a combined effort to bring them altogether and sort them out between them.

Darge, who had been with the Aboriginal people now for several days, explained to the others that they were all to be *coocheed* (painted) red or black, depending on the group to which they were assigned, and they would:

> fetch wood and water for their masters, and also to carry their towrows (fishing gear), when they went on a fishing excursion, and occasionally to carry the spears of the natives.

he looked into his eyes with a penetrating scrutiny, after which he uttered a violent scream

Curtis provided a description, purportedly from Eliza Fraser herself, of how her husband had called over one of the old Aboriginal men with a long beard, assuming him to be the 'chief' and made signs that he wished to talk to him. The Aboriginal elder had approached Captain Fraser:

> with an air of much dignity, and laid hold of Captain Fraser's chin, and then he rubbed his hands up and down his naked person; finally he looked into his eyes with a penetrating scrutiny, after which he uttered a violent scream, which made the rocks echo, and then made joyful gesticulations to the tribe to which he belonged, and who had halted at a little distance, to watch what was going on with an apparently anxious curiosity; in fact, wonder and amazement seemed to pervade their minds.

Another senior Aboriginal man then stepped forward 'and subjected Mrs. Fraser, Brown the Chief Officer, and Baxter, to the same ordeal'. After this, the people settled between themselves who was to go with whom. The white men were then led away into the bush, but Eliza Fraser was left alone on the beach.

And there she remained until late the next afternoon when (in her account as recorded by Curtis) 'a great number of naked female savages' came to see her:

> Her position and destitute state caused derision and mirth to these heartless brutes, and after some fierce, shrill yells, they one and all began to gather handfuls of wet salt sand from the beach, and throw it all over her person, until (to use her own expression) she was completely stuccoed all over; and the sand being of an adhesive quality, caused an excoriation of the skin, which became in a short time excruciating almost beyond endurance.

> The female savages, however, exercised some forbearance, as they did not maltreat her by any further act of violence.

These Aboriginal women were clearly playing with Eliza Fraser and laughing hysterically. Quite possibly they were trying to ease her sunburn—in the oral tradition of the Butchulla people of Fraser Island, the women, finding her 'brundy' ('not all there') due to stress and sunburn, rubbed her with ointments and medicine for her sunburn. Whatever their intentions, Fraser for her part failed to see any fun or goodwill in the exercise.

The women eventually went back into the bush, Fraser pathetically following them, until they met an invalid woman, covered with ulcers, who had a young child and an infant. According to Curtis, Fraser was directed to attend to the needs of this woman. In another version of her narrative, published in 1837, Fraser had not stayed on the beach but had decided to follow the people who had taken her husband, when a 'crowd of black women' approached her. Being 'displeased' by the difference between her complexion and theirs, they had compelled her 'to rub herself over with gums and herbs, which had the effect of making her nearly as dark as themselves', before setting her to work nursing the infant of the invalid woman. It seems that nobody was quite sure what to do with her.

The various accounts offer drastically conflicting versions of Fraser's experiences as an attendant-nurse. Fraser herself did not mention it at all in her original statement. In a lurid version of her story—a pamphlet, published for a North American audience, that built heavily on the established tradition of blood-curdling Indian captivity tales—Fraser complained bitterly about being forced to look after 'the disgusting and ill-humored brat', and claimed that she was beaten whenever it cried by her 'squaw-mistress, who professed to be its mother':

An abject Eliza Fraser being taunted by dancing Aboriginal women.

Great was the abuse that I received from this savage monster, who, in her fits of rage, would, beast-like, gnash her teeth, and sometimes seize me by the throat until I became nearly strangled! and at other times would seize me by the hair, which she would pull to that degree as to prostrate me upon my back.

In this story, Fraser was only protected from her mistress' violence by the interventions of the woman's kind-hearted brother, a man who 'although a savage, evidently possessed a better heart than many who claim a rank among a more humane and civilized race'.

Curtis' representation of the relationship between Fraser and the invalid woman was very different. His version had Fraser as nurse to the woman herself, not to the baby, and described the 'compassion' shown by the woman in response to Fraser's strenuous efforts to 'assuage her sufferings' and, as 'proof that this wild untutored being possessed a sense of gratitude', presented the evidence that the woman 'always interposed' when Fraser was attacked by other Aboriginal people. In covering the woman's sores against flies and insects with leaves, Fraser explained how she was reminded of the English nursery tale in which a red robin bird covered lost children in the woods with leaves, and thus began calling the woman 'Robina', which is a hint that she felt some closeness towards her. Both women were bound together by their marginal and weakened status and Curtis' version had 'Robina' existing on the 'vermin' that preyed on her flesh, 'such was the scarcity of provision', and prevailing upon 'her nurse to do the same!'

It was during this time that the captain died. In her original statement, Fraser said that her husband had become so weak through lack of food that he was:

> totally incapable of doing the work that was required of him, and on being on one
> occasion unable through debility to carry a large bag of wood one of the natives
> threw a spear at him which entered his shoulder a little below the blade bone.
> Of this wound he never recovered, and being soon after seized with a spitting
> of blood he gradually pined away until his death, which took place eight or nine
> days afterwards. During this time which he was laying on the ground incapable
> of moving, I was always prevented from approaching him or rendering him any
> assistance, when he died they dragged him away by the legs and buried him.

Various other published versions were considerably embellished and had the captain accidentally meeting his wife while moving wood, and then being speared before her eyes by an angry Aboriginal man (inflamed by a recent warring dispute); Eliza then, leaping from her hiding place in the bushes to comfort her dying husband, marshalled incredible strength to pull the spear from her husband's body before he mouthed his final words, 'O Eliza! I am gone!'

Following his death, as such versions continued, Fraser was pressed into being the wife of an 'old chief … one of the most ugly and frightful looking Indians that my eyes ever beheld'. She was saved by the brother of her invalid mistress chivalrously defending her honour, but he was killed as a consequence. Eliza Fraser was then supposedly treated more severely than ever, and made to climb tall trees to retrieve honeycomb from wild bee hives:

> she was slow in her movements, and awkward in the use of the sharp
> instrument put into her hands for the purpose of incising the bark, to make

scotches [notches] for her feet. In order to make her quicken her pace, these worse than blood-hounds followed her, and applied fire-brands to her person, in order to make her climb with greater facility.

Here is an English woman, having survived a shipwreck, given birth to a child that dies immediately, endured a lack of adequate food and water, walked for days, suffered excruciating sunburn, witnessed her husband being suddenly speared to death in front of her, but has learnt to climb trees blackfellow style in such a short space of time. Fraser probably never even got off the ground—she had certainly witnessed the way Aboriginal people procured honey, but that would have been the limit of her input.

In her original statement, Fraser said that she and first mate Brown were taken over to the mainland three days after the captain's death. Brown, unable to carry wood, had been burnt by the Aboriginal people on his legs and back 'in a most dreadful manner by rubbing them with fire brands'. The flesh had come off his legs and he was completely unable to walk. After making it to the mainland, Brown died.

In the Curtis version, the ordeals of Brown were transformed into a gory spectacle, the horrified Fraser watching him writhe in agony as he was slowly roasted over a fire, bound hand and foot to a tree. Though this episode is particularly far-fetched and unlikely, it may be that Fraser had either witnessed an attempt to cauterise Brown's wounded limbs or even just to heal him using some kind of smoking method; or, as some have suggested, maybe his ordeal was intended as a warning to the others and that he had indeed been subject to physical punishment for some transgression or offence, but we cannot know.

Published many years later, again for an American audience, crew member Harry Youlden's more measured account of his experiences corroborates Fraser's to some extent in terms of the harassment of the survivors, but it also implies that the white people acted inappropriately, without understanding their position as mendicants among their hosts.

Youlden described how the five dissenters (including Robert Darge), who left the captain and the others behind, took with them 'light bundles of fancy shirts, and similar articles suitable to trade for fish', confirming that the shipwreck survivors from the outset believed, mistakenly, they could trade their clothing for food. Before they had gone very far, 'the natives, by force or artifice, had helped themselves to our whole stock in trade, without any equivalents'.

When they followed some fishermen back to their huts, begging for food, they were given nothing but water, and then:

> one of them very deliberately took possession of our blankets, lying by us
> on the ground, and carried them off. Not pleased with this proceeding, and
> satisfied that the company was not good where such things could be, we all
> made haste to the beach. The whole tribe, old and young, men, women, and
> children, followed, pelting us with stones, which often hit hard; and the aged
> women, hideous to see, seemed most eager to hurt us.

The men's troubles continued over the following days as every group they encountered 'plundered us of what they liked'. Youlden, driven to distraction, eventually seized a handful of spears that had been left in the ground and threw them to his companions, calling them to fight or be killed. But the others were not inclined to go into battle:

> Provoked at their want of courage, I rushed alone, spear in hand, among
> our tormentors, who knew better how to avoid the stroke than I to make it;
> and soon, discomfited, though not subdued, I was compelled to give up the
> unequal contest.

An imposing and fit Butchulla Aboriginal man, with boomerang held aloft.

Walking on, the men met some more fishermen and 'telling my companions it were better to trade our drawers for fish than have them taken without equivalent', Youlden promptly offered his underpants to one of the fisherman in exchange for two fish:

> the bargain was struck. My shipmates did the same; and there we then were, black and white, all mixed together, naked, and I am sorry to confess we cut much the most pitiful figure.

From this point, Youlden's group's interactions with the Aboriginal people began to take a turn for the better. The following day, they found a deserted camp and spent a night sleeping on sheets of paperbark in the relative comfort of a hut. The next day, they encountered another group of people who again 'took particular delight in tormenting us', though now Youlden admitted that some of his companions:

> rather deserved it, for instead of defending themselves manfully, or breaking away, they actually remonstrated with the savages in good English, which, as not one word was intelligible to them, was all thrown away.

The men reached the shore of a river, where they were approached by yet another group. 'Fearing fresh annoyance', the white men took refuge in a hut nearby but, for the first time, they were treated with kindness, the people coming 'forward in a most courteous and friendly manner, bringing fish and roots, which we most thankfully accepted'. It also may have been the first time that the men had not tried to make a trade for food. Youlden's party stayed in the huts with the people for some days.

It was during this time that they were joined by the captain and his wife. The narratives now diverge markedly. Fraser's account, as we have seen, has them being taken captive by a large group of conglomerated clans. In contrast, Youlden wrote that he and the others of the original dissenting group soon grew impatient and were determined to continue on their journey back to Moreton Bay, indicating that they, at least, were not being held against their will. In an attempt to swim across the channel to the mainland, two of Youlden's friends drowned but, soon after, the steward, Corallis:

> crossed with the native at whose hut he was staying, and three others and myself went over with my own particular host in his canoe ... It looked frail, but carried five of us very safely.

Once on the other side, Youlden and one of the men (probably Darge) decided to go on. Eight days later, and near death, 'kind providence' showed up in the form of a group of Aboriginal people, including a man who knew them from the island, who gave them food and with whom they stayed for the next three weeks. Corallis also joined up with them again at this point. Having recovered their strength, the three men decided to continue on, until they came to a place where some men were returning with their day's catch. By now, Youlden had learned how to win favour with the people he met. He described with disarming satisfaction how he took his place 'modestly' by the fire of a man whose fish were the best:

> and we broiled and ate, and for lack of other mode of conversation, looked at each other pleasantly. The laugh of the natives is very peculiar, expressive and contagious, ending with an abrupt explosion and a rapid restoration to gravity.

This particular man apparently found Youlden amusing enough to invite the three men back to his village to stay the night. Evidently, these villagers had some knowledge of Europeans, as Youlden observed their greeting to white people was '"Name yo," the only English they seem to possess, and without waiting for a reply, they mention their own names'. They also knew where the British settlement was and understood that the white men needed to go there.

The laugh of the natives is very peculiar, expressive and contagious, ending with an abrupt explosion and a rapid restoration to gravity

The next morning, Youlden's host indicated that it was time for the white men to be on their way:

> Upon this the poor steward [Corallis] began to cry; and when I explained by my best pantomime, and the few words I had caught, the cause of his distress, that we might lose our way, a generous young brave seized his spear, and volunteered to pilot us to the English settlement.

They had not gone far when Youlden's feet became so sore he could not go on, pressing the others to continue without him as 'it was important to get tidings of us to the settlements'. Alone, Youlden, 'crawling, rather than walking', returned to the village, 'where the old men and women left in charge kindly received me'. The next morning, two Englishmen with two Aboriginal men came into the camp and an old man raised Youlden to his feet 'with an expression of kindness and sympathy' to meet them. Corallis and Darge had found the camp of Lieutenant Charles Otter, an officer of the Moreton Bay garrison, who was shooting the game of Bribie Island, and had asked him to send someone back to get Youlden.

How different Youlden's account of the people who sheltered him was from that of Eliza Fraser, who he described with startling venom, as:

> a very vixen; but as I do not feel she is worth the ink, to say nothing of time
> and paper, I shall only add, she was a terrible liar, and the most profane, artful,
> wicked woman that ever lived; indeed, coming very near my idea of the Devil.

It has been surmised that the people with whom Youlden spent the greater time were more hospitable than those with whom Eliza Fraser had remained, but it is worth noting that Fraser's group had joined Youlden's who, at the time, were with the first Aboriginal people who had shown them kindness. So, we might expect that she too was given some care. Possibly, because she was a woman, she was expected to contribute more in terms of food gathering than was demanded of the white men. Or, perhaps, she just continued to behave in ways that alienated the Aboriginal people and made them impatient with her.

A narrative account of Robert Darge's experiences was provided at the back of the Curtis publication. Darge had given testimony before a mayoral inquiry into Fraser's experiences and the circumstances of her rescue conducted in London after her arrival. Curtis drew directly from this testimony for his narrative and felt obliged to explain why Darge's account differed from that of Fraser's:

> It is the opinion of Darge, that the tribe to which he was attached was more
> humane than that with which Captain Fraser, his wife, Baxter, Brown, and
> others were connected.

Asked whether the people 'delighted' in annoying him he replied that the adult men did not, but that the young ones:

> from 10 to 14 or 15 years old, used to annoy me deliberately with goads and
> fire-sticks. I was unable to sit cross-legged like a tailor, as they used to sit,

and they could not bear to see that, so they used to torment me. When they sat down, they looked like a nation of black tailors, but I cannot call them cruel people.

Here we have an explanation for Brown's injuries and even Fraser's stories of being 'goaded' with firebrands to her legs. Darge further explained (much to the incredulity of his interrogators) that he had never had any apprehension of being killed by the Aboriginal people. He did tell them that he had been made aware of:

> a general deep-rooted hatred in the breasts of the natives to the white men; and the reason for which he assigns for its being engendered is the fact of their having been frequently and sometimes very wantonly fired upon by the soldiery and constabulary force connected with the colonial settlement.

He gave the example of one of the men of the group that had taken him, who had lost a leg from such a shooting, rendering him 'wholly unfit' for hunting and fishing and causing 'him often to be worked up to a fit of frenzy'. It may indeed be that Fraser and the other survivors were on the receiving end of a growing generalised hostility towards all Europeans. Indeed, Darge also implied that Corallis, of African descent, was given favourable treatment by the people, 'but he dared not to throw me anything [food] in their presence'. Their 'dogs, too,' he stated, 'had a great aversion to white men, and used to howl at me.'

Darge did talk about two white men living among one of the tribes that he met, both English convicts, one of whom had been in the bush five years (he was called Tursi) and another, 'a person of great altitude' (called Tallboy). Neither had any interest whatsoever in returning to white society and Tursi talked of his anxiety during the winter when his people went to the coast that he might be recaptured by the whites, and his delight that, as summer was soon approaching, they would soon be on their way to the mountains 'in quest of honey and kangaroos'. Obviously, these two men were more than happy to live the rest of their lives with the Aboriginal people, yet willing to help Darge and Youlden return by explaining that the white men were their own 'countrymen' (and thus, presumably, should be assisted).

On 21 August 1836, the rescue party, led by Lieutenant Otter and guided by former convict runaway John Graham, returned to Brisbane in two ships containing the last four survivors, including Eliza Fraser. There are various stories about Eliza Fraser's rescue and it is impossible to know the truth behind them, as we shall discuss below. The different versions highlight the great problem of credibility that persists with the Eliza Fraser story. After her rescue, Fraser secretly remarried and sailed back to England, where a scandal erupted around her, the accusation being that she was simply an opportunistic fraud on the take for money. Many years later, Queensland Protector of Aborigines Archibald Meston stated:

> She must have either had a serious quarrel with truth or else her head was badly affected by her experiences ... Certainly she gave a wildly improbable tale in Brisbane, accusing the blacks of deeds quite foreign to their known character, and quite unheard of before or since in aboriginal annals.

Davis and Bracefell insisted her tales were purely invention, and old Aboriginal people in the 1870s had told Meston 'a story very different from that of the lady', that the Europeans 'were received in a friendly manner ... and passed on in canoes to the mainland at Inskip Point, to be forwarded to the white people at the Brisbane Convict Settlement'.

We can read the Eliza Fraser story as a demonstration that Aboriginal people expected, indeed insisted, that the pale strangers who came among them had to accept and adopt their manners and customs—sharing food, taking part in the collective labour of the group and shedding their clothing. It is often understood that Aboriginal people had little interest in taking on white/British values and modes of behaviour. By the same token, it has been too easily assumed that Aboriginal people did not expect the Europeans to take on their ways of life and values. He 'knows how to live as well as us', Graham claimed they had said in support of his being allowed to remove Fraser. It is quite likely that they were relieved to deliver this difficult and unassimilable woman into his hands.

Today, fact cannot be separated from fiction in the Eliza Fraser story. All we can say with certainty and without fear of contradiction is that she did not enter willingly or happily into Aboriginal society, and that her legacy has been one of only resentment and confusion. No doubt she will remain a perplexing enigma in the annals of Australian history.

The Many Stories of Eliza Fraser's Rescue

Historian Elaine Brown has provided a succinct summary of what is generally accepted as the events that followed Joseph Corallis and Robert Darge's arrival in the camp of Lieutenant Otter. Within 24 hours, Commandant Foster Fyans had put together an expedition of volunteers, led by Otter and guided by former convict runaway John Graham, to find the remaining survivors. Two crew members of the *Stirling Castle* were soon discovered by Graham after he had been advised by local Aboriginal people of their whereabouts. With information that John Baxter was still on Fraser Island and that Fraser was somewhere in the Wide Bay area, Graham crossed from the mainland to the island and retrieved Baxter from a camp near Hook Point. Then, Graham set out to look for Fraser, eventually finding her at a camp at Fig Tree Point, on the edge of Lake Cootharaba on the mainland.

However, within the broad account, there are many small conflicting details, and a number of others—including Davis and Bracefell—have been suggested as Fraser's rescuers. These conflicting accounts imply the existence of elaborate networks and connections between Aboriginal groups and the white people who lived with them.

RESCUED BY GRAHAM

After Fraser was taken 'across Wide Bay', Baxter, the second officer of the *Stirling Castle*, remained with the Aboriginal people at the old campsite on K'gari. Now nicknamed 'Curri' (meaning 'hungry'), Baxter went on a hunting trip with the Aboriginal group, which met up with another group, among whom was a former escaped convict who had been living with them for several years. This man— described as a 'tall, athletic man' about 37 years of age, painted black, white and yellow, and wearing his hair in a 'huge bunch' on top of his head—might well have been one of the men described by Darge. In any case, on Baxter's return to the coast of the island with his group some days later, he was startled to hear a chorus of cooees coming from the beach. There, walking towards them was a white man, wearing nothing 'but a pair of canvas trowsers'. This was John Graham, who told Baxter that he had been sent to rescue the survivors

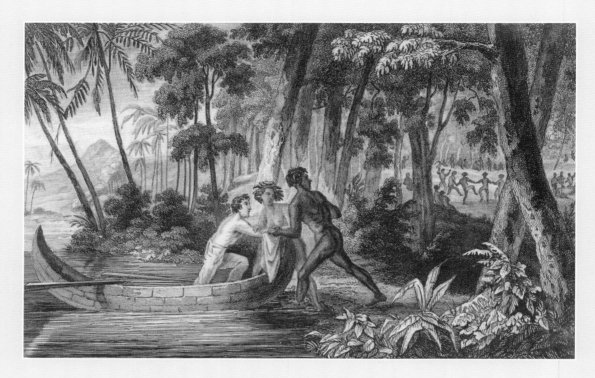

The daring 'rescue' of Mrs Fraser—the details
of her return remain a mystery.

of the *Stirling Castle*. He relayed that Lieutenant Otter was camped close by, and informed Baxter that three other members of the shipwreck had reached Moreton Bay. Graham himself had lived with the local people previously and was instantly recognised by them. Overjoyed at his return, they immediately organised a celebration. Graham told Baxter to prepare to make their getaway that evening during the corroboree but to make no attempt to flee before he gave the warning, or 'they would both suffer instant death':

> At length the much desired moment arrived; the signal was given; and while the natives were engaged upon the giddy mazes of their rude dance, Graham and Baxter ran with all speed to the waterside, when they got into a canoe, and the paddles thereof were instantly put into full play, so that by hard tugging they got over to the other side of the bay in about forty minutes.

On reaching the military camp, Baxter met the two other shipmates from Youlden's group, whom Graham had previously located. As Graham had been offered a full pardon if he managed to safely procure all of the captives alive, he soon:

sallied forth in quest of one in whom the party felt a more particular interest than any of the others, in consequence of her sex and the dreadful sufferings she was said to have undergone.

Some 12 hours later, Graham arrived in the military camp with Mrs Fraser, a pathetically striking figure, with her 'lacerated feet' and her sunburnt skin hanging 'in scales' from her shoulders, clad in the torn waistband of a pair of trousers tied around with vines and wearing a battered sou'-wester on her head, 'the smell of the paint' having 'kept the Blacks from taking it'. In Curtis' account, Graham had told Fraser, on the return trip, of how he had effected her daring rescue, with a plan that involved enlisting the help of an Aboriginal man he called 'Gormandy'. Graham told Gormandy that he was related to the white female who was being ill-treated by the people she was with, and that if he would help Graham abduct her from them, Graham would see that he was rewarded with axes and tomahawks, and with Fraser as a wife for himself. Gormandy, pretending to be 'hostile' to Graham, helped to distract the people's attention during the corroboree, allowing Graham to get away with her. Curiously enough, Darge would later state that 'Gurmonday' was the name of one of the people of the group he was with on the island of K'gari, and one of three individuals who experimented with exchanging names with him—'a thing they delighted in'.

In Graham's own evocative narrative, given in his formal report to the Moreton Bay commandant, Foster Fyans, he stated that he had carried her some 40 miles, with the assistance of four Aboriginal people, to Otter's camp at Wide Bay. Graham explained how the people Fraser was with saw her as a 'female spirit' and that she had been claimed by a man named Mothervane, as Mothervane's wife's sister. But Graham resolved to convince them that she was actually the spirit of his deceased Aboriginal wife, Mamba. He drew upon his existing connections within Aboriginal family networks to win over the people who had her. He had brought his two adult 'sons' with him (no mention of Gormandy) and, on seeing Fraser in the camp, he called to them:

Is your eyes blind, dont you know your Mother, upon whose neck I fell, fancying to cry. My Father in law jumped to his knife, saying, no crying, go up and take her, This mans name is 'Mootemu.' Upwards of 400 Blacks had seized their spears when 'Mothervane' came forward, to whom I said, 'do you claim a Spirit? and she my wife,' she can't speak to tell having lost her speech, and I who have got sense do tell the truth and here are her two sons and Father ... I told them ... if 'Mothervane' would be cross I would call a challenge. Here throwing off my trousers ... I impeached them with being stupid in not knowing her, all the coast Blacks here stood on my side, and said I allways told the truth. Saying give her, she is his, being now satisfied that she was 'Mamba.' ... 'Mothervane' said it was a pitty to let that Spirit go, but here 'Mootemu' said they are 2 ghosts and no men has any right to separate them 'Moilow' has good sense and knows how to live as well as us, he must have his wife.

By good fortune it turned out that the man guarding Fraser was one of Graham's Aboriginal nephews, who told him: 'come uncle I was watching my Aunt; that the Mountain Blacks should not come near, whilst you were talking, I fear none. I'll give her to you'.

Fraser's original and much simpler account made no mention of such details. Graham had come into the Aboriginal camp directly 'and told me he had been sent for me ... he spoke to the Natives for some time and after a good deal of altercation succeeded in getting me away', whereupon they walked a distance of some nine or ten miles until coming to Otter's party, and then 'immediately' set off for Moreton Bay.

A group of Aboriginal people appeared at Otter's camp a few hours after Mrs Fraser's arrival, according to the Curtis account. The lieutenant had ordered his men not to fire unless they were attacked: he 'was induced to act with lenity and humanity to them, from considering that there might yet be some of the crew belonging to the pinnace along the coast, with whom the natives might fall in, and revenge themselves for any casualty which might have arisen, had martial force been resorted to'. They instead distributed axes and food (bread and meat) among the Aboriginal group; Curtis describing how the Aboriginal women joined the feast, and constantly cried out 'Curri, Curri' to Baxter, expressing surprise that in such a short time he had acquired clothing.

Although, on the surface, everything was friendly enough, the following day two convicts from Lieutenant Otter's party were wounded by spears while felling a tree, and another convict was stripped while looking for shells and 'sent back to the camp in a state of nudity'. As a consequence, Otter put his men on alert and, at midnight, when 'the savages came down in a body upon the camp with a mighty rush', a volley fired at short range sent them back into the bush 'and the blood which was discovered next morning told a tale of suffering, if not death', recorded Curtis. Otter's own report does not mention being charged at midnight. One would expect that such an event would have made it into his report.

RESCUED BY DAVID BRACEFELL (WANDI)

There is yet another story. As we have seen when the surveying party led by Andrew Petrie with Henry Stuart Russell met with a group of Aboriginal people at Wide Bay in April 1842, almost six years after Fraser's return, they discovered a white man among them—David Bracefell, or Wandi, who became their interpreter in their dealings with the local people and helped them to find James Davis (see chapter 4). Bracefell told them how he had met Eliza Fraser when she was with Eumundi's group (where he had been, too), and that he had helped her escape from them. Once they reached the outskirts of the settlement, he claimed, she had turned on him and threatened to 'complain' of him rather than support in him in getting the pardon he sought as reward, and he 'turned round and ran back for my life!' Russell believed Bracefell wholeheartedly (though many others since have disputed his claim) and speculated that Fraser had not in fact been collected by Otter's party, but had found her way back to Brisbane with Bracefell, Graham rescuing only Baxter.

RESCUED BY JAMES DAVIS (DURAMBOI)

And still another intriguing version comes to us from the Butchulla oral tradition, recorded more recently by Olga Miller, whose family was relocated by Meston to Fraser Island at the end of the nineteenth century. In this account, from Miller's maternal grandmother, the Aboriginal women on the island did not want to keep Fraser with them and took her to 'the Clever Man', who sent messengers to locate none other than Duramboi. They had him collect Fraser from them at a particular point on the mainland, her body marked with ochre signs indicating that she was not to be harmed and to let her proceed. Duramboi duly took charge of her and took her south to where the white rescue party was, sending her on her way alone once they neared the camp. Later, Duramboi was 'taken to task' by the elders because of claims that had filtered back to them that the white woman had complained Duramboi had raped her (which he denied).

we acquired some knowledge of their language and customs. They seem to pay due respect to family duties. The mothers are devoted to their children, and attached to their husbands

The rich and healthy lifestyle of Aboriginal people on the coast.
A successful harvest of school fish is shown underway at Sandy Beach,
on the northern tip of K'gari (Fraser Island).

Fraser's Aboriginal Life

The many versions of Eliza Fraser's ordeals are all but useless for trying to get a sense of the Aboriginal ways of life she so briefly, and reluctantly, shared. Harry Youlden, who appreciated the humanity of his hosts to a much greater extent, explained how, after getting over to the mainland with Corallis and taking up residence with a group of people there for three weeks:

> we acquired some knowledge of their language and customs. They seem to pay due respect to family duties. The mothers are devoted to their children, and attached to their husbands ... Their fights are man against man; they evince a good deal of chivalric feeling, and will not attack an unarmed foe ... Some possess an expression of great intelligence, but they are never comely, according to our standard.

In his testimony reprinted by Michael Alexander, Robert Darge gave some small snippets of insight into Aboriginal life. He described the skill of the people in fishing with both spears and nets, the latter 'spun across their knees with bark they call *corrigin*', and explained that sometimes the Aboriginal people were happy to turn in runaway convicts to the white authorities in exchange for an axe, or a fish hook. He described how the people bored a hole through the septum of their nose and plugged it with a piece of kangaroo fur, and painted their faces and bodies, encouraging him to do likewise:

> They put cockatoo feather at each side of my head, and stuck small feathers of the most beautiful birds all over it, and they sometimes drew red streaks across my eyebrows, sometimes they rubbed my cheeks with red stuff, and they used to do so with themselves. They put me to a great deal of pain in plucking out my beard and whiskers, which they could not bear. They plucked out their own always; and after they pulled me about and daubed me all over, they would point to me to look in the water at myself. Although we could see ourselves in the stream, they used to take up water in a sort of a bucket made of the bark of trees to see their faces in and they made me do the same.

They put me to a great deal of pain in plucking out my beard and whiskers, which they could not bear

Darge also reportedly claimed (in the version of testimony recorded in Curtis) that while the children 'were indulged in every way in their power', the Aboriginal men treated their wives very brutally. If he really did make this claim, it was a marked change from Thomas Pamphlett's report the decade before, and could reflect some of the social upheavals in the wake of the establishment of the British settlement.

Of the perennial question of cannibalism, Darge stated that he had heard that some of the people along the coast were cannibals, 'but he saw nothing to induce the belief that the tribe with which he located was; at all events, if the fact was so, he never saw any human flesh served up in their repasts'. About Aboriginal religious beliefs, Darge gave no information other than that:

> If they worshipped anything it was the moon. When it was new they used to dance the *corroburo*. That was all I could observe.

7

Barbara Thompson—'Giom'

Barbara Thompson, reputedly the only survivor of a shipwreck in 1844 on the far northern Queensland coast, spent four to five years living on Muralug (Prince of Wales Island) with the Kaurareg Islanders and the Aboriginal people of Queensland's far north. She was known as 'Gieowma', or 'Giom' for short, a senior Islander man's favoured daughter, returned from the dead.

Five years later, in 1849, the crew of HMS *Rattlesnake* would unexpectedly discover her at the tip of the Cape York Peninsula, and take her back with them to Sydney. Captained by Owen Stanley, the ship was on a surveying voyage, its aims including finding another secure entrance through the Barrier Reef for ships travelling between India and the Australian colonies. On board was the artist, Oswald Brierly, who meticulously recorded long interviews with Thompson during their nine-week journey back.

Barbara was about six years old when she came to Australia with her large family in 1837, on an assisted passage from Aberdeen in Scotland. Her father, Charles Crawford, was a tinsmith, and hardship in the family perhaps explains why she ran away from home around 1843, with a William Thompson. The couple made their way to Moreton Bay, where some accounts say they were married. Barbara was probably no older than 12—at this time, under British law (which applied in the colonies), the age of consent for girls was ten, and the minimum age girls could legally marry was 12.

The couple lived in and around the small settlement of Brisbane, where William Thompson met a shipwreck survivor from the Torres Strait area, who convinced him to sail north with him in his cutter to salvage the wreck's cargo of oil casks. In September 1844, the two men, Barbara Thompson and a two-person crew set sail for the Torres Strait.

Near Cape York, the two crew members drowned when the cutter's dinghy overturned and sank. Later, during stormy weather, the cutter was smashed apart on the reef just off Horn Island (Madjii Reef). It was the middle of the day and there were Islanders nearby catching turtles on a reef. Thompson told Brierly:

> The blacks held up their hands and called out Toomah, Toomah—'Bye and bye', for me to hold on. The men were weak from hunger, they fell down from that. They were trying to swim to the shore.

Once the storm subsided, three Islander men—Boroto, Alikia and Tomagugu—rescued Thompson and:

> took me in the canoe to their own island [Prince of Wales Island] and gave me some turtle soup, boiled in their pot, the alupa, a large shell.

By her own account, Thompson was adopted immediately into the family of a highly respected elder named Pequi:

> Pequi was my chief friend or 'father' as he called himself. Others called themselves my fathers and mothers, but Pequi and his wives were considered my real relatives. Pequi said I had his daughter's chin and eyes. Directly I was taken into the camp, when first I was wrecked, Pequi and his wives all jumped out and caught hold of me, calling me after his daughter.

Having an elder like Pequi claiming her as his departed daughter had a marked impact on her reception and acceptance into the group. 'The natives appear to have treated her quite as a pet,' recorded Thomas Huxley, a scientist on the *Rattlesnake,* 'she never shared in the labours of the women but stayed in the camp to look after the children.' The ship's second master, George Inskip, (who recorded, evidently with some confusion, that she had been taken under the charge of an old woman who recognised her as the spirit of her daughter) likewise wrote in his diary that she 'used to look after the children while the women were getting their husbands dinners'.

Above: HMS *Rattlesnake*, the ship that returned Barbara Thompson to colonial society, leaving Sydney Heads.

Left: The ship's artist Oswald Brierly's sketch of an Islander man being entertained at the captain's table.

The men of the *Rattlesnake* were curious as to whether Thompson herself had a husband among the Kaurareg. John MacGillivray, a naturalist on the ship, later asserted that an Islander named Boroto 'took possession of the woman as his share of the plunder; she was compelled to live with him'. Thompson herself denied Boroto was her husband or, indeed, that she had had any husband in the islands.

In his journal, Brierly refers to the old man who named the Kaurareg babies; one he named 'Ootzoo':

He must be an old wag in his way, to judge by the following names: first child, a girl—Ootzoo = muddy water.

Some historians since then, including Thompson's biographer Raymond Warren, have speculated that the baby's name was a reference to her fair skin and that the child was in fact Thompson's own daughter (and that possibly, Thompson had also had a son). European delicacy on such a subject meant that this was glossed over in the records, and there is no way of knowing the real story.

The overwhelming evidence from all accounts is that Thompson was treated with the greatest kindness and love by the Islanders. Brierly left a particularly touching account of the relationship between one of the elders, Sallalli, 'a most worthy character', and Thompson after she had been on board the *Rattlesnake* for a few days:

He comes and sits cross-legged by the hour talking in such kind tones to the white woman, calling her his child and looks with quiet wonder as she displays before him all the gowns which she has been making up from cotton handkerchiefs in the piece, the only thing on board which would serve. There is something so calm and good about the old man.

Nevertheless, life with the Islanders was not all plain sailing and at times Thompson was tested. She had indicated to the white men on the *Rattlesnake* that, although the Islander men treated her very well, for 'a long time' many of the women, 'jealous of the attention shown her ... evinced anything but kindness'. In an incident that occurred while the women were preparing food, she ended up in a physical fight with a woman named Yuri. It was expected that when a woman made an oven of heated stones, she invited others to use it as well. Giom had neglected to do this. Yuri hurled a large shell at her and, in retaliation, Giom filled the shell with water and threw it in her face. Giom then grabbed Yuri by the hair and began punching her about the face. The Islander woman could only cry out: '*Giom, warmera [let go], Giom, warmera*'. 'None of the people took her part', Thompson told Brierly in one of her interviews with him:

> but they called out to me Giom perkee, etc.—'Strike, Giom, strike'. They said I was a stranger amongst them and that the woman should not hurt me. Her daughter, a woman, stood by and did not say anything.

Old Pequi had to be restrained from getting out his 'bamboo beheading knife' and assisting his daughter, crying to all those listening, 'why did they strike his child who had only just come back to him?' While Yuri was incensed by Giom's lack of manners, the others, women as well as men, were prepared to make allowances for the 'stranger'. Afterwards, Yuri became Giom's friend and 'would take me out to dig the *koti* [yam]'.

Although Huxley had recorded that Giom never shared in the women's labour of food gathering, by her own account she did, vividly describing, for instance, collecting food at the onset of the wet season:

> [the rain] will come down heavier than ever. I know it well—my body used to be quite sore all over with the heavy rain beating upon me when I was out in the scrub with all the other women looking for biyu.

Thompson recounted how, at one point, she had tried to make contact with the crew of a passing ship. Three boats carrying white men had come ashore and Boroto had gone to meet them, returning to show Giom the tobacco that they had given him in exchange for 'the women and for tortoise shell'. She 'could not believe him' but recognising the European tobacco, she decided to wait until the transactions had been processed before going down to the beach herself, telling her 'father' that she was going for water. She saw that the men had returned to their ship and were setting sail. In vain she tried to attract the crew's attention, then watched the ship move out 'very slow'. Giom went down to the waterhole well then and 'sat down and cried', while her people cooeed to her in the bush. Eventually she returned. Brierly asked if her group was displeased with her:

> Oh, no, they did me no harm. Glad that I'd come back and jumped around me, but I cried and did not eat anything for two days. If I'd gone with them—the natives—the first day [when Boroto took the women down to meet the white men], then I would have got away. But I was afraid they would keep me back.

At another time, Giom spoke of how people from islands further north from Cape York, who regularly came to Muralug to trade ornaments for the *koti*, had tried to persuade her to go and live with them:

> They used to take great notice of me and said if I would go with them to their island I should sit on the merzallie—the work mats … beautiful mats. I tried to get away from the island to go with them.

She snuck away from her 'sister', who was cooking, to meet the visitors and their canoes, but her 'brothers' foiled her plan, coming 'running round the other way to stop me … They said they would have killed me sooner than I should go'.

In another episode, some Badu people came to visit and asked to meet with the white woman. An old woman called Nuadji tried to convince Giom that she should come and live with them, promising her that she would be protected and given special status (*tubada ogada*), and saying that, if she wanted to come, the Badus would kill the Kaurareg to help her get away. 'I was very much frightened when she told me this, but would not agree to go with her.' Instead, Giom hid with some of the Kaurareg women over the next couple of days, as more and more Badu men as well as men from another island came ashore. Although they demanded to see her, the Kaurareg men protected her, telling the unwanted guests that Giom was frightened and that they could not find her.

Living on the islands at this time was another non-Indigenous person, a man named 'Weenie'. Giom described him unflatteringly as a 'tall elderly man with light hair, marked with the smallpox, with lumps growing out of different parts of his body'. He apparently 'belonged' to two Badu Island men since arriving around 1840 in a small boat, and was quite useful. Giom's people were envious of the Badu's white man: 'Our people say they would like to get a white man who could mend their canoes in the same way as Weenie does for the Badoos'. The Kaurareg women tried to tempt him by sending him gifts of meat, but Weenie would not have anything to do with them, being 'afraid the husbands would spear him'.

Weenie had 'quite forgotten' his own language, whatever that might have been, so he and Thompson spoke in the language of the Islands. He seemed 'quite happy with the Blacks and does not care about leaving them'. Thompson told Brierly that Weenie had suggested that she should be his wife, saying 'We are like all the same people'—apparently referring to their respective Islander

An Islander outrigger canoe with an ornate figurehead.

communities rather than their European heritage—but did not clarify whether she had agreed to that. According to Inskip, however, Giom had refused his offer of marriage.

Weenie's identity remains a mystery. MacGillivray insisted that he had become 'the most important person in the tribe' by killing and intimidating the people, gaining ascendancy as a warrior provided with several wives and property. This led to MacGillivray speculating that Weenie had to have been a Britisher, no doubt a 'runaway convict, probably from Norfolk Island'. Inskip recorded that Thompson believed him to have been 'an Englishman a Runaway Convict', that he was a '*bloodthirsty* villain' who turned the natives against the white men, and that:

> he prefers his Savage life to a civilised one—as he could go on board any vessel he pleases that happens to be passing—he went off to one & they of course wanted him to go with them, but he made an excuse to go on Shore again to get some things & instead of going back hid himself away lest they should come back & look for him.

Thompson, unlike Weenie, did not stay with her Islander hosts. She was about 17 when the crewmen of the *Rattlesnake* first saw her on the beach at Cape York, so deeply tanned that at first they did not realise she was a white woman. Thompson would explain to Brierly that news of the *Rattlesnake*'s arrival at Cape York Peninsula had travelled through the Aboriginal and Islander networks early in 1849. Giom told the Kaurareg women that she wanted to go to meet them, assuring them that the white people would not want to keep her, saying:

> Oh no, I was too black. They would not
> have me now. That I only wanted to
> go over and get medicine for my knee.
> And to let them know there was a white
> woman on the island.

Even so, the women tried to prevent her from making contact in a number of ways, including insisting that she remain back to attend to the cooking when the others rowed across to the mainland:

> I said, 'Oh yes, I shall cook the turtle for
> you and get the wood.' I was very much
> vexed and meant that I would not cook
> it. When they went away in the canoes,
> I began to cry, and I told old Soanna
> that they were keeping me from seeing
> my people.

Islander men approaching the *Rattlesnake* to trade.

Eventually, Tomagugu (one of her original rescuers, an Aboriginal man from the mainland married to a Kaurareg woman) persuaded the others to let her visit, and said he would tell the white people he would be bringing a white woman to 'shake hands with them'.

> Tomagugu was the best man among them. He used to tell me long before in Moralug ... by myself, not to mind them, that he would sometime take me off and old Pequi and Baki, one of the chiefs and Manoon and one or two of the elder men were always willing and used to say that I should go off when I got well. But most of the women and men said that I should die amongst them.

so dirty and wretched an appearance that some people who were out shooting at first mistook her for a gin

The next afternoon, Giom managed to get onto the last canoe that was heading off to see the white men, together with Tomagugu and his wife, Sibi, a mainland Aboriginal couple, Den and Koletta, and two old Kaurareg men, Ylla and Tami. They paddled across the bay (Evans Bay) and secured the canoe, and then followed a track to where the white men were doing their washing in the waterholes. Some mainland Aboriginal people came towards them with some white men, 'shooting birds' as they came, and went up to Thompson.

MacGillivray wrote that she:

> presented so dirty and wretched an appearance that some people who were out shooting at first mistook her for a gin, and were passing by without taking further notice, when she called out to them in English, 'I am a white woman, why do you leave me?'

Huxley's diary account described her as crying out, 'I am a Christian—I am ashamed' while Inskip recorded that she was '*perfectly naked*' apart from a scrap of seaweed and it was 'some minutes before she could speak & her first words were I am a White Woman—I am ashamed'. (None of these men, of course, had been witness to the first encounter between Thompson and the sailors, but reported only what the crewmen had told them.)

An entry, mentioning Barbara Thompson, from the log of the
Rattlesnake under the command of Captain Owen Stanley. The log
was kept by midshipman James Thomas Stanton.

In Thompson's own account, as documented by Brierly, Tomagugu was the
first to speak, 'telling them in his own talk how I had been wrecked and how
he had taken me up out of the water'. Giom interjected, telling the white men
herself that:

> I had been wrecked and pointed out Tomagugu to them and told them he was
> my brother and had saved my life. They asked me if I was from England, or
> Ireland, or Scotland and would I like to go back to England or whether I would
> rather stop here with the Blacks. I told them that I was a Scotch girl and that
> my father and mother were in Sydney.

1849 Oct

... She is about 21, it appears
she was wrecked in a boat with
her husband & a few others,
the boat was only 10 tons & all
were lost but herself. She was
<u>perfectly naked</u> having only a
small bit of sea weed, which very
barely covered her modesty. She
was some minutes before she
could speak & her first words
were I am a White woman—I
am ashamed, poor woman She
thinks it is about 4 years she
has been with them, they have
treated [her] very kindly & were
loth to part with her. She had
to tell them that she was only
going to see her Country-men
& would then go back—Her
name is *Crawford [her maiden
name] Thompson & she calls the
Natives who have been kindred
to her, Brothers & one old man
her Father. The sun has burnt her
back & face & her hair is quite

Cape York.

et Short - The Sergeant of Marines <u>washed</u> her & parted her hair - & the washing party gave her a couple of shirts to put on - She says the Natives have often brought her biscuit that they have got from this Ship & others & that she knew we were here & by the Natives description that we have watered & that officers were with the Men. but they would not let her come. We or rather the Capt intends taking her on to Sydney with him. - This is a strange discovery & I am very thankful that this expedition has been the means of releasing some poor Creature from such a state. - Went on board the Ship for a short time in the evening - Three years to day since I joined the Rattlesnake in Portsmouth. Two more I hope to see happy Old England again

short. The Sergeant of Marines <u>washed</u> her & parted her hair, & the washing party gave her a couple of shirts to put on. She says the Natives have often brought her biscuit that they have got from this Ship & others & that she knew we were here & by the Natives description that we have watered & that officers were with the Men, but they would not let her come. We or rather the Capt intends taking her on to Sydney with him. This is a strange discovery & I am very thankful that this expedition has been the means, of releasing one poor creature from such a state ...

Pages from the diary of George Inskip, second master on the *Rattlesnake*, describing the unexpected appearance of Barbara Thompson.

The white men took her to where the others were washing and:

washed me and combed my hair and dressed me in two shirts, one below as
a petticoat, the other over my shoulders. I was so ashamed ... As I went along
I could hardly speak for crying. All our own people who had gone over in the
canoes before us were at the washing place. They asked me what I wanted to
go off for. I said that there were women on board that I wished to see.

Taken on board the ship, Thompson was given tea, meat and apple-pie and
was then asked whether she would like to stay with 'the Blacks' or to go to
Sydney: 'To this she simply answered, "I am a Christian"'. MacGillivray noticed
how she 'beat her forehead with her hand' when asked if she wanted to leave
'as if to collect her scattered thoughts', stating at last, 'Sir, I am a Christian, and
would rather go back to my own friends'.

The various accounts of the time of her return give the impression that
Thompson was ambivalent about leaving, and that the Kaurareg were very sad
to see her go. MacGillivray recorded that from the time she came on ship:

hardly a day passed on which she was not obliged to hold a levee in her cabin
for the reception of friends from the shore, while other visitors, less favoured,
were content to talk to her through the port.

Brierly described how old Aburda, Sallalli's wife, who had been reluctant to
let Giom go to the ship in the first place, came up to him and 'told me she had
been crying for Giom, the white woman, and talking a great deal, which I could
not understand, about her'.

Sir, I am a Christian, and would rather go back to my own friends

At another time, a party of women from Muralug came to visit Giom,
bringing plenty of mats for sitting on while they talked, and grass for making
baskets together. Among them was an older woman, Gameema, who:

showed the greatest joy at seeing Mrs T. at the port and stood up in the canoe
till she might take hold of her hand, which she kissed with great affection,
at the same time showing a shell which had belonged to Mrs T. while on the

land, saying Giom meeno no [meaning not known] and in which she had
bored a hole and now wore round her neck as a remembrance, saying Giom,
ye noosa eena—'Giom, this is yours', and at the same time kissing it.

Once Thompson was on board the ship, she never returned to the shore.
MacGillivray claimed that this was because she feared Boroto would attack her,
he having left the ship in a rage when he could not persuade her to come back
off the ship, and threatening that, if she ever did come ashore, he or one of his
friends would 'take off her head to carry back with them to Muralug'. Brierly, on
the other hand, made no mention of such threats, and Inskip wrote:

> The natives fancy she is kept against her will & advised her to get out of the
> Cabin port & swim on Shore, they said only look at these poor ghosts they
> have scarcely room to move in this overgrown canoe, they hardly know where
> to sit down—Come on shore with us & there you have all the woods to Roam
> in & we will get you provisions—here you have to wander about to get your
> daily food, you had much better come back.

What became of Giom once she returned to white society is completely
unknown. She was 'handed over to her parents in Sydney in excellent condition',
stated MacGillivray, and promptly disappeared from view. Unlike those white
men in former years who had been given roles of translators and intermediaries
on their return, that option was not available to her (although she did help the
expedition party in their encounters with Aboriginal people and Islanders for
the remainder of its stay, some nine weeks, in the region). One account has
it that a public benefit raised funds for her, but that her relatives 'squandered
the money and left her destitute', and there is an idea she, or members of her
family, may have relocated back to Aberdeen, while various researchers have
claimed that she remarried in Sydney, perhaps twice, bore a daughter and lived
into her eighties.

Whatever path she took, it would have been very difficult for Thompson to
re-enter white society, her previous experiences certainly arousing the prurient
curiosity and ridicule of both friends and strangers. If she thought to publish
her own account of her experiences, she would have needed assistance, being
illiterate. Thompson's story has been confused by some writers with Eliza
Fraser's and, in her own lifetime, she would have been constantly confused with
the other 'wild white woman'. It is not surprising that she chose obscurity.

Within the next few decades following Giom's departure, the Kaurareg way of life would be almost totally destroyed. In 1863, a white settlement, Somerset, was established in the northern reaches of Cape York. Hostilities began here when an Aboriginal man of Cape York refused to hand over an axe that he was accused of stealing. He was subsequently violently flogged, though it turned out that he was completely innocent and had received the axe as a gift. Two marines were speared in retaliation, one recovering quickly and the other dying of complications nine months later. There was no comparison to what came back to the Aboriginal people in response—three weeks later, eight Aboriginal people were shot dead.

In 1867, two missionaries visited the Somerset settlement and described the Aboriginal people of the far north and the Islanders as 'a kind and affectionate people', who were deeply caring for their children: 'They are kind both in word and look to each other and many a Christian family would be put to shame by them'. One of the missionaries, the Reverend F.C. Jagg, added that the Aboriginal people at Somerset were being defamed by the police magistrate and others as 'the most degraded, treacherous and bloodthirsty beings in existence' and that their 'only idea is to shoot them down whenever they were seen'.

Within the next few decades ... the Kaurareg way of life would be almost totally destroyed

The missionaries also visited the Prince of Wales group of islands on a couple of occasions and found that some of the people mentioned by Thompson were still alive and remembered her. Two years later, the violence of colonialism reached the Kaurareg when they were targetted for revenge for a supposed massacre of the crew of the wreck of the *Sperwer*. It was claimed that Islanders were holding the captain's wife (Mrs Gascoigne) and child captive. With little time for detail, the settlers in the region were hell bent on revenge and rampage. A punitive party sent out to look for the white woman in April 1870 destroyed the main Kaurareg camp and their canoes, and captured visiting Kulkalaig men from Mount Ernest Island (Nagir), who were identified as the perpetrators and executed on the spot. As it turned out, Mrs Gascoigne had not even been on that voyage. Very likely, there had been a confusion with Thompson's dimly remembered story—a tragically ironic twist for the people who had so kindly cared for Giom.

Thompson's Aboriginal Life

Unlike William Buckley and James Davis, Thompson willingly shared stories of her life with Indigenous people. As a young white woman, she had had an entirely different experience to that of Fraser; she had been accepted into the Indigenous community and indeed had been warmly embraced by them. She was attuned to the social nuances of relationships with her hosts and, through her narratives, we are able to get a vivid sense of how the Kaurareg regarded her and she them.

Described as the 'Kowrarega' (and other variations) in the original accounts, the people who hosted her had probably had their 'first significant contact' with Europeans in August 1836 when the party looking for the *Charles Eaton* survivors landed on Wednesday Island, part of the Prince of Wales group of islands, and exchanged gifts with Islanders there. Thompson's insights into their lives in the next decade have been made much more widely accessible through the painstaking work of archaeologist David R. Moore, who transcribed and published the Brierly journals, along with other relevant contemporary sources, and who included his own detailed commentary, in 1979. Today, her testimony about Kaurareg culture and customs remains particularly valuable to scholars of Torres Strait Islander history and cultures.

CONNECTION TO NEIGHBOURS AND LAND

Thompson's views of the Kaurareg were far removed from her white contemporaries' understandings of 'natives' as 'savages' with no connection or rights to their own country. Her anecdotes highlighted considerable interaction between the Kaurareg of the Prince of Wales islands and the people of other islands in the Torres Strait, as well as with the Aboriginal people of Cape York, the Gudang, some of whom were married into the Kaurareg or lived among them without losing their separate identity.

Everyone was spiritually connected to their 'own ground, the place on which he was born'. Every couple had a place where they cultivated yams, called a *pod*, and when they died, they passed on their pod to their children:

> Girls get as much land sometimes as boys. The parents will give most land to
> a favourite child; there is no particular rule in that respect. But if the parents
> die without making any division, the youngest gets the most.

Inskip recorded that Thompson said that there was 'no hereditary chieftanship amongst them but the strongest and bravest takes the lead'. She also revealed they 'have no kings or queens, nothing of the sort', but she did talk of a group of elders, who met to discuss whether to make war against other Islander groups:

> They stand up when they speak and when one has said what he thinks, and so on until they have all spoke. Quiqui, the oldest man on the island, speaks first. Quiqui is so old and infirm that they carry him about on a thing like a handbarrow, when they move from camp to camp. Then Perqui and Manu and Baki stood up in turn—first Baki, then Perqui and Manu.

CULTURAL LIFESTYLE

Thompson's detailed accounts of everyday life describe a rich and fulfilling cultural lifestyle that incorporated entertainment, such as song and dance, and also sport and games, including 'a team game remarkably like hockey, known as *koi teape,* and another, similar to hide and seek, played with children'.

During the height of the wet season, the whole group lived together in a large, specially built long house made of bark and cane, and in the dry season each family set up their own smaller huts, with pandanus mats for sitting and sleeping on. Thompson stressed the sophistication of their tools, weapons, utensils and craft, proudly comparing them with the technology of the mainlanders. According to her: 'Their [the Kaurareg's] canoes are much more neatly made. My brother's canoe is beautiful'. She described how canoes were constructed.

> They go into the bush and select a large tree and cut it down with axes—axes they get from the ships that pass. When the tree is felled, all the people, men, women and children, all help to drag it down to the waterside. They make a cut at each end of the log, then chip it all out with axes out of the middle. They don't use fire ... Some work at the outrigger poles, some at the float. All going on at once. They call a canoe 'gool'.

Opposite: An Islander man from Muralug photographed
in the 1890s, wearing an elaborate mask.

PRINCE OF WALES ISLAND MAN WITH MASK
(1364)   KERRY. PHOTO. SYDNEY.

Among the Kaurareg, it was the woman who made presents for the man. 'The women used to ask me if it was so in my own country. I said no, the women had more attention than the men,' Thompson said.

While MacGillivray and Huxley depicted marital relations between Islanders as being harsh, Thompson, on the other hand, provided Brierly with examples of affectionate family relations. She also described the way a husband who mistreated his wife expressed remorse:

> they will sit down and cry and say, What made me beat my wife? ... Then she will perhaps lay in the camp all next day and he will go and get fish for her and try to make it up again.

Sexual violence was frowned upon—the Badu men had a very bad reputation among the Kaurareg for doing 'what they pleased' with their women. There were also strict regulations regarding the behaviour of sons-in-law and mothers-in-law, who were never to speak to each other. Thompson had laughed at this code, telling the women that white people always spoke to their parents-in-law. The Islander women were quick to respond: *'Markibat era girure adjinge irare—It is the white people: they have no mother-in-law and no shame'*.

Thompson told Brierly that a man could have four or five wives but that the first wife distributed the meat he had brought, and only the first and last wives had his company at night, the remaining wives obliged to enjoy his attention 'only in the bush at daytime'. If a woman was unfaithful, her husband was within his rights to spear both her and her lover; however, 'if the *liee*, basket, be full, he says nothing, whatever he may know'.

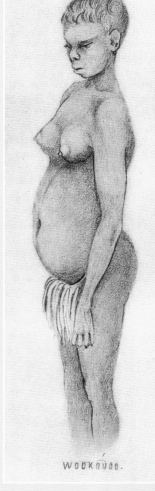

WOOKOUOO.

A sketch of an Aboriginal woman, presumed to be from the Cape York region, in the diary of *Rattlesnake* scientist Thomas Huxley.

Thompson provided vivid descriptions of the Kaurareg men's seafaring hunting techniques. Sometimes, they speared turtles from canoes with the harpoon *(wap)*, but they also had an ingenious method of employing sucker fish *(gapu—remora)* to catch them:

> the gapu was leashed on a strong thin string of coconut fibre, known as egali, tied to its tail and lower jaw ... once the sucker had attached itself to the turtle, the men pulled the line taut and then one of them dived down, following the line, and secured the turtle on a thicker line tied round its flippers in the usual way, so that he and the turtle could be pulled up to the canoe.

The Islanders preferred the female turtles and did not 'care for the male turtle—it is not fat and has no eggs'. The first turtle caught in a new canoe was *adzarr* (a specifically female taboo) to the women.

Turtles were cooked in a ground oven (an *ami*) using layers of pandanus leaves and hot stones, and finally a covering of sand. The 'captain' of the canoe that caught the turtle divided and shared out the meat. There was an elaborate method for the cooking and sharing of dugong.

The people also lived on fish (the men using spears and the women handlines), goannas, flying-foxes, birds, eggs and 'a considerable variety of fruit and nuts'. During the difficult wet season, they subsisted on edible mangrove sprouts and another kind of tuber, both of which had to be carefully prepared to remove toxins.

RITUAL ANTHROPOPHAGY

Thompson described to Brierly an elaborate ceremony that took place after a revenge attack for a senior man's murder. When the revenge party returned in their canoes, complete with a collection of six heads, the men placed the heads in a circle and paced around them, shouting and yelling. After two hours, they put the heads on stakes and painted themselves for a mourning dance for the avenged man which went on all night. The next morning, they took the heads and baked them in a ground oven, and when the heads were cool enough to handle, the men sat around in a circle, away from the women:

First they took the eyes out and then cut the flesh from round the eyes, the men who cut it passing bits round to the rest. When they eat it they would throw their heads back with their mouths open, holding the bit ready to drop in, call out to their wives, Areen idoo eenama, 'Our food, look at it'. They eat the eyes and fat first. Then they cut the bits off the cheeks and handed them round.

After this, the warriors painted themselves and dressed in ornaments for another dance (*karnbub*), all in their weaponry. Then they replaced the defleshed skulls on the stakes and, on the following day, another dance took place.

Similarly, one of the Somerset missionaries, W.C. Kennett, recorded that 'cannibalism' as practised north of Kennedy River on Cape York and the Torres Strait Islands entailed the eating of 'the eyes of cheeks of their fallen enemies, under the impression it will add to their bravery'. Of such practices, the literary scholar, Robert Dixon, has written:

In traditional Islander society, warriors were admired for their fighting skills, and the taking of enemies' heads was a token of personal and clan prestige. The technique of removing an enemy's head was highly ritualised, and warriors carried a special bamboo knife and cane hoop to perform ritual decapitation. The severed heads were cooked, preserved, and made life-like by the addition of beeswax noses and eyes of nautilus nacre, and then placed in a skull house, a sacred place. For the Islanders, these practices were an expression of their belief in life after death, of the spirit world interacting with the living. Through ritual anthropophagy, the marki or spirit of the dead might be imbibed by the living to enhance their potency.

In Thompson's account, her description so closely tallies with John Ireland's account that it may well be that the massacre a decade earlier of survivors of the *Charles Eaton* had been in retaliation for a previous attack by white men (see chapter 5).

GHOSTS OF THE DECEASED

Thompson explained to Brierly that the Kaurareg 'think that white men are the spirits of blacks come again in a new form' and that she, recognised as the returned daughter of Pequi, was a 'ghost' of a Kaurareg. (And white people's dogs likewise were the dogs of the Islanders returned to life.)

White people had already been incorporated into the Islander world view by the time Thompson arrived. She described an elaborate new *'marki angul kowb*—ghost ship dance' that had recently been brought to the Kaurareg by the Kulkulaga people of Nagir (Mount Ernest). The dance involved them wearing the shirts they had been given by white men, and songs about the ships returning 'to their own land' and coming back with:

> biscuits, tobacco, and knives and shirts, the two marki [men acting as Whites] imitate the motion of a white man, holding up and shaking their hands.

At another time, she explained that her people 'think that white fellows in ships live on sharks and whales, porpoises, etc. and are always sailing about in ships'. (Sharks and dolphins were protected by the Islanders, who would not harm them, so this was a significant marker of difference.) George Inskip also referred to the beliefs that the Islanders held about white people in his diary account of Thompson's information:

> It appears they think us to be the ghosts of departed natives. They pity our unfortunate case as they imagine we are obliged to roam about for provisions, that we live on Sharks & Whales & that the Pork & Beef are those fish preserved in a peculiar way.

Evidently, some of the women, at least, recognised white people as people with their own ways and customs, rather than as ghosts of themselves. When talking about babies, Thompson informed Brierly that:

> They used to ask me ... whether white women put their child into a bag when it was born. They thought something of this kind must be done to make them grow up white and how often they took it out to wash it.

Thompson indicated that it was the white people's perceived lack of compassion that made them something other than fully human, in the eyes of the Kaurareg. When she would not cry at the death of an old man, the Islanders told her:

> Your people are like ghosts. They don't cry, they have no feeling. We are people, *garkigi*, we cry.

A studio portrait of an Islander man from Muralug about 1852.

8

James Morrill

A naked man perched on a fence and, in fear, stammering out to two armed settlers not to shoot him—'I am a British object'—is surely one of the most vivid symbols of the terribly perilous position of those who had crossed over the colonial frontier. The experiences of this man, James Morrill (or Murrells), over 17 years with Aboriginal people in the Townsville–Bowen region of northern Queensland, traversed the dramatic and catastrophic changes wrought upon Indigenous culture and society by invasion.

Morrill was about 22 when his life among the Aboriginal people of northern Queensland first began. The son of an Essex millwright and engineer, he had run away to sea as a youth and wound up in Sydney. In February 1846, he joined the crew of the *Peruvian*, setting sail from Sydney for China. The ship was under the command of Captain George Pitkethley and carried seven passengers: the captain's wife, Mr and Mrs Wilmott, their infant and nursemaid, and James Quarry and his young daughter.

A few days out of port, the ship struck a storm. On Horseshoe Reef, at the southern end of the Great Barrier Reef, the *Peruvian* was picked up by waves and became stuck fast on top of a rock. One lifeboat and a seaman were washed overboard and disappeared. The crew and passengers rode out the tempest until

James Morrill, having spent 17 years 'with the Blacks'.

first light, when 'a terrible scene presented itself, for as far as the eye could reach there were the points of rocks awash, but no friendly land in view'. The ship's jolly boat was lowered into the water, but was smashed to pieces in the heavy seas and, when the only other lifeboat hit the sea, it immediately filled with water. No crew member except the captain's brother, First Mate John Pitkethley, was prepared to lower himself down to the boat to bail out the water. Pitkethley had only managed to clear two buckets of water when the boat was torn free and carried away by the current, with him in it.

Those remaining constructed a rough raft out of the ship's masts and crowded onto it. The 21 survivors had intended to stay near the wreck for a few days while trying to build a stronger raft from the ship's boards, but during the night the current tore the raft from its ties. More than 40 days later, the raft was blown into shore, at the southern point of Cape Cleveland, a promontory jutting out just south of present-day Townsville. Only seven people were left alive, having lasted as best they could on seagulls and sharks, caught using the dead bodies as bait.

The survivors—the captain and his wife, Mr Wilmott, sailmaker Jack Millar, sailor James Gooley, a cabin boy and Morrill—were so weakened by their ordeal that they could barely crawl about to gather oysters from the rocks. Wilmott and Gooley died of exhaustion and starvation, 'nobody being equal to provide for more than their own absolute necessities'. The captain, who was the strongest, ventured further and discovered an Aboriginal canoe with fishing lines and spears nearby. On bringing the news back to the group, the sailmaker took the canoe the next morning, not to be seen again by Morrill (he would later learn, from Aboriginal people, that the man's body washed up on the shore of the next bay). Meanwhile, the captain and Morrill had spotted a full-rigged ship running close to shore, but they were unable to signal to it.

The Townsville region in the late 1870s, showing Mount Elliott in the distance.

It was some two weeks after reaching land that the survivors were finally discovered by the local Aboriginal people. Morrill later learned how they had been found. For several nights before, some Aboriginal people had noticed falling stars in one direction—'the direction of the rocks on which we were'. They decided to walk in the direction of the falling stars. Finding the tracks of the boy, who had camped separately from the others, they followed them until they came to the others' camp, where they saw the captain's wife alone. At this point, the Aboriginal investigators left to get more people. When Morrill and the captain returned after a day foraging, the captain's wife told them that she 'beheld a number of naked blackfellows on the rocks' and cried out to her husband—'Oh George, we have come to our last now, here are such a lot of the wild blacks'.

after awhile we neared each other, they came among us, and felt us all over from head to foot to make sure we were human beings like themselves

Morrill observed that these people were 'as afraid of us as we were of them'. In what must have been something of a comic scene, when the survivors held up their hands in surrender, the Aboriginal group mimicked the gesture and raised their arms in surrender as well:

> and after awhile we neared each other, they came among us, and felt us all over from head to foot to make sure we were human beings like themselves; of this they seemed to be satisfied.

Ten of the old Aboriginal men in the group insisted then on entering the camp that the four white people had made under some overhanging rocks, 'but they kept us separated by lying between us'. The old men talked together, leading to:

> a more minute examination of our person, this time evidently to ascertain our sex, which seemed necessary on account of our being clothed. The captain's wife naturally shrank from such scrutiny, but they persisted, and when they found we were like themselves—male and female—they seemed satisfied, and did not further molest us.

The following morning, it became clear that the survivors' visitors were from two different groups. One group (from the Cape Cleveland area) claimed the captain and his wife, while the others (people from Mount Elliott, a large mountain about 30 kilometres south of present-day Townsville) took charge of the cabin boy and Morrill.

The Aboriginal people generously provided the newcomers with food, some small roots that Morrill reported 'tasted like nuts'. They then indicated that if the white people would come with them they would be given 'plenty to eat and drink'. Gratified when they received a positive response, they quickly set up a corroboree to signify the decision, and encouraged the survivors to join in the dancing. Not being strong enough, the wreck survivors decided to 'please them by singing a hymn'. The popular hymn, 'God Moves in Mysterious Ways', was an appropriate choice in the circumstances and 'amazed them very much', plainly sitting well with Aboriginal cultural protocols.

As everyone set off for the Aboriginal camp, Morrill was impressed by the compassion of these people towards the four strangers:

> Seeing the boy was unable to walk, one of these stalwart fellows picked him up, put him on his shoulder with his legs hanging down, the same way as they carry their children when on a journey. And noticing how weak we were two of them helped us along.

Morrill was led up to three men who were sitting around a small fire. He saw that they were senior men with authority and was gripped with fear, thinking (as had Buckley many years before) that he was going to be slaughtered, cooked and eaten. Seeing Morrill shaking in terror, the men warmed their hands at the fire and gently placed them on Morrill's face and body, as a reassurance to him, he believed, that all was well. The captain, his wife and the boy were led through a similar process of acceptance. Historian Bruce Breslin notes that the customary practice of the laying on of hands that had been warmed in the smoke of a fire was intended to protect people from dangerous spirits and effects. This welcoming solace extended to the strangers—not a cannibal feast—was the reality of Aboriginal culture.

Messengers were sent ahead to the main camp to inform them to prepare a feast of celebration, and in the meantime the people with the survivors danced, again encouraging the white people to join in, without success. The culmination of this celebration would be another, much bigger corroboree, although with the survivors still unable to take part except as items to display.

The main Aboriginal camp ground was five to eight miles away and it was sundown when the large group arrived there. The survivors were directed to lie down and were covered with dry grass to conceal them until the right moment for their unveiling. About 50 to 60 men, women and children were then seated in a large circle, and the discoverers of the white survivors, now dressed in some of the European clothes, told the story of the mysterious white people. The introductions now over, the four white people were led into the centre of the ring 'in triumph'. Their unexpected appearance caused more than a little excitement and fear:

> The first sight of us—having white skins and being fully dressed—produced
> a panic, and they scattered in all directions. After a little while, however, being
> reassured, they returned in twos and threes, and ... by and bye they came
> nearer, felt us all over, examined us more minutely, and satisfied themselves
> there was no need to fear.

The white people were given plenty of food and drink and, after the evening corroboree and feasting were over, the hosts eventually drifted off to bed.

The introductions and celebrations of the strange newcomers' arrival would continue for several nights as more distant groups were invited to observe them. After some time, the camp returned to normal and the survivors were adopted into the everyday life of the tribal groupings. At first, the Europeans, being so weak, were not allowed to gather their own food, but had it brought to them: 'Eventually we went with them, but they dug the roots up for us till we learned to do it ourselves'.

After some five or six months, they were also joining hunting and fishing expeditions and had begun to pick up the Aboriginal language. Now somewhat acculturated, they learned that a much larger gathering was being planned where many more people would be coming to see them:

> When they all arrived they numbered considerably over a thousand souls:
> there were a larger number present than I have ever seen in one place since.
> They belonged to about ten different tribes.

At the ensuing three-day ceremony, Morrill observed how about 70 'lads were made men' and instructed in 'their duties towards the women'.

The serene setting of the Port Bowen region many years earlier, in 1802.
James Morrill would be witness to incredible changes in his lifetime.

Observing, also, that some of the groups there had travelled from the south, the Europeans concluded that if they went back with them, they might be able to reach a white settlement. Morrill and the captain 'stole away' with a group, the captain later turning back to 'fetch his wife and the boy'. The boy was given to another group going further south, and it seems that Morrill, the captain and the captain's wife were also split up, but remained near enough to see and hear of each other regularly.

Morrill had been with his new group at the site of Port Denison (the town of Bowen) for two years when he heard that the boy had died and his remains cremated according to Aboriginal custom. Some time after hearing this news, the captain also died. Morrill believed that he had been brought down by the worry he felt about his distressed wife, who died only four days later. Morrill asked the people looking after the captain to see that he was buried rather than burnt, which they agreed to.

Morrill, now left alone 'in a strange tribe', did not have a particularly easy time with these people. In one account, written after his death, he had reportedly described how they would 'roughly expel him' from shelters he built himself, forcing him to sleep in the open, so he 'discontinued laboring for their comfort'.

Morrill decided to return to the people who had originally taken him in. Several months later, when he reached the Mount Elliott area, his original rescuers welcomed him back. But they were very upset at the news of the deaths of his companions and 'laid all the blame on me, and said I deserved a crack on my head' for having coaxed them away in the first place (as the Aboriginal people saw it). Morrill was probably lucky to escape without some severe punishment being administered, but after a short time his acceptance back into the group was complete. The years went by without change or incident. 'I lived on year after year in the tribe, as one of themselves,' he told his biographer Edmund Gregory.

Morrill had been living contentedly with the Aboriginal people for many years before his thoughts turned to seeking out white society again. By this time, the existence of strange—and often very aggressive—white people in the country had come to be known to the people of the coastal region of northern Queensland. For several decades, news had been travelling along the grapevine, not only of the earlier white blackfellows like Pamphlett, Duramboi, Fraser and perhaps Thompson, but also of the white settlements further south. Of course, there were also the increasing sightings of strange animals, the new and valuable trade goods of iron and glass, and the ships passing by along the coastline.

It appears that the people who adopted Morrill into their group at Mount Elliott recognised that he had originated from elsewhere and some were willing to help him get back to his own people—despite the great danger to themselves. This they tried to do in an incident in 1860 (Morrill by then had been with the Aboriginal people for 14 years), which was documented in the records of a government schooner conducting a survey of the land near Cape Cleveland. The ship's report stated that the captain hoped that a 'small party of natives' he had noticed on shore would give him information about the mouth of the Burdekin:

> Such hopes, however, were soon blighted, for upon an increase of their party they suddenly made an attack, which was instantly repulsed, when they retreated with great rapidity.
>
> Observing a canoe passing round one of the points into a lagoon, we gave chase; and after it was deserted, we … broke it to pieces so as to … prevent any immediate increase to the force of the aborigines, already numerous and violently hostile.
>
> [The next day] we observed considerable numbers of natives about the beaches and hills, shrieking and yelling most diabolically.

This report points to the great difficulties that Aboriginal people had in their interactions with white people. In Morrill's account, the Aboriginal people, recalling Morrill's request that they make the white men understand that he was there:

> tried their hardest, but seemed to have failed: the white men became alarmed and thought they meant mischief, whereas it was only their earnestness in trying to make them understand.

Morrill was outraged by the turn of events that followed and their omission from the official report that he would be shown after his return to white society:

> Nothing … is mentioned in this report about shooting the natives; one stout able bodied black-fellow, however, was shot dead by someone in a boat, and another was wounded; and the hideous yelling was the noise they usually make over their dead.

In contrast to the kindness shown to shipwreck survivors by the Aboriginal people, the British responded to the sight of strangers with fear and ignorance. 'Savages' could be shot on sight with little or no feeling and, in most instances, such action was not even considered worthy of recording.

In another shocking incident, reported to Morrill by some Aboriginal people and noted by Breslin, a family had been conducting a funeral and mourning the loss of an old man when a white man with two horses had suddenly come upon them and fired his gun directly into their midst, killing the son of the deceased man, who had been embracing the body of his father. The murderer was probably a new settler in the area, searching for suitable farm land. The Aboriginal people tracked him down, coaxed him off his horse somehow and, at 'a preconcerted signal, they struck him down'.

The killing times in the region had well and truly begun. In 1861, as Breslin reports, the people with whom Morrill had spent his first couple of years at the site that would become Port Denison (later the township of Bowen) were summarily driven off their land and a settlement of white people established there. The newly appointed Police Magistrate, Commissioner for Crown Lands and Commander-in-Chief of the Native Mounted Police, George Elphinstone Dalrymple, led an initial charge on horseback 'designed "to clear off Aborigines" from the land which had always been theirs'.

The 'plan' thereafter pursued at Port Denison was, Breslin records, 'to hunt out of sight everything in the shape of a blackfellow, and when the intruder has not been sufficiently agile to elude his pursuers he has been without mercy shot'.

The Aboriginal people stayed well away from the new settlement, but throughout the region violence had been intensifying, with the notorious and highly skilled Native Police giving the settlers the edge in their determination to take the country by terror. (The Native Police were young Aboriginal men, mostly from the south of the colony, with no affiliations to the people they were attacking. They were the armed 'black fellows' that Morrill feared encountering.) Even as Morrill was galvanising his courage to make contact with the whites, a fishing party from his own group, some 15 people, were shot dead—'a sad reward for all their kindness to us', he told Gregory.

A sense of fear and mistrust was now a part of the Aboriginal understanding of the white people coming into their territory. Morrill, for his part, realised that his survival largely depended on getting back into the white community.

Morrill travelled some way south with his group to the Burdekin (Mall Mall) River, thinking his chances of meeting up with white settlers might be greater there. He stayed there while his people kept travelling between him and their own camp:

> They were always asking me why I did not return with them, as I had lived with them for so long. They evidently began to suspect something unusual would happen.

The Aboriginal people tried their hardest to discourage Morrill from seeking out the whites, telling him he would 'be taken for a blackfellow and treated accordingly, that is shot'. To explain his 'strange' desire to get away, Morrill spun a tale that he had a wife and two children waiting for him back in the white world. His people beseeched him to stay with them, but he told them:

> I was anxious to see the white men myself—to see if they knew my people at home—and to get from them clothes, guns, and old iron, but that I would come back again.

They eventually accepted that he was 'bent on going' and 'left me to my own sweet will'.

The Aboriginal people tried their hardest to discourage Morrill from seeking out the whites, telling him he would 'be taken for a blackfellow and treated accordingly, that is shot'

From that time forward, Morrill recounted, he received almost daily reports of white people. He persuaded his hosts to show him where the white people were, so that he 'might be the means of saving their lives'. A discussion was held and it was agreed that 'what I said was true', and a group of them set out with Morrill for a hill called Yamarama that was near where the Europeans had been seen.

After two old women 'went to spy out the white men's resting place' and returned with the news that they had seen the white people's hut, Morrill decided to approach it. His people insisted that an Aboriginal woman go with him (it was safer to have women rather than men approach the whites). When the pair got down the hill, they saw some sheep, which frightened the woman so much that she ran back ('never having seen anything of the kind before'). But Morrill continued on and, coming to a waterhole, he washed to make 'myself look as much like a white man as possible'. For some time, he sat and watched the smoke from the fire in the house ascend into the sky. Eventually, he overcame his fear and, climbing onto the fence to escape the barking dog, called out: 'What cheer, mates?' When the two men in the hut looked out at the strange naked figure perched on their fence, they went for their guns. Morrill cried out, 'Do not shoot me, I am a British object—a shipwrecked sailor'. Morrill later stated he meant to say subject but 'in the excitement of the moment I did not know what I said'.

The two men motioned Morrill to come around the stockyard where he was 'cross-questioned' about the shipwreck and his experiences since. He was able to tell them the year of the shipwreck and they calculated he had been in the wild for 17 years—he was surprised, he had not thought it 'half so long'. They took him into their hut and fed him bread, which stuck in his throat, and gave him tea that 'was too sweet'. After so many years without sugar, the taste was repulsive to him. He declined an offer of clothes, telling the men he needed to 'go back to the natives who were on the hills in the distance' to tell them to go away to the coast, and he would return to the hut the next morning. The white men agreed and instructed him:

> to tell them, that if they did not interfere with us, we should not interfere
> with them. They also told me that if I did not come back in the morning
> they should conclude I had told them a lie, and that they would put the black
> trackers on our track and shoot us.

Morrill must have carried deeply mixed feelings and concern when he went 'back to the hills to the blacks'. On reaching his people, he responded to their excitement and inquisitiveness:

> I told them as I thought for their good: so as to intimidate them I told them
> there were a great many people, many more than themselves; that they had
> plenty of guns, and that if they went near they would be killed. I told them that
> they had come to take possession of their land.

It must have been a harsh message to deliver, but Morrill (or possibly Gregory on his behalf) reassured his readers that Aboriginal people always adhered to the principle that 'might gives right' and were therefore prepared to believe what Morrill had said of the white outlook and attitude. Perhaps they were simply realists in the current situation. The people asked Morrill to return to the whites with a placatory offer:

> they told me to ask the white man to let them have all the ground to the north
> of the Burdekin, and to let them fish in the rivers; also the low grounds, they
> live on to get the roots—ground which is no good to the white people, near the
> sea-coast and swampy.

Morrill told his friends that he would stay the night, but that in the morning he would return to the whites, explaining their threat to track down the whole group and kill them if he did not. His people, very concerned, questioned whether the white men were already on the way. Morrill assured them that they were not, but that 'we had better move further away'. The next morning, Morrill informed them that he would be away 'quite three or four moons'. As described by Morrill, an emotional scene played out:

> the man I was living with burst into tears, so did his gin, and several other gins and men. It was a wild touching scene. The remembrance of all their past kindnesses ... quite overpowered me. There was a short sharp struggle between a feeling of love I had for my old friends and companions, and the desire once more to live a civilized life, which may better be imagined than described.

Not all may have been gracious upon his departure, though. Another account claimed that some of his people were angry at his determination to leave, telling him to go, and 'saying he would be drowned with the rest of the white men'—a reference to their prophecy that a great flood would destroy all the white people.

Morrill remained at the white men's hut for a fortnight, just 'in case any of the natives should put in an appearance, but none of them ever came in sight'. Eventually, he made it to Bowen on 20 February 1863, and was welcomed there by some of the prominent citizens, who took up a collection for him. He was then provided with a passage to Rockhampton, where he was examined by the police magistrate, and then to Brisbane where he was introduced to the governor in Brisbane (and joined the Baptist faith). In both places, he was reportedly 'besieged by those curious to see the man who had lived such a strange and eventful life'.

Morrill himself, described as 'a plain, unpretending, and kind-hearted man, intelligent, reasonable, and moderate in his views and expressions, even where deeply interested', apparently intended to press for a policy of conciliation towards the Aboriginal people, in which he could play a key role in using his influence to 'benefit and protect the aboriginal blacks ... [who] have so long benefited and protected him, and at the same time to make the white settler feel secure'. Morrill's stated mission in going to Brisbane was to see how far:

> the Queensland Government and Queensland people will further and facilitate this object—an object noble in itself, creditable to him, and certainly well worthy the consideration and patronage of the Government of a Christian people.

The pamphlet in which Morrill describes his life with the Aboriginal people was published in 1863 and also appeared in a number of colonial newspapers, complete with his impassioned call for land rights and gifts as rewards for the people who had taken him in:

> I would just call attention to what I previously mentioned, almost their last wish to me was with tears in their eyes that I would ask the white men to let them have some of their own ground to live on. They agreed to give up all on the south of the Burdekin River, but asked that they might be allowed to retain that on the other, at all events that which was no good to any body but them, the low swampy grounds near the sea coast. It would be no good to send them flour, they would not eat it ... they know nothing of the use of tobacco. But as the cold season is coming on, a good blanket would be invaluable, so would some small tomahawks, knives, old iron hoops and fishing hooks.

In the wider white community—at Maryborough and the Wide Bay region to the south, the site of Fraser's ordeals almost 30 years earlier—Morrill had supporters. An editorial in the *Maryborough Chronicle* that appeared at the time commended the plan to have Morrill take on a role of intermediary between black and white:

> There is something hideous in the fact that when exiled he dared not show himself to his own countrymen, even though he went unarmed, lest he should be shot down like a ferocious beast. If only some medium of communication can be established, many a deed of blood may be stayed.

Morrill would be appointed colonial storekeeper at Bowen and, courtesy of the Brisbane governor, he was able to distribute fishhooks and tomahawks to his friends, while some blankets were dispatched by government order to Port Denison (Bowen). In doing so, another sympathetic journalist wrote, 'he will, to a certain extent, be able to carry out his original intention with respect to his Mount Elliott protectors'.

But, locally, there was staunch and unequivocal opposition to Morrill's stance, and many in the settler community viewed him as being in league with the Aboriginal people against them. One man threatened to give him 'a small piece of lead' were he to appear in his vicinity. Morrill would never be able to put

Opposite: James Morrill became something of a celebrity
on his return, but there were many who opposed his call for land
rights for the people who had protected him.

into effect his plans of leading negotiations that would enable the Aboriginal people he knew so well to keep land in their own country. The answer to the request he brought back from his people—to be allowed to retain the swamps and salt-water creeks—'was sent from the rifle, and those who had protected and fed one of our fellow-beings for so long a time were shot', as one journalist put it.

In May 1863, an infuriated 'influential settler' on the Burdekin wrote from Bowen to the editor of a Rockhampton newspaper. This settler was none other than Police Magistrate Dalrymple. In his letter, he set out the 'serious depredations ... committed by our sable brethren', in order to:

> prove how very incorrect is the statement made of the innocent character of
> the natives, by the man Morrill—as I believe these blacks belonged to the tribe
> he lived amongst.

Dalrymple had landed some five or six tons of goods at the 'landing-place' on the Burdekin and, although the river had risen in the night flooding the banks, leaving the bottom layer of bags damaged, the rest could have been saved if the Aboriginal people had not deliberately destroyed the lot. Dalrymple described how his bullock driver and a worker had gone in a dray to collect the goods and had found 200 Aboriginal people at the landing place, 'determined on mischief'. He was sure that the two men 'would undoubtedly have fallen victims to the blacks', had it not been for the 'riding party' appearing at the time.

Morrill reportedly dismissed the incident as reflecting any hostile intent on the part of the Aboriginal people, saying it was simply what they would do out of 'mere curiosity and ignorance' on discovering the 'abandoned stores'; but one could read it as a message from the Aboriginal people about their opposition to settlement on the north of the river, and indeed the squatters north of the Burdekin thereafter began pressing for another port to be opened, to avoid the necessity of crossing the river to get down to Rockhampton.

In that enterprise, rather incredibly, Morrill entered into an alliance with Dalrymple. In January the following year, he accompanied Dalrymple as his interpreter on an expedition to open a new port at Cardwell. 'I told them, through Morrill,' Dalrymple reported, 'that we had come to take possession of the coast from a point on the north-west shore of the bay to a point opposite Haycock Island, and that we were going to settle there and possess it.'

They said, 'they hoped we were not going to war with them.' I replied, 'No: that we did not wish to hurt them, but that we wished to be left alone; and that if they would keep off and not molest us, we would not injure or interfere with them in any way.' They seemed to understand this ultimatum, and retired slowly into the mangroves; Morrill having explained it to them over and over again, and told them to inform the neighbouring tribes accordingly.

Dalrymple went on to say that he used Morrill's services to ensure the settlers could come to 'an amicable understanding with these people', to avoid 'bloodshed'. But Morrill's own account suggests the conversation was not as easy as Dalrymple reported it. Morrill said that he told the Aboriginal people there that:

> we came as friends, but as we were going inland we wished them to keep away, or if they did not we would make war ... I then said that they must clear out and tell others to do so, as we wished to occupy the land, and would shoot any who approached ... They told us to leave and not to return, and then they went away.

Three days later, on 24 January 1864, according to Morrill but omitted from Dalrymple's report, a group of armed Aboriginal men found near their camp were 'set upon suddenly by Mr Dalrymple's men and rather cut up'.

In April 1865, Morrill was put in charge of a delivery of the first bonded goods to the new settlement on Cleveland Bay (the site of his original shipwreck and, later, Townsville). In June:

> when the first land of the new town was sold, a quarter of an acre was knocked down to Morril at the upset price, no one being disposed to bid against him, and thus he obtained an allotment of land in what he termed his own country.

Morrill was now back on the white side of the frontier. Yet in his two years in Bowen, he had remained an outsider and a stranger. A former officer of the Native Police, Edward Kennedy, who befriended Morrill, described the strange figure Morrill cut in the streets:

> It was curious to watch him as he sauntered along one of the grassy streets of the town; ever and anon would he cast his eyes aloft and scan the spouts of the gumtrees within view looking for 'sugar bag'—wild bees' nests—never, in fact, did he lose this or other wild man's habits ... I went on several excursions with Morrill and was put up to much bush lore ... but he would not open his mouth much until he knew you a bit. In most of his ways he much resembled a black fellow and was pretty nearly as dark as they are.

Having acquired the land at Townsville, Morrill chose to remain in Bowen. A settler who knew Morrill 'sensed some of the inner turmoil', saying that he 'would much have preferred going back to his wild life with the blacks'. But, by this time, Morrill had a new wife—Eliza Ann Ross, the Bowen police magistrate's servant—whom he had married in 1864. With his wife pregnant, Morrill may have envisaged a calmer future. But, in October 1865, at the age of 41, he died suddenly in Bowen, leaving behind his wife and their unborn child.

He always maintained that the aboriginals might be better managed by kindness than by harsh treatment

The funeral was attended by most of the town's residents and the flags of the ships in harbour as well as those in the town stores were lowered at half-mast. He was 'a frank and open-hearted man', it was reported, 'who won the respect of all who knew him, and he will be missed by his numerous friends at Bowen'. A longer account of his life, published in the *Port Denison Times* at the time, hinted at the suspicions that others had of him: 'Although Jemmy never expressed a wish to return to the haunts of his black friends, his sympathies continued with them'. The journalist continued:

> He always maintained that the aboriginals might be better managed by kindness than by harsh treatment, and would willingly have accepted office in the police where he could have acted as mediator between the whites and the blacks, but the Government appears to have been afraid he might again join the natives, and act, perhaps in unison with them to the injury of the flocks.

It was also said, sentimentally, that the 'old men of the tribe' who knew Morrill claimed that he had 'died of a broken heart because the white men continued to ill-use the natives'. In fact he had died at a surprisingly young age for one who was in notably good physical health two years earlier. His cause of death was said to be infection in his knee, possibly an effect of an old 'spear-wound'.

We cannot help but wonder if Morrill had been called to account in some way, by those people to whom he had made a promise that he could not keep.

Morrill's Aboriginal Life

While Morrill attained a certain celebrity status on his return from his Aboriginal life, there was not the same level of outpouring of sensationalised accounts that had marked the return of those who had come before him. However, an interesting narrative, taken down and published by the Brisbane printer, Edmund Gregory, in 1863, the year of Morrill's return, has been republished many times since. While Gregory's account provides a rare sympathetic insight into the experiences of a white man who lived with Aboriginal people, like other 'wild white men', Morrill remained reticent on the subject of Aboriginal tradition and customs, and Gregory later expressed his regret at having obtained only 'trifling information on this subject'.

In one of the earliest accounts that would appear on Morrill's return to white society many years later, he was reported as saying that he had been given the name of 'Karekynjib-Wombil-Moony, after one of their chiefs', but as this name never reappeared in any of the various versions of his life, including Gregory's work, we cannot be sure it was not an imaginative creation of the journalist at the time. Nor did Morrill provide a name for the Aboriginal people he lived with in his accounts, instead identifying them by their place—Mount Elliott. In an interview with the police magistrate at Rockhampton, Morrill reportedly gave the rare piece of information that 'the name of my custodiers was "Baarberuggedy"'. Historian Iain McCalman has identified the people he lived with at Port Elliott as the Bindal clan of the Birri Gubba (or Biri) people, and those based around the site of Port Denison the Jura, or Gia (Guya) people.

Morrill was well integrated into Aboriginal society, if not fully accepted. He could speak no less than eight dialects. He learnt to hunt and fish, and claimed that he eventually became 'very expert' in snaring birds, 'much more so than the natives themselves ... which made them very attached to me'. If he developed any kind of close familial relations within the group though, this was never made clear. There are no accounts hinting at Morrill having ever had any recognised companion, or children. On his return to white society, Morrill explicitly denied having had any sexual relations because of the 'jealousy' of the men, and his wish to avoid trouble: 'hence I fought shy of the seductions of female blandishments'. The settler Thomas Murray-Prior claimed in his diary, on the other hand, that Morrill had privately boasted to him that although he had never been allowed 'a regular wife', he had been 'a greater favorite [with the Aboriginal women] than was good for his constitution'—trading the ducks he had caught for their favours. No accounts describe Morrill bearing cicatrices in the way that Davis, for instance, was always described, implying that he had not undergone the initiation ceremonies that would have given him full manhood status among the people.

DAY-TO-DAY LIFE

Morrill provided some information to Gregory about day-to-day life with the Aboriginal people, including details of various medicinal plants and the abundant and often 'very nice eating' food that they lived on:

> They can eat almost anything, sharks, snakes, crocodiles, shell-fish and fish of all kinds, kangaroos, rats, wallabies, grubs, snails, all kinds of creeping things, wild ducks, geese, turkeys, and several kinds of roots, one of which called (moogoondah), growing on the tops of the highest hills, is the best eating.

Bark from a particular tree and its root was used to stun fish, and they used nets and snares for hunting kangaroo and birds. So generously supplied was the country around Mount Elliott where he lived (and where there was 'a never-failing spring of beautiful water') that it could provide for all the Aboriginal people from the country all around.

CANNIBALISM

The ubiquitous question about cannibalism was raised as soon as Morrill first reappeared in white society. In Gregory's narrative, Morrill stated that the flesh of young warriors killed in battle or by accident, 'also young women and children' was occasionally consumed by the Aboriginal people, but 'never' that of enemies. It is unclear whether this was an embellishment by Gregory to heighten the book's saleability. A newspaper account at the time of his return quoted Morrill as saying that Aboriginal people 'often eat their own children fancying some benefits are derived from it', but this seems a fabrication. Later, the former Native Police officer Edward Kennedy would write that Morrill was his authority for the statement that the Aboriginal people of Queensland were 'not cannibals in the usual sense of the term' (that is to say, they did not kill people for the purpose of eating them, but rather for ritual funerary purposes), which accords also with Murray-Prior's record of what Morrill said about it. As ever, it could be that, if Morrill actually described any anthropophagy practice, he was referring to mortuary rites.

BELIEFS

The Aboriginal people with whom Morrill lived had various beliefs about the world around them. Morrill reported that there was a 'large open space' surrounded by very dense scrub on Mount Elliott that the people told him had been created by the moon ('a human being, like themselves' who sometimes visited earth and accompanied them on fishing trips—they measured time by the cycles of the moon) clearing a circle with its boomerang.

Morrill/Gregory continued:

> They think all the heavenly bodies are under their control ... They think the natives have power over the rain (durgun), to make it come and go as they like. The rainbow (terebare), they think, is the clouds spewing fish in the lagoons, also roots on the hills— something for their good, wherever the ends touch the horizon.

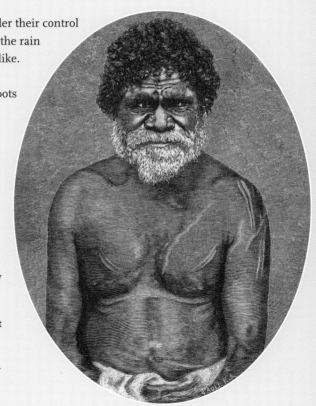

The Aboriginal people had told Morrill of how their ancestors had witnessed a very great flood in which nearly everyone was drowned, except those who made it to the top of a very high mountain, Birriringda—Morrill conjectured that this was the biblical flood. There was a prophecy

An Aboriginal elder of Townsville. It was claimed that some of the old Aboriginal men said that Morrill had died of a broken heart, due to the continued mistreatment of Aboriginal people by the white men.

that another flood would return to deliver them from the settlers. The people also thought that 'the falling stars indicate the direction of danger', an echo of the episode of the original discovery of the survivors, and that:

> comets are the ghosts or spirits of some of their tribe who have been killed at a distance from them, working their way back again, and that they come down from the clouds on the coast.

RETURNED DECEASED RELATIVES

While Gregory alluded to the Aboriginal people having 'some idea that after death they will arise as whitefellows', on record Morrill never said anything explicit about being taken for a returned deceased relative. But there is an account given by a local Townsville historian, Frank Reid, in 1929, based upon the papers of the journalist Frederick Raynor (founder of the *Port Denison Times*), in which the writer states that Morrill at first would have been killed 'but for the interference of the women, with whom he became a great favourite', one 'old woman' going so far as to recognise him as her 'dear departed son'. Perhaps this was an invention of the journalist, or perhaps the women had indeed protected Morrill, but he was not comfortable in making that account public.

FEAR OF WHITES

In his interview with the police magistrate, John Jardine, at Rockhampton, Morrill had been expansive on the subject of the Aboriginal people's fear of the whites. Explaining why he was always circumspect in asking the Aboriginal people for information about where the white people were, and why he felt it 'imperative for my own life's sake, to feign utter indifference on the subject', Morrill had been called upon to justify why he had stayed so long at a distance from the settlers. He told them that the Aboriginal people held the white men in 'great dread' and regarded them as 'enemies'; further noting that the whites had 'certainly given them much cause' to do so. They 'abominate a white man being near them', Morrill told Jardine and the other gentlemen settlers who had been invited to meet with him, 'as they fancy his only object is to destroy them from the face of the earth'.

9

Narcisse Pelletier—'Anco'

The story of French cabin boy Narcisse Pelletier remains one of the most intriguing and least known accounts of a white person living among Aboriginal people in Australian history. Pelletier spent many years with Aboriginal people, who had welcomed him, and in return he embraced Aboriginal culture and became deeply acculturated.

As a 14-year-old boy, Pelletier was marooned on Cape York in 1858 and was taken in by the people of north-east Cape York Peninsula, north of Princess Charlotte Bay. He grew to manhood among them, until he was found 17 years later. An account of his story, taken from conversations with the French-speaking Lieutenant John Ottley (a passenger on the ship that took Pelletier to Sydney before he was returned to France), appeared in Australian newspapers in 1875 and, back in France, he was interviewed by Constant Merland, who had the story published a year after Pelletier had left the Aboriginal people as *Dix-sept ans chez les sauvages: adventures de Narcisse Pelletier* (*Seventeen Years with the Savages: The Adventures of Narcisse Pelletier*), providing Pelletier with an income. Merland's account was republished in a new French edition in 2001, but it was not until 2009 that an annotated English-language translation by Stephanie Anderson brought the story to the attention of an Australian audience again.

Pelletier was born in 1844 in the seaport of Saint-Gilles-Sur-Vie near Bordeaux. The sea held a magnetic fascination for him and, at the age of 12, he embarked on a life on ships. The cabin boy soon discovered a life that was harsh and dangerous. He was stabbed with a knife while serving on the *Reine des mers* in 1857, in an act of so-called discipline by the first mate, and left the ship at Marseilles. Soon after, he served on the *Saint-Paul*, a French ship that had originally set sail from Marseilles for India with a cargo of wine, before sailing on to Hong Kong. There, it took on some 300 Chinese men, recruited to work on the Australian goldfields by the enterprising captain, Captain Emmanuel Pinard.

One evening in September, the ship ran aground on a reef near Rossel Island, part of the Louisiade Archipelago, off Papua New Guinea. All efforts to refloat the ship proved fruitless. Initially, the survivors set up a camp on a small island that had no fresh water. The European crew and the Chinese men were confronted by local Islanders who made their hostility obvious. The crew decided to 'leave the Chinese to shift for themselves' and, as reported in a widely published newspaper article that would appear years later, headed to Rossel Island:

> the Europeans made for the neighbouring Island, where, however, they were attacked by the blacks, and forced to retire, leaving behind them in the hands of the savages, three men—the second officer, a sailor, and an apprentice. During this attack Narcisse received a violent blow on the head from a stone, but managed to reach the boat.

> Much as the crew dreaded the Chinese they dreaded the savages more, and accordingly returned to the island which had first afforded them refuge. Once more in comparative security their former fears returned ... it being finally decided to embark at dead of night when all the Chinese should be asleep.

Captain Pinard and a number of his men managed their secretive departure from the island and set off in the longboat in search of a British settlement. They survived an arduous 600-mile voyage across the Coral Sea and made it to Cape York. On first making land on the Australian coastline, Pinard's party could find only a small waterhole, from which the men drank, 'leaving none for the little cabin-boy, already half dead with hunger, thirst and exposure, and with feet cut to pieces by the sharp coral of the reef'. Expecting him to die, they left him 'to his fate'. Pelletier believed that they had tricked him into waiting by the waterhole, telling him it should shortly refill with water after they had exhausted its supply. When no water came, he quickly retraced his steps to find he had been abandoned.

Left all alone, Pelletier was in need of a virtual miracle to survive. Exhausted and in pain, he ventured further into the bush in the hope of finding food and water. At the point of giving up, he came across three Aboriginal women who fled, terrified. When their husbands appeared, both holding spears, Pelletier was fearful but far too weak to hide or take flight. Fortunately, if unknowingly, the boy followed ritual convention by offering his tin cup as a gift. Noting that both men acknowledged this action favourably, he then presented them with his handkerchief. Wrote Merland:

> From this moment the alliance was made: it was never to be broken. In exchange for the presents that they had received, they gave him water, held out their hands to him to help him walk and tried to make him understand that they were going to give him something to eat.

Left all alone, Pelletier was in need of a virtual miracle to survive

The men, who were brothers-in-law, took him back to meet with the women. The boy was given food and water and taken to a spot where they provided a warm fire. Early the next morning, the two Aboriginal men left Pelletier sleeping while they went in search of food for him. When Pelletier woke to find himself alone again, he burst into tears. He could not comprehend that the men who had shown him such kindness the day before had left him. But they quickly returned with his breakfast, a meal of fruit, *muungkal* or the Wongai plum, a staple food.

In Merland's account, Pelletier had run along the shore in distress and did not at first see them coming back to him; but when he saw them 'responded to them as best he could', and one of the men, Maademan, gratified by his response, 'adopted him as his son' and named him 'Amglo'. In her carefully researched translation of Merland, Anderson argues for 'Anco' instead—the name used in the first official report on Pelletier to the Colonial Secretary, which accords more closely with the Uutaalnganu language the people would have spoken. Pelletier, wanting to show his gratitude, took them to where his shipmates had landed and where they had left behind several blankets.

His new family were delighted and so 'seeing these declarations of affection, whose sincerity he could no longer doubt, all fear was banished from his heart'. Maademan left the young French boy in the care of his wives and went ahead to tell the rest of his people, camped some distance away. When Maademan returned and Pelletier was sufficiently rested, they all set off for the main gathering.

little by little, he completely regained his health and strength; and little by little, too, he took on all the ways of the people with whom he was living

On arrival at the main camp, the women and children hid in fear. Some of the women, suspecting that the young boy with his hairless face could be of their own sex, overcame their fear and set about making sure, but on 'confirming their mistake, they burst into laughter and took themselves off very quickly'. There is no mention of any special ceremonies being held to acknowledge his presence among them. But, as Anco, Pelletier was quickly accepted. Merland wrote that he became used to the diet of the Aboriginal people:

> and, little by little, he completely regained his health and strength; and little by little, too, he took on all the ways of the people with whom he was living. After a certain time all that distinguished him from them was the colour of his skin and the shirt and trousers which covered his body. It was not long before this last feature disappeared. One day while he was bathing, the savages tore up his clothes and shared out the shreds of material to use as a decoration for their foreheads.

Merland also noted that:

> The children especially often made fun of him because of his colour ... He went so far as to wash his hands every day. While this habit did not make him any enemies, it had left him open to teasing by all and sundry, who would laugh heartily and point at him. He also attracted the jealousy of those who could not easily forgive the superior skills that he had developed in the art of making arrows [spears].

In his conversations with Lieutenant Ottley, Pelletier recalled that:

> for a long time—a very long time—after his desertion by the captain, his
> thoughts continually reverted to la belle France, and to his father, mother, and
> little brothers; but that, as years rolled on, they faded from his memory, and
> he became thoroughly identified with the blacks.

Meanwhile, the men who had left Pelletier to die alone had ended up
marooned on the Cape York coast, where they were found several weeks later.
They returned to the French settlement at New Caledonia at the end of 1858.
Pinard immediately sailed back to recover his Chinese cargo but found just one
Chinese man, who told him that only a few of the Chinese men had survived.
Stories inevitably circulated that they had all been eaten by 'the cannibals of the
Louisade Islands'. Author Eric Johns' research has revealed that another two
Chinese men from the wreck were found many years later, living among the
Islanders on Piron Island and that they had been well treated.

Pelletier, remaining in the remote coastal paradise of islands and coral cays,
experienced many years that were rich in adventure. He told Merland that his
adoptive father Maademan was 'devoted' to him and that, while Maademan
regularly carried out physical acts of punishment against others in the group,
'only once' did he inflict any such punishment on Anco (what this was for was
not specified, although elsewhere in the narrative is an account of him suffering
an injury inflicted in secrecy by 'a person whose identity he never discovered',
after eating a fish that was reserved for old men only).

Anco also developed a deep friendship with Sassy, the son of Maademan's
brother and thus his adoptive cousin, who was close to him in age. On one
occasion Anco's cousin saved his life. A disagreement over the distribution of
turtle meat resulted with one man on the verge of driving a spear into Anco
before Sassy intervened. Merland commented:

> feelings of rancour are almost unheard of. They are like big children who,
> after giving each other some hearty clouts on the head, think no more about it
> and return to being the best of friends.

In April 1875, after 17 years of living with his Aboriginal clan, Pelletier's
life as Anco came to an abrupt end. By then the pearl shell and bêche-de-
mer industries were opening up in the Torres Strait and there was regular

lugger traffic along the coast of Cape York, with trading occurring between the Indigenous people and the occasional passing ship. An English pearling lugger, the *John Bell,* cast anchor in sight of the little island where Pelletier, Maademan and some other men happened to be. The captain sent a longboat ashore to the island to trade, crewed only by 'Negro' sailors from among his crew as a way of ensuring that they would be 'favourably received'. (Possibly the pearling crew included African workers—more likely, they were Melanesian workers.)

Surprised to see a white man among the Aboriginal people, the sailors returned to the ship and reported their discovery. The captain directed them to return and to 'offer the most dazzling objects they had ever seen', if Pelletier would accompany them back to the ship. Maademan told his adoptive son that he should go to collect the gifts but to 'swim away' as soon as he had received them and bring back to him what he could.

Anco, for his part, was fearful. Ironically enough in this situation, he was concerned that the black sailors were 'cannibals' whose 'friendly gestures' were a trick devised to lure him out to their ship in order to eat him. Out of deference to Maademan's orders only, he agreed to go with them. When in the longboat:

> his fears intensified: the sailors indicated to him with revolvers in their hands, that he was not to move, and the longboat headed towards the John Bell, which had remained at its moorings.

Merland's account described how, once Pelletier was on the ship, he saw white men there and was 'reassured' and realised 'that instead of the death he feared, it was his freedom which was being given back to him'. But a story published in the *Times*, following the ship's return to Sydney in May 1875, had a different take on it:

> The white savage was induced to enter one of the ship's boats, where he was given biscuit to eat and told to sit still, muskets being at the same time pointed at the natives and fired over their heads to induce them to retire, which they were very unwilling to do without being accompanied by the white man, whom they begged to return with them. This, he has since explained, he wished to do, but was afraid of the guns held by the sailors, and thought that they would shoot him if he tried to leave the boat.

Other newspaper reports confirm that Pelletier was taken against his will:

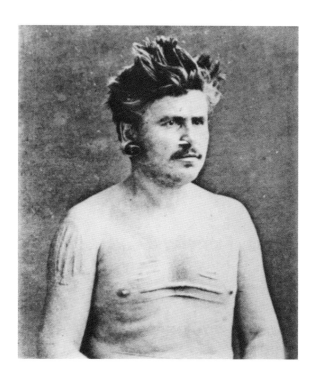

Left: An early photograph of Narcisse Pelletier—'Anco'—displaying cicatrices on his chest and arms.

Following pages: A view of the Somerset settlement on Cape York in the 1870s, where Narcisse Pelletier tried to escape from his white 'rescuers'.

The sailors who brought him off were under the impression that he came willingly, and that the savages understood that he was being ransomed with 'trade'. Narcisse, however, states ... that neither did the natives wish him to go, nor did he himself wish to leave. In fact, at the time, he would much rather have returned to his tribe.

Ottley explained why the men of the *John Bell* had misunderstood Pelletier's wishes:

Unfortunately he knew no English and was unable to talk to the seamen—moreover he gathered that if he did not sit still or if he attempted to escape they would shoot him. In short his view evidently was that instead of being rescued he was kidnapped.

The ship went first to the Cape York settlement of Somerset. Here Pelletier's unsettled behaviour—sitting all day perched on a rail fence 'like a bird' and glancing around him at everything—was noticed by Ottley. It was recorded that in fact Pelletier was 'fastened so he could not escape' and that subsequently he made several attempts to escape from the settlement.

SOMERSET
C YORK

Pelletier's return would have been traumatic, and the language barrier would have made it more so. Not only had he been speaking an Indigenous language for the previous 17 years, but his self-appointed rescuers could not speak his first language and he had to relearn French among these threatening strangers in order to express himself. He rapidly regained his French in conversations with Ottley, who was greatly impressed with his intelligence, noting how Pelletier, by the time they parted, could not only converse freely in French but had recovered his knowledge of reading and writing, and had acquired some English as well.

Ottley described Pelletier as 'about middle height, broad shouldered, and evidently immensely powerful'. A newspaper account based on Ottley's information also provided a description of Pelletier's appearance at the time of his discovery:

> stark naked ... his body burnt by the sun to a rich red color, and having a glazed appearance; his breast adorned with raised lines of flesh, of the thickness of a pencil, while the lobe of his right ear was ornamented with a piece of wood about half-an-inch in diameter and four inches long.

A curiosity, Pelletier spent a month in Sydney and was photographed before sailing to New Caledonia and then home to France in August 1875.

Pelletier's family was shocked and in disbelief with the news that he had been found alive after so long. Anderson tells us his mother, Alphonsine, had worn a mourning dress since his disappearance. Pelletier was met on his arrival home by one of his brothers and was taken at first to Paris to meet with government officials and to spend time in hospital. His return home was truly an event of some magnitude. The whole town turned out and a large bonfire was prepared for the returning hero. Once he had lit the fire, Pelletier was greeted with prolonged shouts of 'Long Live Pelletier'. Yet Pelletier apparently remained completely detached and disconnected from his family, France and its culture. Local oral history suggests that the warm welcome quickly cooled and his family, being confronted by not only his appearance but his adherence to Aboriginal beliefs, decided to have him exorcised by the local Catholic priest.

Myths emerged back in Australia that Pelletier had actually returned and found his way back to his people, and saw out his days in a beachside paradise. Historian Iain McCalman writes that, in contrast to this idyllic end, local French oral history depicts Pelletier as 'morose and solitary, staring wistfully out to sea

II

Narcisse Pierre Pelletier
Le 11 Juliette 1875

Mon cher Père et Ma cher mère
et maisfrère, Je vous écrie une autre
foi. Je vous embarse De tout Mon
cœur. ci vous êtes vivant. Je suis arriver
à nouméa le consule de sydney Ma
envoyez. je suis A bord du'un navire
De guere. Je partirait Dans un mois
à bord Du autre navire qui est venu
il y à trois jour, je me Porte Bien
J'ai toujour mal à la gambe
Droits. il y à Bien longtemps que gai
mal, J'ai vait et Bien de la misère
avec eux. il mon en Poissonnez la
gambe. Mais seulement je me
Porte Bien.

Je vous dit Bonjour
Narcisse Pierre Pelletier

Narcisse Pelletier rapidly regained his own language, as shown in one of the letters he wrote to his parents, before going home to France. 'I embrace you with all my heart if you are alive,' he wrote.

A studio portrait of a brooding Narcisse Pelletier, highlighting the extended lobe of his right ear.

and flying into rages when villages taunted him with his nickname *"le sauvage"'*. Anderson's research found that he had actually married a seamstress, Louise Desiree Mabileau, and worked as a 'signalman' or clerk at the harbour of Saint-Nazaire. It seems that he was a reclusive man and it is easy to imagine that Pelletier wanted to be near the sea, spending time gazing out over the ocean and thinking of a shoreline on the other side of the world. He died childless in 1894 at the age of 50. Anderson found a much later French account of his death that referred to a story that he had died from a spell cast upon him by 'a black sorceror' at the time the English took him from Cape York Peninsula, but that suggested that he had died of 'nervous exhaustion or depression'.

It is truly remarkable that Pelletier disappeared from the annals of Australian history into folklore and fiction. A mere 50 years after the event, Archibald Meston was adamant that the whole Pelletier story was nothing but fabrication:

> Recently there has been a revival of the discussion on a Frenchman named Narcisse Pelletier, who was alleged to have lived with the blacks for many years on various parts of Cape York Peninsula, and was finally picked up on Night Island. It is a bogus story from start to finish ... Night Island is well known to me ... To the blacks the island was known as 'Oung-Gooboo'. None lived there permanently but all the blacks of the adjoining mainland were known as the Night Islanders and their reputation was not the best. The whole story of Pelletier was sifted by me down to the bedrock among the old men of the wild tribes, and they knew nothing of any white man ever being among the blacks of the Peninsula.

Anderson notes that for the people of the Lockhart area today, while 'familiar with Pelletier's story, his life with their ancestors has not been passed down as part of their oral tradition'. Yet, as anthropologist Athol Chase points out, if Meston back in the 1920s had known how to ask the right questions, he might have received different answers:

> First we can assume that Meston and Night Island people could converse in a basic manner by means of the 'Pidgin' Aboriginal English then in use. But what would Meston have asked about? A 'Frenchman'? Someone called 'Pelletier'? Someone who had landed in a boat? These terms would have meant little to Aboriginal people of the area. Meston would have apparently had no knowledge of Pelletier's Aboriginal name to use for more precise enquiry. Second, we can assume that after approximately thirty years any particular memory of a European living among them (particularly if he had left no children) may well have become lost against the growing stream of Europeans coming and going in the area through the expanding marine industries, mining and sandalwooding activities over the intervening period. Third, it is possible that all those who had known Pelletier intimately had disappeared in the maelstrom of intensive contact, reprisal killings and increased mortality through introduced disease.

Narcisse Pelletier remains an elusive figure in the history of the Europeans who lived with Indigenous people. Although he never returned to the men and women who embraced him on the shores of Cape York, perhaps in some ways he never really left.

Pelletier's Aboriginal Life

The area where Pelletier found himself on Cape York Peninsula has been identified by Athol Chase as 'a coastal strip of the Peninsula about 60 kilometres long between Lloyd Bay in the north and a point somewhere around Cape Sidmouth to the south'. It included the territories of three linguistic groups, these being, from north to south, the Kuuku Ya'u, the Uutaalnganu (known in Aboriginal English today as the 'Nightisland' people) and the Umpila. They were collectively known as Pama Malngkana ('people of the sand beach') and had a strongly marine-oriented economy.

Pelletier was part of a clan group within the Uutaalnganu linguistic group, consisting roughly of about 30 people, whom he called the 'Ohantaala' (the name of a site) in Merland's account, and who are now identified as the Wanthaala. He was incorporated into a strict kinship system of belonging and connection. The people were spiritually connected to their clan country, both on land some seven kilometres along the shore and inland about six to ten kilometres, and extending over 40 kilometres out into the sea and Great Barrier Reef. Pelletier came among them on 'the very cusp of contact', as Chase observed. The people who took Pelletier in were evidently gaining some familiarity and experience with white people. As such, his account published by Merland is a valuable resource for ethnohistorians of the far north.

But, like other white people who had lived with Indigenous people, Pelletier was guarded about the knowledge he would reveal to those who interviewed him after he returned to white society. As Lieutenant Ottley noticed, Pelletier gave 'very vague replies' to those who questioned him, 'that left us under the impression that he knew more than he chose to confess'.

A Cape York Aboriginal man prepared for ceremony, photographed in the 1930s.

Anderson writes that it was unlikely that Pelletier, as Anco, became an initiated man. He chose not to undergo the tooth evulsion rite (which was connected to an individual's maternal line). As he never mentioned having an adoptive mother, this may be the reason and may reflect that he was not fully incorporated into the Indigenous social and cultural world at the time he was found. Even so, Pelletier did submit to scarring operations (resulting in cicatrices across his chest), which were apparently for the purposes of enhancing male attractiveness, not initiation.

In the latter years of Pelletier's time with the Aboriginal people, Maademan arranged for him to be provided with a wife from a neighbouring group. Pelletier's betrothed was only a child, aged seven at the time Pelletier was found again, when he was 32. It was a marriage of duty for Anco, if the way Merland recorded it reflected his recollections, and not much welcomed by his promised wife. 'The bride seemed to feel more antipathy towards her husband than liking,' Merland wrote. 'Most of all she was unable to forgive him for the whiteness of his skin.'

Earlier, Merland's account had explained that girls were contractually married at the age of three or four years old, and from the age of seven until puberty the spouses were not able to have much in the way of interaction with each other, except that from this age (seven) 'until the day she is handed over to him the husband is obliged to provide her with food'. This arrangement suited the fathers-in-law, ensuring that elderly men had strong adult men who were obliged to 'come to his aid whenever he asks for it'. If her husband died, she was passed into her brother-in-law's charge, and the only 'properly independent' women were older widows.

What other relationships Pelletier may have been able to have with women are unknown. There were rumours that Pelletier had fathered children, and the French scholar, Marcel Baudouin, recorded that Pelletier later confided that he had three children. Pelletier had a keen awareness of the 'jealousy' of men and women in his community, explaining that a man held 'absolute rights over his wife, or wives' and that both the men and women were 'extremely jealous, the women perhaps even more than the men'. On being asked by Merland whether there was 'sexual promiscuity' in Aboriginal society, he stressed the opposite:

> the feeling of modesty happens to be even more pronounced than in civilised societies.

> Men and women, except for spouses, barely go near each other. The distance separating them is almost always at least eight metres. Several times throughout the day they will move far enough away not to be seen, and the women will disappear at the slightest indisposition, not returning until any sign of their condition has ceased. There are never any improper conversations, never the slightest indecency of behaviour or tone of voice. It is quite true that this extreme reserve is also imposed by another sentiment, that of fear.

GATHERING AND HUNTING ON THE LAND

Where Pelletier lived, there was an endless supply of seasonal fruits and estuarine and reef shellfish to harvest. There were also crocodiles and snakes (including the large scrub python capable of growing up to eight metres in length). The crocodile was a much sought after food item and Pelletier described the skills and strategy employed to bring one to the table:

> The eye of the hunter can easily detect the tracks left by the crocodiles ... he arms himself with a sort of pike made from a very hard and resistant wood. Throwing himself upon the animal as soon as he sees it, he will strike it on the head and attempt to gouge out its eyes. With every blow that it receives the poor crocodile cries out with a sound like a dog barking, until mortally wounded, it lies motionless on the ground ... He will not leave without looking for its eggs, which he usually finds quite easily. What he obtains from this hunt allows him to feed himself and his family and friends for several days.

The Uutaalnganu hunted birds of every variety, including ducks, parrots, cockatoos, hens, doves, pigeons and 'ostriches' (Anderson explains that Merland was referring to emus or cassowaries, describing the former as 'white ostriches' and the latter as 'black ostriches'). Only the black ostriches were hunted while the eggs of the white ostrich were particularly prized—but only adult men and old women were allowed to eat them (the emu egg was thought to have 'abortifacient properties').

The Uutaalnganu, masters of their marine environment, centred most of their activities on the beachfront. Athol Chase describes their boats:

> The canoes ... could hold three or four adults; they had double outriggers for seaworthiness and stability; and were propelled by paddles. They featured a short platform on the bow, from which a harpooner could launch himself and the harpoon at a turtle or dugong.

Such craft were well able to travel to the outer reaches of the Great Barrier Reef. Dugong and turtle were a valuable food source and the meat from these catches provided 'a large amount of succulent meat', and to the present day 'a skilled and successful hunter becomes a man of renown (*pama watayichi,* or 'dugong man') who has command over the necessary hunting magic, as well as possessing outstanding hunting skills'.

Merland noted that the clan Pelletier belonged to 'only devoted their time to fishing'. The men went out in canoes to fish, usually three men to a boat. They used no nets, lines or baits but only special fishing spears with splayed and barbed hooks, for fish, and iron-pronged harpoons for the dugong. It was only the men who fished; once women used to play a role, but this practice ended after an alarming incident:

> One day when the catch had been abundant and the husbands had returned to land, leaving their wives to bring back the fish which they had caught, ten women boarded a canoe and landed on the little island where the men had left the fish. Barely had they set foot on shore when they noticed an English ship which was heading in their direction. Very frightened by the sight of it, and not

An array of the specialised fishing spears.

having time to get back to their canoe, they made a hasty escape and hid in the woods covering the island. The English landed straight away.

Nothing which had just occurred escaped the eye of the savages and they were therefore extremely fearful: they were convinced that their wives were going to be taken from them and that they would never see them again. When night had fallen, the men, taking the greatest precautions, went to the island. How great was their surprise and joy in finding their dear wives again! They soon consoled themselves about the loss of their canoes and the fish, which the English had seized.

they were therefore extremely fearful: they were convinced that their wives were going to be taken from them and that they would never see them again

NEW TOOLS OF IRON

The people who took Pelletier in were evidently gaining some familiarity and experience with white people. As with those people who had taken in Buckley years earlier on the Victorian coast, and the Islanders who took Ireland and the D'Oyley boys from the wreck further north in the Torres Strait, the Uutaalnganu also found that shipwrecks provided a useful source of iron (in the rings of barrels), which they used to replace their traditional shell saws and knives. With the new tools, they found that the construction of canoes 'became very much easier and took much less time'. Pelletier witnessed too the replacement of emu and kangaroo bone barbs on the spears with barbs of glass and iron, and the making of razors from glass.

WARFARE AND RETRIBUTION

Pelletier described staged battles between different groups over abducted women (or runaway wives), but 'The campaign is always a short one'. During his 17 years, he said that he had seen, and fought in, 12 such 'wars', though managed to escape injury.

As with descriptions from other Europeans who lived with Aboriginal people, the conflicts Pelletier described more closely resembled a medieval tournament than any full-scale war. The two groups, rarely numbering more than 80 people, would advance on each other openly and then at a distance of some 30 yards, begin to hurl their spears. The older, senior men, rushed between the combatant groups, trying to 'prevent them from reddening the soil with their blood'. The women also entered the fray, trading blows with one another directly. After 'a certain number of soldiers' had been wounded and some killed:

> the army that has come off worst takes flight, leaving the field of battle to the victors. The latter are ruthless; they never take prisoners. They finish off the poor soul lying on the ground, even if it means returning his body to his family or his tribe.

The most important outcome to consider in these exchanges was that peace was obtained 'without a ransom being paid, without lands being ceded ... Often peace is reached without the purpose for which the war had been waged having been achieved'. After the engagement, the old men 'resume their peace mission, and each tribe goes back to its own territory, without clinging to the hatreds which with us perpetuate wars between nations'.

RETRIBUTION AFTER MURDER

Punishment through law was a deterrent to crime. Murder was the ultimate crime and severe retribution was enacted:

> If, for example, a man is guilty of murder or of causing serious injury, he must stand at about thirty metres from those whom the family of the deceased or of the wounded man has appointed to exact vengeance. Armed with arrows [spears], they fire about thirty of them at the guilty man. These can deliver a fatal blow but it is very rare for this to happen.

The accused did his best to avoid the spears, assisted by a friend who used a stick to ward them off. Surviving the shooting gallery was not the end of the court proceedings. The individual had to then go to the victim's relatives and endure having a spear thrust into his thigh, followed by a painful operation to extract the barb. Thereafter, the guilty one was under an obligation for some time to provide food 'of the highest quality' to all the relatives of the victim.

There was much ceremony and significance attached to death and funeral rites and it was 'essential that the corpse was buried within country of close relatives, where the grave and spirit could be cared for, and recognised by following generations'. Lengthy mortuary ceremonies ensured the preservation of the corpse allowing it to be carried as a relic for 15 to 18 months before final burial (except in the case of elderly people, who were buried immediately). The people had a designated burial ground for their dead, called *Manillecaglo,* where the interred body was 'covered over with shells, fishbones, and animal and whale bones, and on top of these, by way of tombstone, there is a turtle's head'.

Pelletier explained, also, that his clan believed that 'every black person, without exception, returns to life by changing colour and that, once they have become white, they go and live in a land situated to the west of theirs'. As far as his adopting group was concerned, Pelletier was, therefore, 'merely a black person who had come back to life'.

Questions about cannibalism, a topic that had morbid allure for 19th century Europe, caused him to close up immediately

On the subject of cannibalism, Pelletier provided Merland with a curious anecdote about how one of his friends had promised Pelletier that if he were to die before him, he would consume him—although his friend 'had no taste for cannibalism'—as a way of ensuring that he (the friend) would become a great fisherman. The story indicates the existence of mortuary rites involving anthropophagy. Yet as Chase noted, Pelletier was otherwise very resistant to such discussions:

> Questions about cannibalism, a topic that had morbid allure for 19th century Europe, caused him to close up immediately, even later, in his life back in France. Was this because he had engaged in some kind of ritual cannibalism where a small part of a deceased body is eaten ritually? There is no record of

cannibalism in later anthropological research. Or was it because he found the European mode of categorising the 'savages' in the Hobbesian mould as primitive, brutish and animal-like extremely distasteful, given his deep knowledge of the very human qualities of his adopted families?

SPIRITUAL BELIEFS

It is fairly obvious from an Indigenous perspective to realise that Pelletier was tied to strict rules and obligations regarding what he could speak about. The people he lived with, according to Chase, called the Dreaming or creation period *yiilamu*. This was the time when the ancestral creator beings had created the world and everything in it. As Anderson has argued, Pelletier's failure to mention these spiritual beliefs of the people he lived with or any of their complexity could simply reflect the constraints he felt upon him, 'in his *Uutaalnganu* identity, as the Aboriginal person, or *pama,* he had become, about imparting secret and sacred knowledge'.

Instead, Pelletier talked about his inability to convince the Aboriginal people of the Christian beliefs he had been tutored in. As reported by Merland, when Pelletier tried in vain to impart his own religious beliefs about an omnipotent, all-seeing and punishing God, the people told him:

> we know as well as anyone else who created the earth. Look up above, can't you see the moon which is looking down at us? It is to the moon and to the moon alone that the earth owes its being. The earth is the moon's child, no other power can lay claim to its creation.

> If Pelletier replied, 'But who then made the moon?' they remained silent, not wanting to continue the discussion, or else they ridiculed him and treated him as a fool.

A finely decorated ceremonial drum from the Cape York region, complete with crocodile mouth.

Conclusion

Throughout the nineteenth century and since, the narratives of the wild white men and women who lived with Aboriginal and Torres Strait Islander people have more often than not been presented as tales of melancholy. But in re-presenting them here, we hope that readers do not feel the kind of sense of despair that often permeated the contemporary accounts, with their suggestions of inevitability, extinction and surrender of the Indigenous people. Instead, we have highlighted the complex interactions 'on the other side of the frontier' between white men and women and the Aboriginal people who found them and gave them a place in their own world.

These stories hold immense importance in providing a glimpse of the possibilities of what might have been and what still can be. The majority of these narratives reveal that Indigenous people were prepared to accept and embrace outsiders if they took on local ways and learned to abide by local laws and customs: still today, other Australians can learn that it is worth thinking of how to adapt to Aboriginal and Torres Strait Islander ways, instead of requiring Indigenous people to adapt to the white world. This message is profound in this chaotic and violent world we experience today, where climate change, rampant multinational companies and religious extremism of all persuasions are a major threat to the environment and humankind itself.

Tragically, so much Indigenous knowledge was recklessly devalued and destroyed at the time of invasion and since, but the stories here reveal a rich cultural lifestyle that those who experienced life with Aboriginal groups recognised for its all-encompassing value. As Germaine Greer pointed out some years ago: 'Blackfellas are not and never have been the problem. They were the solution, if only whitefellas had been able to see it'.

Unknowingly, and ironically, across the nineteenth century the country's new inhabitants had been adopting what was normal practice for Aboriginal Australia in pursuing a successful egalitarian society, as the push for equality, better working conditions and hours established the concept of the 'fair go' and standing by your mates (although that did not include Aboriginal Australians). Ninety years ago, John Maynard's grandfather, Worimi activist Fred Maynard, recognised that everything that the trade union movement was then fighting for had already 'existed in our country at the time of invasion by Europeans—the men only worked when necessary—we called no man "master" and we had no King'. He wrote to New South Wales Premier Jack Lang that, in the 1920s, the state government was only just catching up with what traditional Aboriginal society had in place for thousands of years. There was a strict policy of looking after the elderly and children, and 'your present Old Age Pensions was obtained from our ancient code, as likewise your Child Endowment Scheme and Widows Pension'.

the state government was only just catching up with what traditional Aboriginal society had in place for thousands of years

This collection of stories of white people who lived with the Indigenous people of Australia reveals that many of them recognised and appreciated the worth of Aboriginal culture and society. Everybody was provided for: you did an honest day's work and you in turn profited from a shared return. It was not only a sustainable and equitable system but also a rich and embracing way of life.

It is also clear that many who came back felt indebted to their former hosts; and furthermore, obligated to conceal much of what they observed and had experienced. There was the reticent William Buckley from whom 'it was impossible to get any connected or reliable information'. Duramboi was just as obdurate: 'No one will get anything from me about the blacks,' he declared. And the Frenchman Pelletier, who 'knew more than he chose to confess'.

Given the unquenchable thirst of their interrogators for the goriest details of life 'among savages' we cannot help but feel sympathy for their position. There is little evidence that contemporary white colonial Australians were interested in hearing about the fullness and importance of Indigenous social and cultural life. Instead, those who returned to colonial society were generally regarded with a mix of fascination and revulsion, forever marked as untrustworthy outsiders, whose loyalties were permanently divided. Pressed for details of Aboriginal social life that would confirm white superiority and the legitimacy of dispossession and extermination, those who had returned were often unhappy and out of place.

In writing this book, we could not shirk dealing with complex issues arising from constant disturbing references in these accounts to violent conflict and cannibalism. Wild and sensational distortions within the original accounts have impacted through to today and continue to reverberate when racial and political tensions run high.

those who returned to colonial society were generally regarded with a mix of fascination and revulsion, forever marked as untrustworthy outsiders

Some accounts have been used by historians and other commentators as evidence to argue that pre-contact Aboriginal society was intensely violent and war-like. However, even as these were sometimes described as battles or even wars, they seem to be something rather different; and despite the fact that often large numbers of Aboriginal combatants were apparently involved (both men and women), in all of these accounts only a handful of people—two or three at most—were killed in the course of combat. Such small numbers of casualties in these perceived 'battles', and the formal ceremonial processes that were typically associated with them, are more consistent with 'payback' reprisals or even law enforcement procedures, than with full-scale wars. To construe these incidents as 'warfare' is like describing the British legal system of the time—with all its intrinsic punitive violence, including executions—as warfare.

Many of the large gatherings of organised conflict that we see described in the accounts are also similar to large sporting events, comparable to medieval jousting, archery and sword fighting events of yore—or even to some of our high-contact sporting events today. Olga Miller, who gives us an Aboriginal oral tradition about Eliza Fraser (see chapter 6), provides an interesting insight into the 'mock battles' that people fought on Fraser Island in her grandfather's time:

> It has been recorded that the Butchulla people were always fighting among themselves, especially on the Back Beach where there seemed to be four miles of Aborigines just fighting. I asked my grandfather about this, and he said 'Oh, you can't fish all the time'; he said, 'What about when the tide goes out', he said, 'You've gotta do something.' And so they would pit the young warriors against each other. Each area would put up their champion men and this one would fight that one, and the winners would fight somebody else. And so it was like an elimination system of winner fighting somebody else in these mock battles. And the reason I asked about this was because every winter my grandfather would come around and he had rheumatism (we call it arthritis today). And I'd rub his leg and knee (he had a terrible scar) with liniment. And I said to him, 'How did you get this? So he told me about these mock battles, and I said to him 'Why did you have these mock battles if you could get speared in the knee?' And he got very huffy. He said 'Humf—Why do white fellas play football?' So it was the same thing, it was a sport.

Large gatherings where combat fighting took place for sport and spectacle were depicted by the convict artist, Joseph Lycett, with his images in and around the Coal River, present-day Newcastle. These games were instrumental in honing hunting skills and maintaining fitness, and Lycett shows everyone enjoying themselves, including women and children, who sat on the sidelines, urging on the competitors.

Historians who view these conflicts as warfare rather than legal processes or sport also argue that a chronic state of warfare kept the population of the country low. Such arguments are based upon longstanding theories that the Aboriginal population at the time of the British invasion in 1788 was between 200,000 to 300,000 inhabitants. Others, like the economic historian Noel Butlin, have contended that the population was much bigger, and even in excess of a million people. There is wide evidence to support this. In the area of present-day Newcastle, early settler memories have recorded that the Pambalong clan of the local Aboriginal people had a population of some size, estimated at 4,000 between Tarro and Newcastle (a distance of some 20 kilometres), and that 'the coastal tribes were always numerically strong': their food supply was 'unlimited'. Archaeologist Len Dyall found that the sheer size of some middens in the Newcastle area indicated an Indigenous population of some thousands. Some of those who lived with Aboriginal people also provide evidence of flourishing populations. In Queensland, James Morrill described the large numbers of Aboriginal people at a ceremony: 'When they all arrived, they numbered considerably over a thousand souls, this was a larger number than I had ever seen before'.

disease spread widely throughout Aboriginal Australia in the early nineteenth century ... decimating the overall population well in advance of the actual appearance of white men

Back in 1788, Governor Arthur Phillip recorded that the 'natives are far more numerous than they were supposed to be. I think they cannot be less than fifteen hundred in Botany Bay, Port Jackson and Broken Bay'. The next day he restated the 1,500 figure as accounting for the population within a radius of just 'ten miles to the northward and ten miles to the southward' of the settlement. As the colonial authorities realised that Aboriginal warriors outnumbered the marines by at least two to one, they were suddenly aware of their situation—a fragile enclave in a strange land surrounded by many more Aboriginal people than had been assumed. This encounter may or may not be connected to the mysterious outbreak of a smallpox-like epidemic that swept through the local Aboriginal population some months later, carrying off what the governor estimated to be 50 per cent of the inhabitants of the region of the settlement, but in any case we know that some devastating disease spread widely throughout Aboriginal Australia in the early nineteenth century, along trade routes and waterways, decimating the overall population well in advance of the actual appearance of white men. If we accept that the population of Aboriginal Australia in 1788 was around a million, with people regularly coming together in gatherings of the hundreds, and even thousands, the small numbers of deaths in these conflicts would have been inconsequential.

We have also delivered an honest appraisal of the repetitive accounts of anthropophagy in the written recorded testimonies. Those who recounted these narratives for a wider audience took great license to sensationalise and titillate their readers with horrifying stories of savage 'cannibalism'. Yet unquestionably there is evidence that at least some Islander groups in the Pacific practised rituals involving the consumption of their dead enemies' eyes and cheeks to underscore and mark their conquest, while elaborate mortuary rites of various Indigenous groups sometimes entailed the ritual consumption of portions of

> *In any case, Indigenous people were not out hunting and killing people to eat—they were not 'man-eaters' in the generally understood meaning of the term*

human remains. Such practices seem to relate more closely to ancient customs around concepts of mortality and immortality that served to bind social groups together in the mourning process, and conceivably were more symbolic than actual in practice. In any case, Indigenous people were not out hunting and killing people to eat—they were not 'man-eaters' in the generally understood meaning of the term. It has been argued that the colonial fixation on Indigenous 'cannibalism' might have been connected to the anxieties around the very real spectre of maritime cannibalism that developed in association with European sea exploration, and in that regard it is perhaps predictable that the stories of the shipwreck survivors and convict runaways who lived with Aboriginal and Torres Strait Islander people took the shape that they did. But the heightened prominence of so-called cannibalism in the accounts of those white people who lived with Indigenous people, most powerfully served—and continue to serve—the same purpose as the insistence upon their warlike nature, to justify the exclusion of Indigenous people from a common humanity.

And in that respect we need a new language about the past that is honest and truthful. Rather than retelling narratives of those who shared the Indigenous space, for many decades in some cases, in a way that re-inscribes the dangerous and toxic message they were forced to bear in their first incantations, we have sought to ensure that an Indigenous perspective on these stories cuts through the biases, distortions and sensational embellishments to the original accounts, revealing the acceptance and generosity of Indigenous people that resides at the heart of them. Throughout these narratives, we have noted that on numerous occasions the lost, the shipwrecked and the runaways were accepted into an Indigenous community and cultural life, allotted their place in the social network as returning deceased members of families, and were afforded every conceivable chance to make good their newfound lives. In repeated instances, the Indigenous people genuinely cared for those they had taken in with them and openly lamented when they returned to the world of the ghosts. We have

Indigenous people genuinely cared for those they had taken in with them and openly lamented when they returned to the world of the ghosts

seen also how some of these individuals foresaw or witnessed the catastrophe that was about to be unleashed upon their Indigenous families and hosts. They stood on the cusp of a future from which their Indigenous hosts were going to be brutally excluded for many, many years to come, and of a history of which we are just only now starting to try to understand.

In our book, we hope to make some effort toward re-evaluating encounters in our colonial past knowing that so many previous attempts have found white Australians baulking and turning away from new possibilities. For us, the most enduring message from the stories is the profound and heartfelt feeling of loss expressed by many of the different Indigenous groups when it became apparent that those they had welcomed as family were going to leave their care. The departure of those they had sheltered and welcomed represented the ending not only of an individual's story of connection across a major cultural divide but the closing of a window of great opportunity. The nation itself, even today, has not come to terms with the magnitude of this loss. In the final analysis, we hope that we have delivered a glimpse of what living together with mutual respect might still be like, if we could only imagine it.

A group of Kabi people of Queensland painted for
ceremony at the start of the twentieth century, showing the
influences of the old and the new.

Bibliography

Living with the Locals

Badcock, Ivan, 'Sammy Cox', in Anne M. Bartlett (ed.), *Way Back When ... People, Places and Events: Contributed Stories about the Early Days of Settlement in Northern Tasmania*, Launceston: West Tamar Historical Society, George Town and District Historical Society and Launceston Historical Society, 2012.

Barrett, Charles, *White Blackfellows: The Strange Adventures of Europeans Who Lived among Savages*. Melbourne: Hallcraft Publishing, 1948.

Blomfield, Geoffrey, *Baal Belbora the End of the Dancing: The Massacre of a Peaceful People*. Sydney: Alternative Publishing Co-operative, 1988.

Button, Henry, *Flotsam and Jetsam: Floating Fragments of Life in England and Tasmania: An Autobiographical Sketch with an Outline of the Introduction of Responsible Government*. Launceston: A.W. Birchell & Sons, 1909.

Carr, Julie E., *The Captive White Woman of Gipps Land: In Pursuit of the Legend*. Melbourne: Melbourne University Press, 2001.

Causer, Tim (ed.), *Memorandoms of James Martin*. The Bentham Project, UCL: London, 2014, www.ucl.ac.uk/Bentham-Project/publications/martins-memorandoms/martins-memorandoms.html, viewed 6 November 2014.

Cilento, Raphael and Lack, Clem, *'Wild White Men' in Queensland: A Monograph*. Brisbane: W.R. Smith & Paterson for the Royal Historical Society of Queensland, 1959.

Collins, David, *An Account of the English Colony in New South Wales ...*, vol. 1. London: T. Cadell & W. Davies, 1798.

Farnill, Paul, 'The Background to John Shortland's Discovery: John Hunter's Missing List', Coal River Working Party–Historical Newcastle, University of Newcastle, 13 January 2011, coalriver.wordpress.com/2011/01/13/the-background-to-john-shortland's-discovery-john-hunter's-missing-list/, viewed 10 November 2014.

Huntington, H.W.H., 'History of Newcastle and the Northern District, No. 14', *Newcastle Morning Herald and Miners' Advocate*, 24 September, 1897.

Karskens, Grace, '"This Spirit of Emigration": The Nature and Meanings of Escape in Early New South Wales', *Journal of Australian Colonial History*, vol. 7, 2005, pp. 1–34.

Meston, A. 'Wild White Men: Australian Instances', *The World's News*, 27 October 1923, p. 11, nla.gov.au/nla.news-page14391441.

Monds, T.W., 'Our Tasmanian Centenarian', *Launceston Examiner*, 9 June 1890, p. 2, nla.gov.au/nla.news-article39549941.

Piper, A.K.S., 'Another Cheated Heir? Unravelling a Tasmanian Mystery—The Story of Sammy Cox, Alias "Samuel Emanuel Jervis"', *Australian Folklore*, vol. 20, 2005, pp. 132–141.

Ryan, D.J., 'The Discovery and First Settlement of Newcastle and Genesis of the Coal Industry', *Journal of the Royal Australian Historical Society*, vol. 9, pp. 227–259.

Willey, Keith, *When the Sky Fell Down: The Destruction of the Tribes of the Sydney Region 1788–1850s*. Sydney: Collins, 1989.

1 John Wilson—'Bunbóe'

Baker, H.C., 'Explorer Wilson Speared by Jealous Lover', *The Sun* (Sydney), 26 September 1977, p. 26.

Bayley, Roger. 2003. 'Pemulwy's White Man', ABC Lateline Program, TV Program transcript, www.abc.net.au/lateline/content/2003/hc17.htm, viewed 29 July 2013.

Bladen, F.M. (ed.), *Historical Records of New South Wales Volume III: Hunter 1796—1799*. Sydney: Charles Potter, 1895. Facsimile edition, Mona Vale: Landsdown Slattery & Company, 1978.

Bladen, F.M. (ed.), *Historical Records of New South Wales Volume IV: Hunter and King, 1800, 1801, 1802*. Sydney: Charles Potter, 1896. Facsimile edition, Mona Vale: Landsdown Slattery & Company, 1979.

Chisholm, Alec H., 'The Romance of the Lyrebird', *Royal Australian Historical Society Journal and Proceedings*, vol. 43, 1957, pp. 175–204.

Collins, David, *An Account of the English Colony in New South Wales With Remarks on the Dispositions, Customs, Manners, etc, of the Native Inhabitants of that Country*, vol. 1, 1798 and vol. II, 1802. Fletcher, Brian H. (ed.), Sydney: Reed, 1975.

Cunningham, Chris, *The Blue Mountains Rediscovered: Beyond the Myths of Early Australian Exploration*. Kenthurst, NSW: Kangaroo Press, 1996.

Karskens, Grace, *The Colony: A History of Early Sydney*. Crows Nest: Allen & Unwin, 2009.

McHugh, Evan. *Outback Pioneers: Great Achievers of the Australian Bush*. Camberwell, Vic.: Penguin, 2009.

Price, John, 'Journey into the Interior of the Country New South Wales', *Historical Records of New South Wales Volume III*, pp. 820–822.

Willmot, Eric, *Pemulwuy: The Rainbow Warrior*. Moorebank, NSW: Bantam, 1988.

2 William Buckley—'Murrangurk'

Barrett, Charles, *White Blackfellows: The Strange Adventures of Europeans Who Lived among Savages*. Melbourne: Hallcraft Publishing Company, 1948.

Basedow, Herbert, *The Australian Aboriginal*. 2nd edn. Virginia, NT: David M. Welch, 2012.

Blainey, Geoffrey, *Triumph of the Nomads*. Rev. edn. Melbourne: Macmillan, 1983.

Bonwick, James, *Port Phillip Settlement*. London: Sampson Low, Marston, Searle & Rivington, 1883.

Bonwick, James, *The Wild White Man and the Blacks of Victoria*. Melbourne: Fergusson & Moore, 1863.

Broome, Richard, *Aboriginal Victorians: A History since 1800*. Sydney: Allen & Unwin, 2005.

Buckley, William and Langhorne, George, *Manuscript of Reminiscenses of James Buckley Who Lived for Thirty Years among the Wallawarro or Watourong Tribes at Geelong Port Phillip, Communicated by Him to George Langhorne*. 1837, State Library Victoria, MS 13483.

Dawson, James, *Australian Aborigines: The Languages and Customs of Several Tribes of Aborigines in the Western District of Victoria, Australia*. Melbourne: George Robertson, 1881. Facsimile ed., Australian Institute of Aboriginal Studies, Canberra, 1981.

Flannery, Tim (ed.), *The Life and Adventures of William Buckley*. Melbourne: Text Publishing, 2002.

Hayden, Kevin, *Wild White Man: A Condensed Account of the Adventures of William Buckley, Who Lived in Exile for 32 Years (1803–35) amongst the Black People of the Unexplored Regions of Port Phillip*. Geelong, Vic.: Marine History Publications, 1976.

James, Charles, *A New and Enlarged Military Dictionary in French and English in Which Are Explained the Principal Terms with Appropriate Illustrations of All the Sciences That Are More or Less Necessary for an Officer and Engineer*, vol 2. 3rd edn. London: T. Egerton Military Library, 1810.

Massola, Aldo, *Bunjil's Cave: Myths, Legends and Superstitions of the Aborigines of South-east Australia*. Melbourne: Lansdowne Press, 1968.

Morgan, John, *The Life and Adventures of William Buckley, Thirty-two Years a Wanderer amongst the Aborigines of the Then Unexplored Country around Port Phillip, Now the Province of Victoria*, edited by C.E. Sayers. Facsimile edn. London: William Heinemann Ltd, 1967.

Morgan, John, *The Life and Adventures of William Buckley: Thirty-two Years a Wanderer amongst the Aborigines of the Then Unexplored Country around Port Phillip, Now the Province of Victoria*. Hobart: Archibald Macdougall, 1852.

Nance, Beverley, 'The Level of Violence: Europeans and Aborigines in Port Phillip, 1835–1850', *Historical Studies*, vol. 19, 1981, pp. 532–552.

Orton, Rev. Joseph, 'Letter, August 1836, Hobart Town, Van Diemen's Land', in *Aborigines of Australia*. London: Thoms, 1836.

'Source Documents for William Buckley, the Wild White Man', williambuckleyconvict. wordpress.com, viewed 30 August 2014.

Tudehope, Cecily, *William Buckley*. Prahran, Vic.: Hall's Book Store, 1962.

Willey, Keith, *When the Sky Fell Down: The Destruction of the Tribes of the Sydney Region 1788–1850s*. Sydney: Collins, 1979.

'William Buckley, the Wild White Man of Victoria', *The Illustrated Australian News for Home Readers*, 19 April 1869, p.91, nla.gov.au/ nla.news-article60450161.

3 Thomas Pamphlett, Richard Parsons & John Finnegan

Barrett, Charles, *White Blackfellows: The Strange Adventures of Europeans Who Lived among Savages*. Melbourne: Hallcraft Publishing, 1948.

'Curious Case of Shipwreck', *The Australian* (Sydney), 21 October 1824, p.2, nla.gov.au/nla. news-article37072074

Field, Barron (ed.), *Geographical Memoirs on New South Wales by Various Hands Containing an Account of the Surveyor General's Late Expedition to Two New Ports, the Discovery of Moreton Bay River, with the Adventures for Seven Months there of Two Shipwrecked Men ...* London: John Murray, 1825.

Hornibrook, J.H. 'Pamphlett, Thomas (1789–1838)', in *Australian Dictionary of Biography, National Centre of Biography*. Canberra: Australian National University, 1967 adb.anu. edu.au/biography/pamphlett-thomas-2536/ text3443, 1967, viewed 16 January 2015.

Oxley, John, 'Extract from the Field Books of Mr. John Oxley, Surveyor General of New South Wales, Relating to the Discovery of the Brisbane River on 2nd December, 1823 ...', *Journal of the Historical Society of Queensland*, vol.2, 1823.

Oxley, John, 'Report of an Expedition to Survey Port Curtis, Moreton Bay, and Port Bowen, with a View to Form Convict Penal Establishments There, in Pursuance of the Recommendation of the Commissioner of Inquiry into the Colony of New South Wales', in Field.

Pearce, Chris, *Through the Eyes of Thomas Pamphlett, Convict and Castaway*. Brisbane: Boolarong Publications, 1993.

Steele, J.G., *Aboriginal Pathways in Southeast Queensland and the Richmond River*. St Lucia, Qld: University of Queensland Press, 1983.

Uniacke, John, 'Narrative of Mr Oxley's Expedition to Survey Port Curtis and Moreton Bay, with a View to Form Convict Establishments There, in Pursuance of the Recommendation of the Commissioner of Inquiry'; and 'Narrative of Thomas Pamphlett, Aged Thirty-four Years, Who Was with Two Other Men Wrecked on the Coast of New Holland in April, 1823, and Lived among the Natives for Seven Months', in Field.

Welsby, Thomas, *The Discoverers of the Brisbane River*. Brisbane: H.J. Diddams & Co, 1913.

'Wild Aboriginals Made Brothers of Lost Whites', *Daily Mirror*, 10 July, 1922, p. 22.

4 James Davis—'Duramboi' & David Bracefell—'Wandi'

Barrett, Charles, *White Blackfellows: The Strange Adventures of Europeans who Lived among Savages*. Melbourne: Hallcraft Publishing, 1948.

Brown, Elaine, *Cooloola Coast: Noosa to Fraser Island: The Aboriginal and Settler Histories of a Unique Environment*. St Lucia, Qld: University of Queensland Press, 2000.

Cilento, Raphael, and Lack, Clem, *'Wild White Men' in Queensland: A Monograph*. Brisbane: W.R. Smith & Paterson for the Royal Historical Society of Queensland, 1959.

'Durrumboi or Davis', *The Week* (Brisbane), 11 May 1889, p. 14, nla.gov.au/nla.news-article186196327.

An Eight Years' Resident [Ebenezer Thorne], *The Queen of the Colonies; or, Queensland as I Knew It*. London: Sampson Low, Marston, Searle & Rivington, 1876.

Knight, J.J., *In the Early Days: History and Incident of Pioneer Queensland: With Dictionary of Dates in Chronological Order*. Brisbane: Sapsford, 1895.

Lang, John Dunmore, *Cooksland in North-Eastern Australia, the Future Cotton-Field of Great Britain: Its Characteristics and Capabilities for European Colonization: With a Disquisition on the Origins, Manners, and Customs of the Aborigines*. London: Longman, Brown, Green and Longmans, 1847.

Langevad, Gerry (transcriber), *The Simpson Letterbook*. St Lucia, Qld: Anthropology Museum, University of Queensland, 1979.

Laurie, Arthur, 'Davis, James (1808–1889)', *Australian Dictionary of Biography, National Centre of Biography*, Australian National University, adb.anu.edu.au/biography/davis-james-1965/text2371, published first in hardcopy 1966, viewed 24 December 2014.

Mathew, John, *Two Representative Tribes of Queensland: With an Inquiry Concerning the Origin of the Australian Race*. London: T. Fisher Unwin, 1910.

O'Keeffe, Mamie, 'The Runaway Convicts of Moreton Bay', *Journal of the Royal Australian Historical Society of Queensland*, vol. 10, 1976, pp. 52–71, espace.library.uq.edu.au/view/UQ:204799, viewed 24 December 2014.

Petrie, Constance Campbell, *Tom Petrie's Reminiscences of Early Queensland*. Brisbane: Watson, Ferguson & Co., 1904.

Queensland Legislative Assembly, 'Minutes of Evidence, Wednesday 12 June 1861', in *Report from the Select Committee on the Native Police Force and the Condition of the Aborigines Generally*. Brisbane: Fairfax and Belbridge, 1861.

Richards, Harold John, *Duramboi: A Story of a White Man Who Lived with Aborigines for Fourteen Years*. Bardon, Qld: H.J. Richards, 1973.

Robertson, William, *Coo-ee Talks: A Collection of Lecturettes upon Early Experiences among the Aborigines of Australia Delivered from a Wireless Broadcasting Station*. Sydney: Angus & Robertson, 1928.

Russell, Henry Stuart, *The Genesis of Queensland: An Account of the First Exploring Journeys to and over the Darling Downs ...* Sydney: Turner & Henderson, 1888.

Tynan, Patrick J., *Duramboi: The Story of Jem Davis of Glasgow (1808?–1889)*. Virginia, Qld: Church Archivists' Press, 1997.

Williams, Fred, *Princess K'Gari's Fraser Island: A History of Fraser Island*. Emu Park, Qld: Fred Williams, 2002.

5 John Ireland—'Waki' & William D'Oyley—'Uass'

Barton, Charlotte, *A Mother's Offering to Her Children: By a Lady Long Resident in New South Wales*. Sydney: 'Gazette' Office, 1841.

'Batavia, "Charles Eaton"', *The Sydney Herald*, 20 June 1836, p.4, nla.gov.au/nla.news-article12854571.

Brockett, William Edward, *Narrative of a Voyage from Sydney to Torres' Straits: In Search of the Survivors of the Charles Eaton, in His Majesty's Colonial Schooner Isabella, C.M. Lewis, Commander*. Sydney: Henry Bull, 1836.

'The *Charles Eaton*', *The Sydney Monitor*, 19 October 1836, p. 3, nla.gov.au/nla.news-article32152506.

Ireland, John, *The Shipwrecked Orphans: A True Narrative of the Shipwreck and Sufferings of John Ireland and William Doyley, Who Were Wrecked in the Ship Charles Eaton, on an Island in the South Seas*. New Haven: S. Babcock, 1845.

Ireland, John, *The Young Captives: A Narrative of the Shipwreck and Sufferings of John and William Doyley*. New Haven: S. Babcock, 1850.

Jukes, J. Beete, *Narrative of the Surveying Voyage of H.M.S. Fly, Commanded by Captain F.P. Blackwood, R.N. in Torres Strait, New Guinea, and Other Islands of the Eastern Archipelago, during the Years 1842–1846: Together with an Excursion into the Interior of the Eastern Part of Java, Vol. I*. London: T. & W. Boone, 1847.

King, Phillip Parker, *A Voyage to Torres Strait: In Search of the Survivors of the Ship Charles Eaton ...* Sydney: George William Evans, 1837.

Peek, Veronica, *Charles Eaton: Wake for the Melancholy Shipwreck*, veronicapeek.com, viewed 27 July, 2013.

Wemyss, Thomas, *Narrative of the Melancholy Shipwreck of the Ship Charles Eaton: and the Inhuman Massacre of the Passengers and Crew: With an Account of the Rescue of Two Boys from the Hands of the Savages in an Island in Torres Straits*. Stockton: W. Robinson, 1837.

6 Eliza Fraser

'Account of the Crew of the Stirling Castle', *The Edinburgh Evening Courant*, 24 August 1837.

Alexander, Michael, *Mrs. Fraser on the Fatal Shore*. New York: Simon & Schuster, 1971.

Barrett, Charles, *White Blackfellows: The Strange Adventures of Europeans Who Lived among Savages*. Melbourne: Hallcraft Publishing, 1948.

Behrendt, Larissa, *Finding Eliza: Power and Colonial Storytelling*. St Lucia, Qld: University of Queensland Press, 2016.

Brown, Elaine, 'Convict Brisbane and The Rescue of Eliza Fraser, 1836', Queensland History Journal vol. 21, 2013, pp. 847–854.

Brown, Elaine, *Cooloola Coast: Noosa to Fraser Island: The Aboriginal and Settler Histories of a Unique Environment*. St Lucia, Qld: University of Queensland Press, 2000.

Brown, Elaine, 'Eliza Fraser: An Historical Record', in Ian McNiven et al (eds), *Constructions of Colonialism: Perspectives on Eliza Fraser's Shipwreck*. London: Leicester University Press, 1998.

Brown, Elaine, 'Fraser, Eliza Anne (1798–1858)', *Australian Dictionary of Biography*, National Centre of Biography, Australian National University, 2005, adb.anu.edu.au/biography/fraser-eliza-anne-12929/text23361, viewed 29 September 2013.

Brown, Elaine, 'The Legend of Eliza Fraser—A Survey of The Sources', *Journal of the Royal Historical Society of Queensland*, vol. 15, May 1994, pp. 345–360.

Curtis, John, *Shipwreck of the Stirling Castle: Containing a Faithful Narrative of the Dreadful Sufferings of the Crew ...* London: George Virtue, 1838.

Davidson, Jim, 'Eliza Fraser's Mutating Myth', Eureka Street, vol. 6, 1996, pp. 52–53.

Drummond, Yolanda, 'Progress of Eliza Fraser', *Journal of the Royal Historical Society of Queensland* vol. 15, 1993, pp. 15–25.

Evans, Raymond, and Walker, Jan, '"These Strangers, Where Are They Going?" Aboriginal–European Relations in the Fraser Island and Wide Bay Region 1770–1905', in Peter K. Lauer (ed.), *Fraser Island*, Occasional Papers in Anthropology No.8, St. Lucia, Qld: University of Queensland Anthropology Museum, 1977.

Fraser, Eliza, *Narrative of the Capture, Sufferings, and Miraculous Escape of Mrs. Eliza Fraser ...* New York: Charles S. Webb, 1837.

Fyans, Foster, *Manuscript of Letter from Foster Fyans to the Colonial Secretary*, 6 September 1836. Archives Office of New South Wales SZ976 Misc. 2, Colonial Secretary's Correspondence COD 183.

Gibbings, Robert, *John Graham, Convict, 1824: An Historical Narrative*. London: Faber and Faber, 1937.

Graham, John, John Graham's 'Memorandum of the Real Facts', Written in Sydney, 4 January 1837. Archives Office of New South Wales, SZ976 Misc. 2 Colonial Secretary's Correspondence COD 183, 1837.

Graham, John, Report to Foster Fyans by John Graham, 6 September 1836. In 'Correspondence and Records Relating to the Shipwrecks of Stirling Castle, Neva and Cataraque, Including John Graham's Account of the Rescue of Eliza Fraser and Petition for Pardon, 1835–1846,' DLSPENCER 196, Mitchell Library, Sydney.

Lavelle, Keren, 'Indigenous Legal Scholar Debunks Eliza Fraser Myths', *Law Society Journal*, November 2009, pp. 18–19.

'Loss of the Stirling Castle', *The Edinburgh Evening Courant*, 27 March 1837.

McCalman, Iain, *The Reef: A Passionate History*. Melbourne: Penguin, 2013.

McNiven, Ian et al (eds), *Constructions of Colonialism: Perspectives on Eliza Fraser's Shipwreck*. London: Leicester University Press, 1998.

McRae, Toni, 'Elder Claims Fraser Story is False', *Fraser Coast Chronicle*, 23 October 2010.

Miller, Olga, 'K'gari, Mrs Fraser and Butchulla Oral Tradition', in Ian McNiven et al (eds), *Constructions of Colonialism: Perspectives on Eliza Fraser's Shipwreck*. London: Leicester University Press, 1998, pp. 28–36.

Mulvaney, D.J., 'John Graham: The Convict as Aboriginal', in Reece, Bob (ed.) *Irish Convict Lives*. Darlinghurst, NSW: Crossing Press, 1973.

Otter, Charles, Manuscript of a Report to Foster Fyans by Charles Otter, 27 August 1836, Archives Office of New South Wales SZ976 Misc. 2, Colonial Secretary's Correspondence COD 183.

'Police', *The Times* (London), 19 August, 1837, p. 6.

'Police', *The Times* (London), 24 August, 1837, p. 4.

Russell, Henry Stuart, *The Genesis of Queensland: An Account of the First Exploring Journeys to and over the Darling Downs ...* Sydney: Turner & Henderson, 1888.

Ryan, J.S., 'Captain Foster Fyans and Mrs Eliza Fraser', *Journal of the Royal Historical Society of Queensland*, vol. 12, 1985, pp. 260–263.

Ryan, J.S., 'The Several Fates of Eliza Fraser', *Journal of the Royal Historical Society of Queensland* vol. 11, 1981, pp. 88–112.

Schaffer, Kay, *In the Wake of First Contact: The Eliza Fraser Stories*. Cambridge: Cambridge University Press, 1995.

Statement by Eliza Ann Fraser and Statement by John Baxter: Corroborated by Joseph Corralis, 6 September 1836. Archives Office of New South Wales, SZ976 Misc. 2 Colonial Secretary's Correspondence COD 183, 1836.

'The Stirling Castle', *Bell's Weekly Messenger*, 17 September 1837.

'The Stirling Castle', *The Sydney Gazette and New South Wales Advertiser*, 18 October 1836, p. 3.

Stromness Museum, *Eliza Fraser Castaway: The 150th Anniversary of the Adventures of the Wife of an Orkney Sea Captain, Her Shipwreck on the Great Barrier Reef and Her Enslavement by Aborigines*. Orkney: Stromness Museum, 1986.

The Shipwreck of Mrs. Frazer and the Loss of the Stirling Castle on a Coral Reef in the South Pacific Ocean ... London: Dean and Munday, 1837.

Williams, Fred, *Princess K'Gari's Fraser Island: Fraser Island's Definitive History*. Brisbane: F.R. Williams, 2002.

Williams, Fred, *Written in Sand: A History of Fraser Island*. Milton, Qld: Jacaranda Press, 1982.

Youlden, Harry, 'Shipwreck in Australia', *The Knickerbocker*, vol. 41, no. 4, 1853, pp. 291–300.

7 Barbara Thompson—'Giom'

Austin, C.G., 'Early History of Somerset and Thursday Island', *Journal of the Royal Historical Society of Queensland* vol.4, 1949, pp. 216–230.

Barrett, Charles, *White Blackfellows: The Strange Adventures of Europeans who Lived among Savages*. Melbourne: Hallcraft Publishing, 1948.

Bayton, John, 'The Mission to the Aborigines at Somerset', *Journal of the Royal Historical Society of Queensland*, vol. 7, 1965, pp. 622–633.

Brady, Liam M., and the Kaurareg Community, 'A Middle Ground? Recent Archaeological Investigations from the Kaurareg Archipelago, South-Western Torres Straits, Queensland', *Australian Archaeology*, vol.65, 2007, pp. 17–29.

Brierly, Oswald W., 'The Journals of HMS Rattlesnake October 1848–December 1849', in Moore.

Carroll, J.M., 'Journey into Torres Straits', *Queensland Heritage*, vol. 2, 1969, pp. 35–42.

Dixon, Robert, *Prosthetic Gods: Travel, Representation and Colonial Governance*. St Lucia, Qld: University of Queensland Press, 2001.

Geason, Susan, *Australian Heroines: Stories of Courage and Survival*, Sydney: ABC Books, 2001.

Huxley, T.H. and edited by Julian Huxley, *T.H. Huxley's Diary of the Voyage of H.M.S. Rattlesnake*. London: Chatto & Windus, 1935.

Inskip, G.H., *Manuscript of Diary*, 1849–1850. NLA MS 3784, 1849–1850.

'The Jagg Reports, 1867–1868', in Moore.

Lack, Clem, 'The Story of Cape York Peninsula: Part II: Torres Strait Saga', *Journal of the Royal Historical Society of Queensland*, vol. 7, no. 1, 1963, pp. 132–153.

MacFarlane, W.H., 'Captive Women of the Sea', *Cummins & Campbell's Monthly Magazine*, April 1948, pp. 13, 15, 37.

MacGillivray, John, *Narrative of the Voyage of the H.M.S. Rattlesnake, Commanded by the Late Captain Owen Stanley during the Years 1846–1850 .... Vol. I.* London: T. & W. Boone, 1852.

McCalman, Iain, *The Reef: A Passionate History*. Melbourne: Penguin, 2013.

Moore, David R., *Islanders and Aborigines at Cape York: An Ethnographic Reconstruction Based on the 1848–1850 'Rattlesnake' Journals of O.W. Brierly and Information he Obtained from Barbara Thompson*. Canberra: Australian Institute of Aboriginal Studies; Humanities Press, 1979.

Sharp, Nonie, *Footprints along the Cape York Sandbeaches*. Canberra: Aboriginal Studies Press, 1992.

'Somerset, Cape York, The Massacre at Prince of Wales Island', *The Brisbane Courier*, 27 November 1869, p. 6.

Southon, Michael, and the Kaurareg Tribal Elders, 'The Sea of Waubin: The Kaurareg and Their Marine Environment', in Nicolas Peterson and Bruce Rigsby (eds), *Customary Marine Tenure in Australia*. Sydney: Sydney University Press, 2014.

'Surveying Voyage of the Rattlesnake', *Chambers' Edinburgh Journal*, 10 April 1852.

Turner, George, 'Barbara Thompson's Captivity amongst the Blacks', *Cummins & Campbell's Magazine*, March 1933, p. 31.

Warren, Raymond J., *Wildflower: The Barbara Crawford Thompson Story*. Brisbane: R.J. Warren, 2007.

8 James Morrill

Barrett, Charles, *White Blackfellows: The Strange Adventures of Europeans who Lived among Savages.* Melbourne: Hallcraft Publishing, 1948.

Bolton, G.C., 'Morrill, James (1824–1865)', *Australian Dictionary of Biography*, National Centre of Biography, Australian National University, 1967, adb.anu.edu.au/biography/morrill-james-2484/text3339, viewed 29 September 2013.

Bowen Historical Society, *The Story of James Morrill.* Bowen, Qld: Bowen Historical Society, 1966.

Breslin, Bruce, *Exterminate with Pride: Aboriginal–European Relations in the Townsville–Bowen Region to 1869.* Townsville: Department of History & Politics, James Cook University, 1992.

'Death of Mr James Morrill', *Townsville Daily Bulletin*, 28 November 1907, pp. 2–3.

Dortins, Emma, 'James Morrill, Shipwreck Survivor, Birri-gubba Adoptee and Explorer-in-retrospect', *History Australia*, vol. 9, 2012, pp. 67–88.

Ferguson, John Alexander, *Bibliography of Australia Volume VI: 1851–1900.* Canberra: National Library of Australia, 1977.

'Fifty Years Ago', *The Brisbane Courier*, 15 March 1913, p. 12.

'From Our Own Correspondent', *The Brisbane Courier*, 11 March 1863, p. 3.

George, Neville, *The 'Peruvian' and James Morrill: The Story of the Peruvian Shipwreck in 1846 and the Survivor James Morrill Who Lived with the Cape Cleveland Aborigines for Seventeen Years.* Townsville: Maritime Museum of Townsville, 1989.

Gibson, Ross, *Seven Versions of an Australian Badland.* St Lucia, Qld: University of Queensland Press, 2002.

Gregory, Edmund, *Narrative of James Murrells' ('Jemmy Morrill') Seventeen Years' Exile among the Wild Blacks of North Queensland, and His Life and Shipwreck and Terrible Adventures among Savage Tribes ...* Brisbane: Edmund Gregory, 1896.

Gregory, Edmund, *Sketch of the Residence of James Morrill among the Aboriginals of Northern Queensland for Seventeen Years: Being a Narrative of His Life, Shipwreck, Landing on the Coast, and Residence among the Aboriginals ...* Brisbane: The 'Courier' General Printing Office, 1866.

'James Morrill, Seventeen Years a Captive amongst the Blacks (From the *Port Denison Times*, November 1.)', *The Newcastle Chronicle and Hunter River District News*, 15 November 1865, p. 3.

Kennedy, Edward B., *The Black Police of Queensland: Reminiscences of Official Work and Personal Adventures in the Early Days of the Colony.* London: John Murray, 1902.

Maryborough Chronicle, Wide Bay and Burnett Advertiser, 21 May 1863, p. 2, nla.gov.au/nla.news-article150316967.

McCalman, Iain, *The Reef: A Passionate History.* Melbourne: Penguin, 2013.

Morrill, James, *Manuscript of Statement by James Morrill [Morrell]* (1863), James Morrell Papers, State Library of Queensland, OM74–92, archives.qld.gov.au/Researchers/Exhibitions/Top150/051-075/Pages/055.aspx, viewed 29 September 2013.

Morrill, James, *Sketch of a Residence among the Aboriginals of Northern Queensland for Seventeen Years, Being a Narrative of My Life, Shipwreck, Landing, on the Coast, Residence among the Aboriginals, with an Account of Their Manners and Customs ...* Brisbane: The 'Courier' General Printing Office, 1863.

Murray-Prior, Thomas, *Manuscript of Diary Entry for 12 October 1863*, Thomas Lodge Murray-Prior Diaries, Mitchell Library, MSS 3117/4.

'The New Robinson Crusoe', *Queanbeyan Age and General Advertiser*, 19 March 1863, p. 3.

'Particulars of the Escape of James Morrill', *The Sydney Mail*, 21 March 1863, p. 7.

'Port Denison', *Empire* (Sydney), 19 May 1863, p. 2.

'Port Denison', *Rockhampton Bulletin and Central Queensland Advertiser*, 10 June 1863, p. 2.

'Queensland', *The Sydney Morning Herald*, 22 June 1863, p. 5.

Robertson, William, *Coo-ee Talks: A Collection of Lecturettes upon Early Experiences among the Aborigines of Australia Delivered from a Wireless Broadcasting Station.* Sydney: Angus & Robertson, 1928.

'Rockhampton', *Maryborough Chronicle, Wide Bay and Burnett Advertiser*, 14 May 1863, p.3.

'Seventeen Years among the Aborigines of Queensland', *Geelong Advertiser* (Victoria), 25 May 1863, p. 1.

'Seventeen Years Exile of a White Man amongst the Blacks!—Personal Narrative', *The Courier* (Brisbane), 18 March 1863, p. 3.

Strutton, S. Scott, 'Wreck of the Peruvian', *The Australasian* (Victoria), 12 November 1932, p. 4.

'Tuesday, November 14, 1865', *The Argus*, 14 November 1865, p. 5, nla.gov.au/nla.news-article5780489

Welch, David M. (ed.), *17 Years Wandering among the Aboriginals: James Morrill: With Photographs Published by Eric Mjoberg 1918.* Virginia, NT: David M. Welch, 2006.

Also, various other newspapers of the time: *The Argus; The Australasian; The Courier* (Brisbane); *Maryborough Chronicle, Wide Bay and Burnett Advertiser; The Newcastle Chronicle and Hunter River District News; Queanbeyan Age and General Advertiser; Sydney Mail; Townsville Daily Bulletin.*

Bibliography

9 Narcisse Pelletier—'Anco'

Anderson, Stephanie, *Pelletier: The Forgotten Castaway of Cape York*. Melbourne: Melbourne Books, 2009.

Chase, Athol, '*Pama Malngkana*: The "Sandbeach People" of Cape York', in Anderson.

D., H.J., 'A Page of Forgotten History', *The Brisbane Courier*, 20 December 1923, p. 16, nla.gov.au/nla.news-article20663158.

Hamilton-Gordon, Arthur, 'Seventeen Years among Savages', *The Times*, 21 July 1875, in Anderson.

Johns, Eric, 'The Rossel Island Massacre', *The National Library Magazine*, September 2012, pp. 12–15.

McCalman, Iain, *The Reef: A Passionate History*. Melbourne: Penguin, 2013.

Merland, Constant, 'Seventeen Years with the Savages. The Adventures of Narcisse Pelletier' (originally published in French in 1876), in Anderson.

'Narcisse Pelletier', *The Sydney Morning Herald*, 27 May 1875, p. 7, nla.gov.au/nla.news-article28404713.

Conclusion

Anderson, Stephanie, *Pelletier: The Forgotten Castaway of Cape York*. Melbourne: Melbourne Books, 2009.

Biber, Katherine, 'Cannibals and Colonialism,' *Sydney Law Review*, vol. 27, 2005, pp. 623–637.

Bonwick, James, *The Wild White Man and the Blacks of Victoria*. Melbourne: Fergusson & Moore, 1863.

Butlin, Noel G., *Our Original Aggression: Aboriginal Populations of Southeastern Australia 1788–1850*. Sydney: George Allen & Unwin, 1983.

Dyall, Len, 'Aboriginal Occupation of the Newcastle Coastline', *Hunter Natural History*, vol. 3, 1971, pp. 154–168.

Greer, Germaine, *Whitefella Jump Up: The Shortest Way to Nationhood*. Sydney: Allen & Unwin, 2004.

Historical Records of New South Wales, Vol. I, Part 2, Phillip 1783–1792. Sydney: Charles Potter, 1892.

Maynard, John, *Fight for Liberty and Freedom: The Origins of Australian Aboriginal Activism*. Canberra: Aboriginal Studies Press, 2007.

Maynard, John, 'The 1920s Aboriginal Political Defence of the Sacred "Ancient Code"', *Cultural Survival Quarterly*, vol. 26, 2002, pp. 33–36.

Maynard, John, *True Light and Shade: An Aboriginal Perspective of Joseph Lycett's Art*. Canberra: National Library of Australia, 2014.

Miller, Olga, 'K'gari, Mrs Fraser and Butchulla Oral Tradition', in Ian McNiven et al (eds), *Constructions of Colonialism: Perspectives on Eliza Fraser's Shipwreck*. London: Leicester University Press, 1998, pp. 28–36.

Pickering, Michael, 'Consuming Doubts: What Some People Ate? Or What Some People Swallowed?' in Laurence R. Goldman (ed.), *The Anthropology of Cannibalism*. Westport, CT: Bergin & Garvey, 1999.

Petrie, Constance Campbell, *Tom Petrie's Reminiscences of Early Queensland (Dating from 1837.): Recorded by His Daughter*. Brisbane, Qld: Watson, Ferguson & Co, 1904.

'The Aborigines of the Big Swamp', *Wallsend & Plattsburg Sun*, 17 December 1890.

Welch, David M. (ed.), *17 Years Wandering among the Aboriginals: James Morrill: With Photographs Published by Eric Mjoberg, 1918*. Virginia, NT: David M. Welch, 2006.

List of Illustrations

pages 34–35
Samuel Thomas Gill (1818–1880)
Aborigines and White Men Hunting Kangaroos
c. 1850
sepia wash; 24 x 37.1 cm
Rex Nan Kivell Collection
nla.gov.au/nla.cat-vn1980675

page 39
George Rossi Ashton (1851–1942)
*John Batman's Famous Treaty with the Blacks,
Merri Creek, Northcote, June 6, 1835* c. 1914
b&w photo reproduction of engraving
40.5 x 57 cm
nla.gov.au/nla.cat-vn1815824

pages 40–41
Samuel Calvert (1828–1913)
Buckley Discovering Himself to the Early Settlers
1869
colour wood engraving
handle.slv.vic.gov.au/10381/122478
Courtesy of State Library of Victoria

page 45
Frederick Grosse (1828–1894)
William Buckley, the Wild White Man 1857
wood engraving; 15.5 x 11 cm
nla.gov.au/nla.cat-vn1480164

page 47
Samuel Thomas Gill (1818–1880)
*Native Method of Climbing the Trees When
Hunting Oppossums, So. Australia, Adelaide,
Jany 1849*
wash; 23.7 x 15.7 cm
Rex Nan Kivell Collection
nla.gov.au/nla.cat-vn1980159

page 53
George Henry Haydon (artist, 1822–1891),
Henry Hainsselin (artist) and Charles Risdon
(lithographer)
*Natives Fishing on the Lakes in Gippsland,
Victoria, 1846*
lithograph; 15.7 x 25.3 cm
nla.gov.au/nla.cat-vn1169551

pages 54–55
Joseph Lycett (c. 1775–1828)
*Fishing by Torchlight, Other Aborigines beside
Camp Fires Cooking Fish* c. 1817
watercolour; 17.7 x 27.9 cm
nla.gov.au/nla.cat-vn2428221

page 57
Joseph Lycett (c. 1775–1828)
*Aborigine Climbing a Tree with Two Aborigines
Sitting beside a Fire, Others Spearing Birds*
c. 1817
watercolour; 27.8 x 17.6 cm
nla.gov.au/nla.cat-vn2428151

3 Thomas Pamphlett,
Richard Parsons & John Finnegan

page 65
Walter G. Mason (1820–1866)
*Weapons Used by Natives near Moreton Bay
N.S.Wales* 1857
wood engraving; 11.2 x 14.7 cm
Rex Nan Kivell Collection
nla.gov.au/nla.cat-vn1141045

page 67
Owen Stanley (1811–1850)
Native Huts, Moreton Island
f63 in *Voyage of H.M.S. Rattlesnake: Vol.1*
1846–1849
drawing; 40 x 31 cm
Mitchell Library, State Library of New South Wales
a487063

page 70
The Finding of Pamphlet
page 316 in *Picturesque Atlas of Australasia*,
vol. II, edited by Andrew Garran
(Sydney: The Picturesque Atlas Publishing Co.,
1886–1888)
Rex Nan Kivell Collection
nla.gov.au/nla.cat-vn1654251

page 75
Blackfellow Mending His Net
page 349 in *Picturesque Atlas of Australasia*,
vol. II, edited by Andrew Garran
(Sydney: The Picturesque Atlas Publishing Co.,
1886–1888)
Rex Nan Kivell Collection
nla.gov.au/nla.cat-vn1654251

pages 78–79
Samuel Calvert (1828–1913)
Natives Fishing 1873
wood engraving; 21.5 x 31.5 cm
nla.gov.au/nla.cat-vn2833890

4 James Davis—'Duramboi'
& David Bracefell—'Wandi'

pages 84–85
Henry Boucher Bowerman (1789–1839)
Moreton Bay, New South Wales 1835
pencil; 22.4 x 36.2 cm
nla.gov.au/nla.cat-vn1865914

page 95
*James Davies Poses in front of His Crockery Store,
George Street, Brisbane, c. 1872*
b&w negative
John Oxley Library, State Library of Queensland
SLQ Negative Number 141503

page 127
Mrs Fraser on the Rock
plate opp. page 133 in *Shipwreck of the Stirling
    Castle: Containing a Faithful Narrative of the
    Dreadful Sufferings of the Crew, and the Cruel
    Murder of Captain Fraser by the Savages ...*
    by John Curtis
(London: George Virtue, 1838)
Rex Nan Kivell Collection
nla.gov.au/nla.cat-vn2450767

page 129
*Mrs. Frazer & a Part of the Crew of the Stirling
    Castle Who Had Escaped from the Wreck in
    the Long Boat Being Seize'd & Stripped by the
    Savages*
frontispiece in *The Shipwreck of Mrs. Frazer, and
    Loss of the Stirling Castle, on a Coral Reef in
    the South Pacific Ocean ...*
(London: Dean and Munday, 1837)
Rex Nan Kivell Collection
nla.gov.au/nla.cat-vn902357

page 132
Robert Gibbings (1889–1958)
frontispiece 1937 in *John Graham Convict 1824:
    An Historical Narrative* by Robert Gibbings
(London: J.M. Dent & Sons Ltd, 1956)
Rex Nan Kivell Collection
nla.gov.au/nla.cat-vn2269818
Courtesy Estate of Robert Gibbings and the
Heather Chalcroft Literary Agency

page 135
Butchulla Man about to Go into Battle
b&w negative
John Oxley Library, State Library of Queensland
SLQ Negative Number 4679

page 142
Mrs Fraser's Escape from the Savages
plate opp. page 162 in *Shipwreck of the Stirling
    Castle: Containing a Faithful Narrative of the
    Dreadful Sufferings of the Crew, and the Cruel
    Murder of Captain Fraser by the Savages ...*
    by John Curtis
(London: George Virtue, 1838)
Rex Nan Kivell Collection
nla.gov.au/nla.cat-vn2450767

pages 146–147
Harden S. Melville
Beach at Sandy Cape
plate 5 in *Sketches in Australia and the Adjacent
    Islands* by Harden S. Melville
(London: Dickinson & Co., 1849)
hand-coloured lithograph; 15.6 x 22 cm
Rex Nan Kivell Collection
nla.gov.au/nla.cat-vn1248170

7 Barbara Thompson—'Giom'

page 151
Oswald Brierly (1817–1894)
H.M.S. Rattlesnake off Sydney Heads c. 1848
watercolour; 34.5 x 52 cm
nla.gov.au/nla.cat-vn1984468

Oswald Brierly (1817–1894)
*Men at Table with Native On-board Rattlesnake
    1849–1850*
pencil
State Library of New South Wales
PX*D 82

page 155
Oswald Brierly (1817–1894)
Kai Marrina
plate opp. page 63 in *The Log of a Merchant
    Officer: Viewed with Reference to the Education
    of Young Officers and the Youth of the Merchant
    Service* by Robert Methven
(London: John Weale, 1854)
Rex Nan Kivell Collection
nla.gov.au/nla.cat-vn433776

pages 156–157
*A Native Outrigger Canoe alongside 'The
    Rattlesnake' in the Louisiade Archipelago*
frontispiece in *T.H. Huxley's Diary of the Voyage
    of H.M.S. Rattlesnake* edited by Julian Huxley
(London: Chatto and Windus, 1935)
Rex Nan Kivell Collection
nla.gov.au/nla.cat-vn1613881

page 159
James Thomas Stanton
Log Books 1849–1851
Rex Nan Kivell Collection
nla.gov.au/nla.cat-vn1394645

pages 160–161
G.H. Inskip
Diary, 1849–1850
nla.gov.au/nla.cat-vn271095

page 167
Charles Henry Kerry (1857–1928)
Prince of Wales Island Man with Mask 1890s
b&w photograph; 20.4 x 15.2 cm
nla.gov.au/nla.cat-vn3086766

page 168
*An Australian Woman, Probably from the Cape
    York Region*
plate 8 in *T.H. Huxley's Diary of the Voyage of
    H.M.S. Rattlesnake* edited by Julian Huxley
(London: Chatto and Windus, 1935)
Rex Nan Kivell Collection
nla.gov.au/nla.cat-vn1613881

Index

Page numbers in **bold** refer to illustrations.

Acknowledgements

Our study is based largely on the collections of the National Library of Australia, a rich and infinite treasure house of material for our history, and we have endeavoured to work as closely as possible with original records, and early publications.

However, we have also relied upon the ground-breaking work of more recent researchers, many of whom have devoted many years to meticulously researching the lives and experiences of individual Europeans who lived among Aboriginal or Torres Strait Islander people, and to bringing their stories to broader attention. We are indebted to the historical and biographical scholarship of writers including, among others, Chris Pearce (for Thomas Pamphlett), Patrick J. Tynan (for James Davis), Veronica Peek (for John Ireland and William D'Oyley), Elaine Brown (for Eliza Fraser), David Moore and Raymond Warren (for Barbara Thompson), David Welch and Bruce Breslin (for James Morrill), and Stephanie Anderson (for Narcisse Pelletier).

We are extremely grateful to National Library of Australia Commissioning Publisher Susan Hall and Editor Joanna Karmel. They have provided us with intelligent and thoughtful advice in the research and editorial process that has undoubtedly enhanced the final work (all mistakes and errors, of course, remain our own). We also thank the staff at the Library who assisted greatly by copying material for us, locating sources including visual images, and for designing the book itself.

We acknowledge the assistance received from archival staff and librarians at other repositories, particularly Janette Pelosi of the State Archives of New South Wales, Mitchell Librarian Richard Neville, and Sarah Morley of the State Library of New South Wales, who helped us to locate the long-missing original account of Eliza Fraser's rescue by John Graham. For research assistance, we are also indebted to Lachlan Russell and other staff at the Australian Institute of Aboriginal and Torres Strait Islander Studies, and Sue Paton, Gregg Heathcote and Gionni Di Gravio at the Auchmuty Collection Collections. We thank Iain McCalman and Angela Woollacott, for some helpful advice on sources for the chapter on James Morrill, in particular.

We would also like to take the opportunity to recognise the support of the University of Newcastle and Wollotuka Institute and our colleagues there.

Most importantly, we acknowledge the traditional Indigenous peoples that appear in the stories of this book, and also their descendants today. We offer our deepest respects to the people who so generously sheltered and provided for strangers in their midst, and in many instances saved their lives. We honour their memory, their kindness and their ongoing connections to country.